The Bible Speaks Today

Series Editors: J. A. Motyer (OT)
John R. W. Stott (NT)

The Message of
Joel, Micah & Habakkuk
Listening to the Voice of God

Titles in this series

OLD TESTAMENT

The Message of **Genesis 1—11**
David Atkinson

The Message of **Genesis 12—50**
Joyce G. Baldwin

The Message of **Deuteronomy**
Raymond Brown

The Message of **Judges**
Michael Wilcock

The Message of **Ruth**
David Atkinson

The Message of **Chronicles**
Michael Wilcock

The Message of **Nehemiah**
Raymond Brown

The Message of **Job**
David Atkinson

The Message of **Proverbs**
David Atkinson

The Message of **Ecclesiastes**
Derek Kidner

The Message of the **Song of Songs**
Tom Gledhill

The Message of **Isaiah**
Barry Webb

The Message of **Jeremiah**
Derek Kidner

The Message of **Daniel**
Ronald S. Wallace

The Message of **Hosea**
Derek Kidner

The Message of **Joel, Micah & Habakkuk**
David Prior

The Message of **Amos**
J. A. Motyer

NEW TESTAMENT

The Message of the **Sermon on the Mount (Matthew 5—7)**
John R. W. Stott

The Message of **Mark**
Donald English

The Message of **Luke**
Michael Wilcock

The Message of **John**
Bruce Milne

The Message of **Acts**
John R. W. Stott

The Message of **1 Corinthians**
David Prior

The Message of **2 Corinthians**
Paul Barnett

The Message of **Galatians**
John R. W. Stott

The Message of **Ephesians**
John R. W. Stott

The Message of **Philippians**
J. A. Motyer

The Message of **Colossians & Philemon**
R. C. Lucas

The Message of **1 & 2 Thessalonians**
John R. W. Stott

The Message of **2 Timothy**
John R. W. Stott

The Message of **Hebrews**
Raymond Brown

The Message of **James**
J. A. Motyer

The Message of **1 Peter**
Edmund P. Clowney

The Message of **2 Peter & Jude**
Dick Lucas & Christopher Green

The Message of **John's Letters**
David Jackman

The Message of **Revelation**
Michael Wilcock

The Message of Joel, Micah & Habakkuk

Listening to the Voice of God

David Prior

Director of the Centre for Marketplace Theology
in the City of London

Inter-Varsity Press
Leicester, England
Downers Grove, Illinois, U.S.A.

InterVarsity Press
P.O. Box 1400, Downers Grove, IL 60515
World Wide Web: www.ivpress.com
E-mail: mail@ivpress.com

Inter-Varsity Press
38 De Montfort Street, Leicester LE1 7GP, England

InterVarsity Press® is the book-publishing division of InterVarsity Christian Fellowship/USA®, a student movement active on campus at hundreds of universities, colleges and schools of nursing in the United States of America, and a member movement of the International Fellowship of Evangelical Students. For information about local and regional activities, write Public Relations Dept., InterVarsity Christian Fellowship/USA, 6400 Schroeder Rd., P.O. Box 7895, Madison, WI 53707-7895.

Inter-Varsity Press is the book-publishing division of the Universities and Colleges Christian Fellowship (formerly the Inter-Varsity Fellowship), a student movement linking Christian Unions in universities and colleges throughout the United Kingdom and the Republic of Ireland, and a member movement of the International Fellowship of Evangelical Students. For information about local and national activities write to UCCF, 38 De Montfort Street, Leicester LE1 7GP, England.

USA ISBN 0-8308-1241-5

UK ISBN 0-85111-586-1

Typeset in Great Britain by The Midlands Book Typesetting Company.

Printed in the United States of America ♻

Library of Congress Cataloging-in-Publication Data

Prior, David, 1940-
   The message of Joel, Micah, and Habakkuk: listening to the voice
of God / David Prior.
    p. cm.
   Includes bibliographical references.
   ISBN 0-8308-1241-5 (paper : alk. paper)
   1. Bible. O.T. Joel—Criticism, interpretation, etc. 2. Bible.
O.T. Micah—Criticism, interpretation, etc. 3. Bible. O.T.
Habakkuk—Criticism, interpretation, etc. I. Title.
BS1575.2.P76 1999
222'.9—dc21
                                                      98-54078
                                                        CIP

British Library Cataloguing in Publication Data

A catalogue record for this book is available from the British Library.

20	19	18	17	16	15	14	13	12	11	10	9	8	7	6	5	4	3	2
16	15	14	13	12	11	10	09	08	07	06	05	04	03	02	01			

For Marcus, Daniel,
Emma and Susanna,
as they each find their way
and their calling in the
twenty-first-century marketplace

Contents

Habakkuk

General preface

The Bible Speaks Today describes a series of both Old Testament and New Testament expositions, which are characterized by a threefold ideal: to expound the biblical text with accuracy, to relate it to contemporary life, and to be readable.

These books are, therefore, not 'commentaries', for the commentary seeks rather to elucidate the text than to apply it, and tends to be a work rather of reference than of literature. Nor, on the other hand, do they contain the kind of 'sermons' which attempt to be contemporary and readable without taking Scripture seriously enough.

The contributors to this series are all united in their convictions that God still speaks through what he has spoken, and that nothing is more necessary for the life, health and growth of Christians than that they should hear what the Spirit is saying to them through his ancient – yet ever modern – Word.

J. A. MOTYER
J. R. W. STOTT
Series Editors

Author's preface

Joel, Micah and Habakkuk have no discernible link with one another, in either their historical setting or their content. It is, in any case, impossible to date the book of Joel. Micah dates himself in the opening verse and Habakkuk's dating is clear from his subject matter. All three prophets, as we would expect, emphasize the vital importance of listening to what the LORD has to say in times of disaster (Joel), disobedience (Micah) and destruction (Habakkuk).

It is reasonable to summarize the three books in the following way. *Joel* starts by taking us, painfully and slowly, through the bleakness of national disaster. He moves on to the anticipation of a mighty outpouring of God's Spirit, but against the backcloth of the forthcoming day of the LORD. *Micah* spells out the pervasive disobedience of God's people, particularly in the city life of Jerusalem, and the certain judgment of the LORD which is to fall – a judgment that will be thorough, but will leave a remnant of the faithful under the leadership of God's chosen king.

Habakkuk addresses his message to the LORD in prayer, unburdening himself with total candour in the face of what looks like imminent destruction of the city, the land and the people by a vicious and violent invader. The LORD then reveals that a fundamental truth is being worked out by means of his sovereign activity in history, though usually in a hidden way.

Each book speaks powerfully into a world and a church living on the cusp of a millennium. About five years have elapsed since I began to research the background and study the literature relating to these three prophets. During this time I have moved, after twenty-seven years in the life of local churches, to marketplace ministry in central London – initially in the diverse workplaces of the West End, and more recently in the more monochrome, but highly specialized, world of the City. This transition ultimately came about in response to a London businessman saying to me, 'David, come and stand

11

alongside us with an open Bible.' I had spent the previous twenty-seven years as an ordained minister entrusted with the oversight of different local churches, saying to people like that man, 'Come and help me build a decent church.' It had been demanding, absorbing, exhausting and fulfilling work. My priority, from the time God originally called me, had always been to absorb the Bible and to apply it to the entire life of the church in that particular place.

I am discovering that this priority assumes distinctive characteristics when you spend most of your time standing in the marketplace (the world), rather than the holy place (the church). That is particularly true of these three prophets, who were all standing in a similar position in their day.

We are all, of course, called to stand together both in the holy place and in the marketplace – to live the distinctive life of the holy place in the marketplace. But when we fail to engage relevantly, truthfully and compassionately with the marketplace, the marketplace enters the holy place and begins gradually to take it over. The holy place loses its distinctiveness. It becomes a place for religious acts and religious language by religious people. Such people daily spend significant time in the marketplace but, because their religion touches neither their inner being nor their daily lives, they import the attitudes and behaviour of their marketplace lives into the holy place.

God, meanwhile, wants to meet his people at depth as we gather in the holy place, and then propel us out into the marketplace – to make a difference by being different. That, directly or indirectly, is the thrust of all three prophets. It is the thrust of the whole message of the Bible.

I want especially to thank Alec Motyer for the incisive precision with which he scrutinized the original manuscript. Graciously, but firmly, he passed shrewd and constructive comment on many matters – not least pointing out details connected with the meaning of Hebrew words and phrases, where otherwise I would have made any number of howlers and drawn not a few unwarranted assumptions. There are three or four places where I have ultimately decided to abide by my personal conclusions and so I take responsibility for the final text.

My personal prayer is that these three prophets will encourage every reader, each in his or her own marketplace, to let the Lord speak through them by their daily words, attitudes and actions.

London, March 1998   DAVID PRIOR

Chief abbreviations

AV	The Authorized (King James) Version of the Bible (1611).
NASB	The New American Standard Bible (1963).
NBD	*New Bible Dictionary*, 3rd edn, ed. I. H. Marshall *et al.* (IVP, 1996).
NIDOTTE	*New International Dictionary of Old Testament Theology and Exegesis*, ed. W. A. Van Gemeren (Paternoster, 1997), 5 vols.
NIV	The New International Version of the Bible (1973, 1978, 1984).
NRSV	The New Revised Standard Version of the Bible (1989).
RSV	The Revised Standard Version of the Bible (NT 1946, second edition 1971; OT 1952).
TDOT	*Theological Dictionary of the Old Testament* (Eerdmans, 1974–); trans. by J. T. Willis of G. J. Botterweck and H. Ringgren, *Theologishes Worterbuch zum Alten Testament* (1970–).

Bibliography

Allen   Leslie C. Allen, *Joel, Obadiah, Jonah, Micah*, New International Commentary on the Old Testament (Eerdmans, 1976).

Armerding   Carl E. Armerding, 'Habakkuk', in *The Expositor's Bible Commentary* 7 (Zondervan, 1985).

Baker   David W. Baker, *Nahum, Habakkuk and Zephaniah*, Tyndale Old Testament Commentaries (IVP, 1988).

Boice   James Montgomery Boice, *The Minor Prophets: An Expositional Commentary* (Zondervan, 1986), 2 vols.

Bruce   F. F. Bruce, '*Habakkuk*', in *The Minor Prophets: An Exegetical and Expository Commentary* 2, ed. T. E. McComiskey (Baker, 1993).

Calvin   John Calvin, *Commentaries* 14 and 15, ed. and trans. John Owen (Baker, 1984).

Craigie   Peter C. Craigie, *Twelve Prophets* 1 and 2, The Daily Study Bible (St Andrew Press, 1985).

Dillard   Raymond Dillard, 'Joel', in *The Minor Prophets: An Exegetical and Expository Commentary* 1, ed. T. E. McComiskey (Baker, 1992).

Finley   Thomas J. Finley, *Joel, Amos, Obadiah*, Wycliffe Exegetical Commentary (Moody, 1990).

Goldsmith   Martin Goldsmith, *Habakkuk and Joel: God is Sovereign in History* (Marshalls, 1982).

Hubbard   David Allan Hubbard, *Joel and Amos*, Tyndale Old Testament Commentaries (IVP, 1989).

Kaiser   Walter C. Kaiser Jr, *Micah to Malachi*, The Communicator's Commentary 21 (Word, 1992).

Keil   C. F. Keil, 'Joel', 'Micah' and 'Habakkuk', in

	C. F. Keil and F. Delitzsch, *Commentary on the Old Testament* 10 (reissued Eerdmans, 1986).
Lloyd-Jones	D. Martyn Lloyd-Jones, *From Fear to Faith: Studies in the Book of Habakkuk* (reissued IVP, 1997).
Marsh	John Marsh, *Amos and Micah: Thus Saith the Lord*, Torch Bible Commentaries (SCM, 1959).
McComiskey	T. E. McComiskey, 'Micah', in *The Expositor's Bible Commentary* 7, ed. Frank Gaebelein (Zondervan, 1985).
Morgan	G. Campbell Morgan, *Voices of Twelve Hebrew Prophets* (Pickering and Inglis, no date).
Patterson (*EBC*)	Richard D. Patterson, 'Joel', in *The Expositor's Bible Commentary* 7, ed. Frank Gaebelein (Zondervan, 1985).
Patterson (WEC)	Richard D. Patterson, *Nahum, Habakkuk, Zephaniah*, Wycliffe Exegetical Commentary (Moody, 1991).
Pusey	Edward B. Pusey, *The Minor Prophets: A Commentary* 2 (reissued Baker, 1950).
Robertson	O. Palmer Robertson, *Nahum, Habakkuk and Zephaniah*, New International Commentary on the Old Testament (Eerdmans, 1990).
G. A. Smith	George Adam Smith, *The Book of the Twelve Prophets* (Hodder and Stoughton, 1928), 2 vols.
R. L. Smith	Ralph L. Smith, *Micah to Malachi*, Word Biblical Commentary 32 (Word, 1984).
Stuart	Douglas Stuart, *Hosea to Jonah*, Word Biblical Commentary 31 (Word, 1987).
Waltke	Bruce Waltke, 'Micah', in *The Minor Prophets: An Exegetical and Expository Commentary* 2, ed. T. E. McComiskey (Baker, 1993).
Waltke (TOTC)	Bruce Waltke, *Obadiah, Jonah, Micah*, Tyndale Old Testament Commentaries (IVP, 1988).
Wolff	H. W. Wolff, *Joel and Amos*, Hermeneia (Fortress, 1977).

Introduction to Joel

I remember the first time I saw a locust. We were driving in the family car through the afternoon heat of a sultry Karoo desert road in South Africa. Everything and everyone was fairly sleepy, including the driver. Suddenly there was a shriek, followed by pandemonium, from the back of the car. We halted and investigated. There was a huge locust – or it seemed huge to people more used to ordinary grasshoppers in an English garden.

That solitary locust – and its impact on one family for a few minutes in the 1970s – comes to my mind whenever I read the book of Joel. At the time I recall thinking back to John the Baptist, with his rather unusual diet of locusts and wild honey in the deserts of Judea. I had never been able to understand what nourishment or attraction there might be in a locust. After that South African locust I was thoroughly enlightened: chop off head, tail and legs, and I could imagine a fairly succulent piece of flesh, preferably grilled to perfection and suitably garnished with garlic, as the French (especially) serve proper-sized prawns.

But a *plague* of locusts: that would be rather different. For the people of Joel's day it certainly was different. It was horrific, devastating, overwhelming. They had seen locusts before, probably hordes of them over the years. But this was unprecedented:

> *Hear this, you aged men,*
> *give ear, all inhabitants of the land!*
> *Has such a thing happened in your days,*
> *or in the days of your fathers?* (Joel 1:2).

We have only to read accounts of such locust invasions to catch the feel of the appalling experiences they unleashed. Augustine writes:

When Africa was a Roman province, it was attacked by a large number of locusts. Having eaten everything, leaves and fruits, a formidable swarm of them was drowned in the sea. Thrown up dead on the coasts, the putrefaction of these insects so infected the air as to cause a pestilence so horrible that in the kingdom of Masinissa alone 800,000 and more are said to have perished. Of 30,000 soldiers in Utique, only 10,000 remained.[1]

In about 1960 a grasshopper horde attacked California and was described in the newspaper in terms reminiscent of Joel. In one county 200,000 acres were covered with insects 'over every inch and in some cases stacked on top of each other'. Fields were left 'bare as the floor'. One agricultural official remarked: 'What they don't eat, they cut off for entertainment.'

Today areas having the potential for a locust outbreak are monitored by international agencies using satellite reconnaissance and other technology; incipient swarms are met by aircraft and trucks carrying powerful pesticides. If the locusts are not destroyed or contained soon after they hatch, once the swarm has formed, control efforts are minimally effective even today. In 1988 in a civil war in Chad, the fighting prevented international co-operation in attacking the hatch and a destructive swarm spread throughout North Africa, devastating some of the poorest nations and threatening Europe as well.

Apparently the swarming locust is none other than an ordinary species of grasshopper. When moisture and temperature conditions favour a large hatch, the crowding and unceasing contact and jostling of the nymphs stimulate significant changes, so that the grasshopper nymphs make a transition from solitary behaviour (like our South African friend) to the swarming, gregarious and migratory phases of the dreaded plague. Plagues continue as long as climactic conditions favour large hatches.

Such swarms can cover great distances (they have been seen 1,200 miles out to sea), can be of immense size (an area of 2,000 square miles was recorded around the Red Sea in 1881) and can contain huge numbers in tight density (up to 120 million per square mile). One female grasshopper, which lays her eggs in June, may have 18 million living descendants in October. Swarming hordes often block out the sun, riding high on the wind. A swarm can contain up to 10 billion insects.

Their noise, also, is appalling. Early in 1994 I was sitting in a garden in Montevideo, Uruguay, where I became mesmerized by the strident racket of several cicadas. They effectively destroyed any

[1] *City of God* III.xxxi.

sense of peace and quiet. The noise of locusts in a swarm has been likened to that of a jet engine, due to the twofold sound of whirring wings and crunching jaws. I can well believe it.

They get into houses, even through cracks and chimneys. Pliny[2] claims that they can even gnaw through doors. They strip the bark off trees. When dead, they give out a revolting stench, and their bodies breed typhus and other diseases in both animals and humans.

It is clear that a locust invasion, especially one on the scale experienced by Joel's contemporaries, was a nightmare, like something straight out of hell, the kind of scenario which a film-maker like Alfred Hitchcock or Steven Spielberg might powerfully evoke by imaginative use of special effects and photographic skills. We can hardly begin to appreciate the impact or the thrust of Joel's message unless we enter into something of what he is describing. For most of us it is an alien, unknown experience.

And it raises all sorts of theological questions. Joel addresses these and asks some of his own. This bundle of questions is timeless and relevant to people of any country at any time in the face of any such disaster, 'natural' or brought about by human cruelty or folly. They include such questions as: Why is this happening to us? What has caused it? What is God doing about it? What is God saying to us? Is there anything we can do to stop it now and prevent it happening again?

It is a help, in addressing such questions today, to accept the impossibility, according to the scholars, of dating the book of Joel. It could have been written at any time between the ninth and the third centuries BC, a span of 600 years. It is, simply, *the word of the LORD that came to Joel, the son of Pethuel* (1:1), and it therefore tells us far more about the LORD God than about the prophet Joel. God spoke to the people of Joel's time and Joel's nation, and God spoke effectively: the people responded to the prophet's message – that much is clear within the text itself as it proceeds.

God still speaks today. He speaks as the timeless message of Joel is applied by the Lord's people living and speaking prophetically into our contemporary crises. In January 1994 California was reeling after a succession of disasters – riots, drought, fire, floods, earthquakes. One magazine article (one of many trying to ask and answer the right questions) attempted to address the issue of 'Why California?' Its conclusion, couched in not overly impressive wisdom, was: 'Mother Nature has decreed it so.'

As we pursue God's message through Joel, it will become plain that the prophet's impact was partly due to his rejection of such simplistic paganism: if we write God out of his creation and, in

---

[2] *Natural History* I.ii.12.

particular, out of the unpleasant and unacceptable aspects of the world which he has created, we will end up lost in a meaningless universe with no hope and no direction. There is a way back from the nightmare scenario depicted by Joel, but the issues are deadly serious and the time is necessarily short.

Joel's theology is robust and comprehensive. He sees the hand of God in the totality of human experience. He shares the heart of God for every human action and inaction. He talks of God's personal and direct involvement in all human affairs. He may have been addressing a context and a culture where it was natural to talk in such blunt language, where God-talk was recognized and still reverberated in the souls of his listeners, and we may have moved away from such an atmosphere. The Israel of Joel's day was, however, no less secularized than our own generation. Joel had the courage to talk of God's direct and personal involvement in current affairs and to assert that he and he alone had the answers to the national crisis: that would have been as contrary to contemporary worldviews and received wisdom as it would be today.

Nevertheless, we need to be honest in assessing whether or not we have any philosophy or definition of living which provides significance or meaning to the world in which we live. In other words, it may well be time to return to such a robust and comprehensive theology. If we find it hard to accept Joel's explanation of his particular set of circumstances, what is the alternative? Put bluntly: if God did not send the locusts, who did? We still have to investigate what we mean by such a statement, but we must not rationalize it so far that it becomes an ignored relic belonging to another world. For Joel's agriculturally based economy, the locust plague threatened the basic necessities of daily living and therefore the economic stability of the nation. Where are the locusts today in our technologically brilliant, but ethically bankrupt, society?

One particular phrase acts like a refrain throughout Joel's message: *the day of the LORD*.[3] This is where Joel is most robust and direct. The locust invasion is a prelude to something far worse, probably enemy invasion from the north, and certainly a day of final judgment. Whatever else Joel may or may not be saying, he is emphasizing as strongly as he knows how that that great and terrible day is imminent. Any present or pending disaster, such as the locusts, comes as a warning, a trumpet-blast in the ears of the complacent and heedless. God is speaking and he is speaking personally, directly and urgently.

[3] Joel 1:15; 2:1, 11, 31; 3:14.

Joel 1:1–20
1. Cry to God

1. The prophet (1:1)

The opening phrases make it plain that the book of Joel is *the word of the LORD*. The language is very similar to the opening lines of other prophetic books in the Old Testament.[1] But there is no clue to its date, nor is there any indication about the background and personality of its author. He introduces himself as *Joel, the son of Pethuel*. Interestingly, we can in this case note with profit what the names of Joel and his father mean. Joel means 'whose God is Yahweh' or perhaps 'Yahweh is God'. Pethuel means 'the straight-forwardness or sincerity of God'.

The two names together, in effect, sum up the message of the book. It is entirely focused on God and its message is completely straightforward – God is speaking directly to his people.

Precisely how Joel received *the word of the LORD* remains an open question. The indications are that he was intimately acquainted with the temple at Jerusalem. So the word of the LORD came to him – perhaps audibly, perhaps visually, perhaps a mixture of both, perhaps neither. The Hebrew text says, 'The word of the LORD that *was* to Joel'; it became a reality to him, and Joel believed that his very words were the actual word of the LORD, invested with divine accuracy and authority.

It is in many ways providential that the book cannot be dated or traced to a particular person in a particular setting. The events described in it are, at one and the same time, unprecedented and timeless. The message of Joel is, therefore, relevant to any situation in any generation. 'As there is no certainty, it is better to leave the time in which Joel taught undecided and, as we shall see, this is of no great importance.[2]

---

[1] *E.g.* Micah, Jonah, Zephaniah, Zechariah.   [2] Calvin, Preface, 14, p. xv.

2. The people (1:2–20)

In the space of thirteen verses Joel, speaking with the words of God, gives no fewer than seventeen words of command – to *all inhabitants of the land* (2), to *aged men* or *elders* (2, 14), to *drunkards and all you drinkers of wine* (5), to the *tillers of the soil* and *vinedressers* (11), to the *priests* (13). Joel is nothing if not straightforward as he describes the appalling situation in the nation and what must be done about it.

In each case, it could be argued, the people addressed are commanded to do what they would not, in normal circumstances, expect to do. But these are not normal circumstances, by any stretch of the imagination, and therefore everyone must behave differently. The older men, who in Israelite society were listened to with the immense respect due to their seniority and wisdom,[3] must now *Hear this;* they must become listeners themselves. As *the elders* (14) of the community, they were accustomed to passing instructions to others. Now Joel is passing on instructions to them.

Drunkards spend a good deal of their time fast asleep. Those who enjoy drinking wine are usually merry. Now, says Joel, it is the time to *awake* and *weep*. The appalling situation requires even partygoers and heavy drinkers to *wail* (5). Similarly, those who till the soil and dress the vines (and in a rural community that is most people) are instructed to *be confounded* and to *wail* (11). Farmers normally go to their work with zest and determination. Sitting over a drink today with our local farmer, we listened to him describing that he has no holidays, but that he enjoys his work. However hard it might be, it is rewarding and worth all the effort and anxiety. The farmers in Joel's day were bidden to sing a different tune – to cover their heads in shame and to howl.

The priests, finally, are instructed to go completely against their customary practices: *Gird on sackcloth and lament . . . Go in, pass the night in sackcloth* (13). They normally wore splendid priestly garments and presided over liturgies of celebration. Now they are to wear sackcloth and lead the people in special rites of lamentation. Such unusual actions would not have come easily or naturally to these *ministers of the altar* (13) – and they are to *spend the night* like this, when all good priests were normally sound asleep.

Yes, special circumstances require special action. The situation facing Joel's country was not just special; it was unprecedented. He asks the older men, *Has such a thing happened in your days, or in the days of your fathers?* (2). The importance of remembering the past –

---

[3] See Gn. 15:15; Ex. 20:12; Lv. 19:32; Ps. 71:9, 18 – and, in another but similar culture, Jb. 5:26; 12:20; 15:10; 32:7.

to absorb its lessons and apply its perspective – is paramount in the history and worship of Israel.[4] It is particularly crucial in the weekly supper, when the father of every family tells everyone about the nation's past and the nation's God. There is today an understandable emphasis on youth and the future and so it is particularly important not to allow any agist prejudices or sheer ignorance to make us forget the lessons of the past.

Joel's current disaster is so unprecedented that he tells the older men to include it in what they will, from now on, pass on to future generations. It cannot be allowed to fade from people's memory:

> *Tell your children of it,*
> *and let your children tell their children*
> *and their children another generation* (3).

Such a thing is to take its proper place among all the other acts of God in the history of the nation. It is to be told to the third and fourth generation.

3. The problem (1:4)

So what is this unprecedented disaster? Joel describes it succinctly and memorably:

> *What the cutting locust left,*
> *the swarming locust has eaten.*
> *What the swarming locust left,*
> *the hopping locust has eaten.*
> *What the hopping locust left,*
> *the destroying locust has eaten* (4).

The land has been invaded by a swarm of locusts on a cataclysmic scale. Joel's descriptive powers make it sound almost apocalyptic – which in an important sense, as we shall see later, it is.

Commentators vary in their interpretation of this key verse. Most accept that it describes a literal locust invasion, but they debate the details. Some of these believe that chapter 2 continues with a description of the locusts, opening up into a wider perspective in which the locusts are pointers to, and precursors of, an invading army. A few commentators assert that the whole locust description is figurative and that the invasion by foreign armies is the issue from start to finish.

Such a detailed description is more likely to be the result of actually seeing locusts at work in such profusion. All the descriptions we

[4] See *e.g.* Ex. 12:26; 13:8; Dt. 6:20.

have of this phenomenon substantiate the accuracy of Joel's language. The prophet does not exaggerate the situation one bit. Probably only those who have not experienced locusts on the march cannot conceive such an appalling scenario.

If 1:4 summarizes the locust invasion and its impact on the land, it becomes unimportant whether the four words used of the locusts have particular reference to distinct stages in their development. It is unlikely that Joel would have had any interest in, or access to, biological data about the life cycle of a locust. What he would have known, by observation, is that locusts cut, locusts swarm, locusts hop, locusts destroy. There was simply nothing left after a series of locust onslaughts. The impact would have been utterly devastating and it would have continued long after the locusts had gone; see the phrase in 2:25, referring to *the years* (plural) *which the locust has eaten*. It was a root-and-crop destruction and it took years to recover.

4. The results (1:5–20)

Joel paints a vivid description of this wholesale destruction. A poet, he uses language evocatively and emotionally. He attributes personal feelings to created things. He uses particular phrases more than once. We can catch the force of the description by pondering the verbs in the chapter: *cut off, laid waste, dried up, torn down; stripped, destroyed, withheld; ruined, devoured, burned; fails, languishes, withers, shrivels*. Everything is affected – fields, food, fruit; barley, barns, beasts; ground, grain, gladness. Choice items, such as pomegranate and fig, are eradicated. Important crops, such as wheat and barley, are gone.

Amid this wholesale devastation Joel highlights four events which have particular significance.

a. Life's basic necessities have failed

The grain is destroyed, the wine fails, and *the oil languishes* (10). It is difficult for non-Mediterranean readers to absorb the force of this. For British people an equivalent might be bread, butter and tea. For Americans it might be hamburgers, coffee and gasoline. In China and many countries in the East, the grain concerned would be rice. Grain, wine and oil were necessary for the staple diet of Mediterranean countries – the grain to make bread; the fruit of the vine as daily drink; olive oil for cooking, cleansing, soothing, lighting and much else besides.

So their whole way of life has been destroyed. We can cope with most things until our basic lifestyle is affected. Then we sit up and take notice. In today's western and modernized world we are protected from the impact of such disasters. Modern technology has given us cans and refrigerators. If a shortage looms or threatens, we stock up. But this is not true in other parts of the world, even today. In a recent letter from Zimbabwe, friends wrote, 'We are desperate for rains next season; water-rationing and food handouts are now a common experience.'

It is also likely that Joel focuses attention on grain, wine and oil for explicitly theological reasons. Hosea, for example, likens the unfaithfulness of the people towards God to the adultery of his own wife. God says, 'She did not know that it was I who gave her the grain, the wine, and the oil' (2:8). Joel's compatriots were being forced to face up to the true source of their daily bread, wine and oil, now that these had vanished. In Psalm 104:15 the same essential trio is mentioned, as gifts from God: 'wine to gladden the heart of man, oil to make his face shine, and bread to strengthen man's heart.' Again, should the country be invaded as a consequence of its refusal to serve the LORD, the people had been warned that the enemy 'shall not leave you grain, wine or oil'.[5] Joel is also reminding the people of the land's original and intended fertility.[6]

Only a perverse – and wilfully perverse – idiot could fail to get the message.

God often punishes men and it behoves them to be attentive as soon as he raises his finger. But common punishments are wont to be unheeded. Men soon forget those punishments to which they have been accustomed. God has, however, treated you in an unusual manner, having openly as it were put forth his hand from heaven and brought upon you punishments nothing less than miraculous. You must be more than stupid if you perceive not that you are smitten by God's hand.[7]

'More than stupid' – a verdict which is highlighted by the second event in this wholesale destruction.

b. The reaction of farm animals and wild animals

How the beasts groan!
The herds of cattle are perplexed

[5] Dt. 28:51; cf. Nu. 18:12; Dt. 7:13; 11:14; 12:17; 14:23; 18:4; 2 Ch. 31:5; 32:28; Ne. 10:3, 39; 13:5, 12; Je. 31:12; Ho. 2:10, 24; Hg. 1:11.
[6] See e.g. Ex. 3:8, 17; 13:5; 33:3; Lv. 20:24; Nu. 13:27; Dt. 8:7–9; Jos. 5:6; Je. 32:22; Ezk. 20:6.
[7] Calvin, p. 21.

> *because there is no pasture for them;*
> *even the flocks of sheep are dismayed* (18).

> *Even the wild beasts cry to thee,*
> *because the water brooks are dried up,*
> *and fire has devoured*
> *the pastures of the wilderness* (20).

Cows and sheep depend on good pasture. Farmers take great care to nurture grazing land in order to provide what the animals need all the year round. In the Pyrenees, Basque farmers take most of their sheep up to the higher mountain pastures in the summer months, so that the limited areas of good grazing land lower down around their farms can be maintained for the winter, when higher areas are covered with snow.

Sheep, particularly, will eat anything at all nourishing – the edges of the maize crop and, if allowed, the shrubs and plants in our garden. They spend the whole day in non-stop grazing. Joel certainly understood the mood of sheep and cattle when deprived of their customary pasture. He describes their behaviour in terms of human feelings: they *groan*, they *are perplexed;* they are *dismayed.* The Hebrew word translated *are perplexed* can be more literally rendered 'wander aimlessly', for ever on the move in a vain search for better pasture.

This last word has, in fact, a directly theological motif. It means 'hold themselves guilty' or 'are treated as guilty'. Joel is introducing the notion of the animal kingdom suffering the consequences of human sin, even so identifying with it that they in some sense take responsibility for it. The animals sense that behind the disaster there is an offended God.

Joel's perspective on the oneness of all creatures in the bundle of life is based on the Genesis account of creation.

The whole creation, framed by Yahweh's word and shaped to achieve his purposes, is seen as a unity by Joel, along with the psalmists and the prophets. The literary personifications that depict the pain and shame of scorched land and starved animals are more than artistic devices. They demonstrate the vitality of a creation designed not just as a stage for redemption's drama but as players in it, sharply affected by the changing scenes of judgement and grace. From Eden forward, human beings and the rest of creation have been wrapped in one bundle of life. What touches one reaches the other, whether in bane or blessing.[8]

---

[8] Hubbard, pp. 34–35.

For Joel, therefore, humanity's stewardship and struggle in relation to God's created universe come into sharp focus. He calls on his fellow human beings, the people of God, to do what the animals instinctively are doing – crying out to God in their distress. He hints (to give his words their least significance) that human beings are responsible for the distress of the animals. This perspective is not confined to Joel in the Old Testament, but among the Hebrew prophets he articulates it most powerfully.[9]

All created things depend on human beings, who are created in the image of God, to exercise their God-given stewardship of creation with due responsibility and humility. It is sadly significant that the cudgels wielded on behalf of Earth's resources in recent times have not normally been in the hands of those committed to a biblical theology. In fact, most Christians have lagged behind in the ecological debate. By so doing, we have left the field wide open to others, many of whom make a crusade out of fighting for the 'rights' of animals over against those of selfish human beings.

The following words from a New Age publication make the point eloquently: 'The recent upsurge in volcanic action, earthquakes and unusual weather patterns may well be messages from Gaia, calling us to pay attention to her needs.' In the New Age scenario Gaia is a goddess, an ancient name for Mother Earth. The goddess has been 'seriously wounded' by the expansion of human civilization and now, it is said, there must come a universal atonement for these many millennia of grief on her part.

In addition to their roots in Greek and Roman mythology, the themes of the great mother and the great goddess are grounded in Eastern religions. The great mother goddess was worshipped under any or many of her different names: Diana or Artemis,[10] Isis, Demeter, Hecate, Cybele. In the Old Testament we find reference to (the) Asherah, the female consort of (the) Baal.[11] Basically, this group of names expresses a belief system in which nature itself is deified by worshipping the so-called female in natural processes and energies – a goddess who lives within us and all living things. The trendy word for all this medley of beliefs is ecofeminism.

Such a religion is as old as the hills and, in the promised land, it presented a continuous threat to the monotheism of the people of God. The worshipping practices of the Canaanites are fully recorded in the pages of the Old Testament, and they lie not that deep below the surface of Joel's prophecy. When the people of God became blasé about the claims and commandments of Yahweh, there were plenty of 'other gods' with alternative philosophies and promises.

---

[9] See Pss. 104:10–13, 21; 145:15–16; 147:9.
[10] *E.g.* of the Ephesians in Acts 19:27–37.   [11] *E.g.* Mi. 5:14.

Such a credo was not that far removed from the modern spirituality which, having dispensed with a God who is creator, sustainer, redeemer and judge, replaces him with a 'goddess' who enables us to get what we want from our 'higher selves' within and from the universe around. There is a degree of biblical truth in the New Age emphasis on the inherent powers in the created world, particularly on the imperative of fertility. But, drawing on the ritual magic endemic to religions such as ancient Baalism, New Age practices deliberately disassociate the cultivation of such powers from the call to be holy. So we need a robust creation theology and a celebratory creation spirituality.

Excursus: creation

The key New Testament passage for such a theology and such a spirituality comes in a remarkable chapter in the middle of Paul's letter to the Romans, in which the apostle is writing about the work of the Holy Spirit in the lives of 'those who are in Christ Jesus' (8:1). Intriguingly, in the context of Joel's locust disaster, Paul addresses the reality of *suffering* – the proper suffering which is integral to being children of God in a world dominated by sin and death. It is a suffering which we share with Christ himself (8:17).

Paul continues:

I consider that the sufferings of this present time are not worth comparing with the glory that is to be revealed to us. For the creation waits with eager longing for the revealing of the sons of God; for the creation was subjected to futility, not of its own will, but by the will of him who subjected it in hope; because the creation itself will be set free from its bondage to decay and obtain the glorious liberty of the children of God. We know that the whole creation has been groaning in travail together until now; and not only the creation, but we ourselves, who have the firstfruits of the Spirit, groan inwardly as we wait for adoption as sons, the redemption of our bodies. For in this hope we were saved (Rom. 8:18–25).

It is immediately obvious from this passage that Paul sees an inextricable link between human beings and the rest of God's creation in terms of past, present and future existence – all being together under the overarching control and purposes of God himself. At this fundamental level, therefore, we are bound to be ecologically alert, sensitive and committed. What affects us as human beings affects everything created, and *vice versa*. No Christian can opt out of the environmental debate without, therefore, being deliberately deaf to the word of God.

Our theology and our spirituality will, then, hold together the unity of human beings and all other created beings. We are not free either to rid our minds of ecological and environmental issues, or to accept beliefs which confine God to an existence within the created order, let alone which identify God with the forces of nature. Philosophically, this latter is pantheism; theologically, it is idolatry, involving worship of the creature, not of the Creator. Paul has plenty to say about that in the first chapter of Romans (verses 18–32).

In positive terms, Paul has much to teach us about the Creator's purposes in, for and through the whole of creation. Looking at the past, Paul states that creation 'was subjected to futility' by the express purpose of God. This subjection was 'not of its own will', and so there is an inherent frustration at work in the created order, brought on by a desire to break free from all the limitations imposed upon it.

The word 'futility' is best illuminated by the whole book of Ecclesiastes, which begins with the lament of the Preacher: 'Vanity of vanities! ... vanity of vanities! All is vanity' (1:2). He spends twelve chapters describing this repetitive cycle of emptiness and pointlessness at the heart, not just of human endeavour, but of the whole universe. The psalmist also expressed this futility in a moment of painful awareness:

> Behold, thou hast made my days a few handbreadths,
> and my lifetime is as nothing in thy sight.
> Surely every man stands as a mere breath!
> Surely man goes about as a shadow!
> Surely for naught are they in turmoil;
> man heaps up, and knows not who will gather! (Ps. 39:5–6).

This futility is as real for animals as for humans, and it leads to what Paul describes as 'bondage to decay'. Everything and everyone created is in bondage. Nothing and nobody is free. We need to be liberated from all the limitations of our earthly existence, in order to realize our potential and find our destiny. The world is a glorious place: but it is a grinding prison, full of death and decay. This leads to 'the whole creation ... groaning in travail' together – a description vividly reminiscent of Joel's remark: *How the beasts groan!* (1:18).

Paul sees the groaning as a symphony in which everything in God's creation plays a part – as if the whole world is sending up a long, passionate, unbroken and unending wail to its Creator. At times of special suffering, such as in civil war, plague and pestilence or 'natural' disaster, this groaning is almost tangible. It became a reality in the United Kingdom after the death of Diana, Princess of Wales, at the end of August 1997. Visits I have made to Uganda in the last fifteen years have made me personally aware of its intensity. Those who have spent time more recently in Rwanda tell similar stories. Peru had the same feel when 'Shining Path' terrorists were wreaking havoc a few years ago. You can feel it in the atmosphere. You can see it in the eyes of those, particularly the children, who have witnessed appalling atrocities. Such groaning wells up also out of the concrete jungles of our major cities, and in the continuing agony of Ireland.

This kind of suffering impacts the environment and everything created. Paul's perspective on such wholesale suffering is that it is like a woman in travail – which is a word of hope. The suffering may seem futile, within an earthbound perspective. The groaning may be intense and protracted, but there is a future and a hope: 'the creation itself will be set free from its bondage to decay and obtain the glorious liberty of the children of God'. God subjected it to futility; God will liberate it into glory. The future of the universe is inextricably bound up with the future of God's children, a future which Paul describes as 'the redemption of our bodies'.

This glorious future, in which the key realities are redemption and liberty, is, as Paul explains elsewhere,[12] a resurrection from the dead. There is sin and there is death; there is futility and decay, everywhere in creation. But our physical, mortal frames will, in Christ, be resurrected to live fully, freely and eternally in 'a new heaven and a new earth'.[13] That will reveal what is meant by 'the redemption of our bodies'. This will be the new birth for which the whole of creation now groans in travail together. Redemption, resurrection, rebirth, re-creation: this is the vocabulary of a theology and a spirituality appropriate to the book of Joel and relevant to the tired, polluted, creaking universe in which we live.

The way into this glory is through suffering. The Holy Spirit of God enables us to enter into this future, partially but substantially, in our present groaning. An essential part of this journey is allowing Christ to sensitize us to his suffering. To be a child of God, and to be a joint-heir with Christ of God's resources in the glory of heaven, necessarily involve us in this kind of suffering – that is, to come inside the broken heart of God and to share his pain for all that human sin has unleashed on his creation. So God's Spirit introduces us both to the suffering and to the glory of God. Any genuine movement of the Spirit will take us deeper into both – and this will need expression in the way we pray and worship together, as well as in the way we think and talk: in our spirituality as well as in our theology.

---

[12] Esp. 1 Cor. 15.   [13] Cf. 2 Pet. 3:13; Rev. 21:1.

'Heaven and earth together', therefore, has always been the intention of the Creator – a new heaven and a new earth in which 'righteousness is at home'.[14] We can have only limited hopes for a world in the grip of futility and decay. Jeremiah saw and felt this acutely:

> How long will the land mourn,
>   and the grass of every field wither?
> For the wickedness of those who dwell in it
>   the beasts and the birds are swept away,
>   because men said, 'He will not see our latter end' (Je. 12:4).

But we must allow the Spirit of God, who moved in creative power over the primeval chaos, to help us feel the futility and the decay inherent in our world. We must not ignore it, trivialize it or glamorize it.

Then the Spirit, who is himself 'the firstfruits' of God's *new* creation, will open our eyes to what he is gradually bringing into being, which will culminate in a full revelation of 'the glorious liberty of the children of God'. The prophet Isaiah provides rich insights into what this will mean, in a passage which ends like this:

> The wolf and the lamb shall feed together,
>   the lion shall eat straw like the ox;
>   and dust shall be the serpent's food.
> They shall not hurt or destroy
>   in all my holy mountain,
>   says the LORD (Is. 65:25).

c. Gladness fails from the sons of men

The third event depicted by Joel is clouded by an overwhelming atmosphere of doom and gloom. Nobody smiles. Nobody has any joy: *Surely, joy withers away among the people* (Joel 1:12, NRSV); *Rejoicing dries up from the sons of men* (NASV). Gladness, joy and rejoicing are painfully absent, emphasizing the way happiness can be entirely dependent on material circumstances when people are out of touch with the living God.

This is where the drunkards come in again. They depend entirely on their drink for their happiness. It is artificially stimulated by what they consume. Now their wine supplies have run out. They will have to face up to life's harsh realities without the stimulus (or the escape route) provided by their wine. For many, this will mean an appalling

---

[14] 2 Pet. 3:13, my translation.

descent into the abyss of withdrawal, with all the terrifying symptoms of the DTs – hallucinations, shaking and trembling, nightmare scenarios of hell's torments. Addicts to any drug (be it alcohol, nicotine, cocaine or crack, LSD, heroin or whatever – whether 'hard' or 'soft', prescribed or black-market) live in terror of its no longer being available.

The sweet wine . . . is cut off from your mouth (5) – a sudden, dramatic action: the bottle is brought to their lips and then it is whipped away. This represents a powerful intrusion into a chosen or imposed lifestyle, forcing upon people an experience which deprives them of the one thing that keeps them going. That inevitably leads, not just (as Joel says) to the end of any *gladness*, but (as we can see today) to violence. In today's cities and communities, drugs play the part that drink played in Joel's time. A significant proportion of all violent crime is drug-related. Large areas of major cities throughout the world are controlled by drug barons. This frightening scenario, not that dissimilar from Joel's locust-ridden world, has come about as individuals (from a very young age) look for kicks and 'highs' from artificial stimulants, especially from drink and, at first, 'soft' drugs. They are easy targets for those looking for quick, easy and increasing profits.

An article on teenage suicides brought this letter to the editor:

After reading your article, I felt I had to put pen to paper. As a 16-year-old girl awaiting her exam results, I feel I am well placed to comment. Depression, drugs and unemployment are, in my view, the three main contributing factors for suicide attempts among my peers. The pressure on young people today to succeed socially and academically is intense. This is matched by a growing sense of alienation from society.

I live in a former mining and market town, where unemployment is sky-high. There is a sense of apathy among many young people today. The future looks increasingly black – no jobs, no job security. Many of us have been drawn into crime and drugs and there is insufficient counselling and hope for those with drug problems, which are often dismissed as 'teen-angst' – a phrase that makes my blood boil! Is it any wonder that depression and suicide attempts are on the increase? There is a need for better support for young people with problems.[15]

As this letter clearly shows, the bottom line is a search for happiness or *gladness*. Life is 'boring' – a dismissive catchphrase that speaks of a search for true meaning as well as of the need for constant

---

[15] *The Independent*, 12 August 1995.

stimulation. Young people, in particular, are looking for excitement, something to break the routine, stop the tedium and take their minds off the bleak future. Under-age drinking and reckless experimentation with drugs are bound, therefore, to be rife.

But it is not only young people without many, or any, prospects. This absence of *gladness* has often been stressed to me by those working long hours, under heavy pressure and often with high incomes. In the current job climate there are fewer jobs, more redundancies and greater uncertainty about the future. Those who do have a job often have to do the work of two, even three, people. The atmosphere is highly charged, both with the expectations of employers for greater productivity and commitment, and with the sheer vulnerability of employees' positions. There is, also, frequent incidence of hard drug-taking, including mainline heroin injection and crack, among very high earners in the money-markets of the City of London. It has, for some, become a way of life – all in search of *gladness.*

In such a climate, as one person recently said to me, 'there are not many smiles in the workplace'. *Gladness fails from the sons of men.* It is all a chore and a grind. At another level, the same condition reveals itself (although it is often kept hidden) in the prevalence of depression.

There is, of course, an important distinction to be drawn between happiness and gladness, particularly the joy and rejoicing mentioned by Joel. Today we seem to be involved in a restless pursuit of happiness. Happiness is enshrined in the American Declaration of Independence as one of every citizen's three 'inalienable rights' ('Life, Liberty and the pursuit of Happiness') – 'one of the silliest ideas ever propagated', according to Malcolm Muggeridge. The Dalai Lama has said: 'I believe that the purpose of life is to be happy ... I don't know whether the universe, with its countless galaxies, stars and planets, has a deeper meaning or not, but at the very least it is clear that we humans who live on this earth face the task of making a happy life for ourselves. Therefore it is important to discover what will bring about the greatest degree of happiness.'

Joel, however, is concerned about *gladness*, and he refers to three specific times of rejoicing in the community – at a wedding (8), at harvest (10–11) and at the temple services (9, 13, 16). At all these occasions joy and gladness were normal and expected. Much of the joy was sheer anticipation of all the good things in store. All these high points in life were rooted in celebrating the lavish generosity of a bountiful Creator who has called us, whom he has created in his own image, into a personal relationship of faith and obedience. Apart from such a relationship there may be a degree of happiness, but there will be none of the true gladness and none of the joy to which Joel is referring.

The Old Testament is full of such joy. Psalm 45, for example, is a love song in celebration of the king's marriage to his princess. To the bridegroom these words are sung:

> . . . you love righteousness and hate wickedness.
> Therefore God, your God, has anointed you
> with the oil of gladness above your fellows.

His bride is described in glowing terms:

> The princess is decked in her chamber with gold-woven robes;
> in many-coloured robes she is led to the king,
> with her virgin companions, her escort, in her train.
> With joy and gladness they are led along
> as they enter the palace of the king (Ps. 45:7, 13–15).

This rejoicing has been cut off in Joel's day and has been replaced by wailing and lamentation, akin to the grief of a bride bereaved of her husband-to-be on the brink of her great day of celebration.

The joy of harvest is celebrated vividly in Psalm 65, rising to a crescendo of rejoicing:

> Thou crownest the year with thy bounty;
> the tracks of thy chariot drip with fatness.
> The pastures of the wilderness drip,
> the hills gird themselves with joy,
> the meadows clothe themselves with flocks,
> the valleys deck themselves with grain,
> they shout and sing together for joy (Ps. 65:11–13).

What a contrast with Joel's lamentation! What a shock, for people accustomed to such overflowing abundance, to face such desolation! Now there is absolutely nothing to anticipate, nothing to celebrate.

But the most devastating aspect of Joel's description is the end of gladness in the house of the LORD:

> *Is not the food cut off*
> *before our eyes,*
> *joy and gladness*
> *from the house of our God?* (16).

This brings us to the fourth and last focus of Joel in this opening chapter as he describes the impact of the locust plague.

d. The worshipping life of the people

Gladness has been destroyed at every level – in daily life, on special occasions, at harvest time. But a less obvious impact of the locust plague is the destruction of regular worship in the temple, typified by *the cereal offering and the drink offering* (9, 13), for which the basic ingredients are no longer available.

Cereal (or grain) offerings and drink offerings were made twice daily by the priests to accompany the morning and evening sacrifice of a lamb. This regular daily offering (called the *tāmiḏ* in Hebrew) was regarded as the most important task of the priests on behalf of the community of Israel.[16] It was the essential daily expression of the covenant between the Lord and his people.

If, then, the *tāmiḏ* should cease, it was equivalent to the covenant being rendered inoperative. The *tāmiḏ* was a daily reinforcement of the covenant, as can be seen in a regular refrain in Leviticus, Numbers and Deuteronomy in which it is said to be 'a pleasing odour to the Lord'. Each cereal offering, each grain offering, smelt good to God and also brought reassurance to the people that the covenant relationship was sound and secure.[17]

The Joel disaster meant the eradication of this daily assurance of the actual presence of God dwelling among the people as the Lord their God, and meeting them in order to speak with them. The locusts meant no dwelling, no meeting, no speaking: the apparent absence and the eloquent silence of God.

For a people brought up on the presence and provision of God, this was the ultimate disaster. The priests were indispensable mediators in this life of fellowship with God. Each priest represented all Israel when he ministered in the holy place; hence the focus in Joel on the impact of the catastrophe on the priests:

> *The priests mourn,*
> *the ministers of the Lord* (9).

They are mourning, not for the absence of grain, wine and oil for the offerings, but for this apparent absence of God.[18] The absence of the offerings did not cause God to withdraw, but made the position of the people unsafe in the presence of a holy God.

This perspective also explains the deeper significance of Joel's instruction to the priests to put on *sackcloth* (13). Priestly garments, as has been mentioned earlier, were very splendid, 'for glory and for beauty' (Ex. 28:2). Each garment had symbolic meaning. For example, the twelve precious stones on 'the breastpiece of judgment'

---

[16] See Nu. 28–29.   [17] See Ex. 29:38–46.   [18] See Ezk. 7:25–27.

stood for the twelve sons of Jacob, the twelve tribes of Israel: 'So Aaron shall bear the names of the sons of Israel in the breastpiece of judgment on his heart, when he goes into the holy place, to bring them to continual remembrance before the LORD' (Ex. 28:29). Every detail of every piece of the priestly garb carried similar significance. Now the priests had to put all that to one side and don a black gown woven from goats' hair:

> *Go in, pass the night in sackcloth,*
> *O ministers of my God!* (13).

So the whole elaborate system of maintaining fellowship with God had disintegrated. But the strange thing is that, unlike virtually every other prophet in Israel, Joel does not mention any particular sins in the nation which might have provoked the LORD to anger. This silence has led several commentators to suggest that there is more just below the surface of the text than might be immediately apparent. 'Religious syncretism and pluralism lay at the heart of Judah's problems', and the words of Joel give clear 'hints of the religious corruption which was costing the (temple) cult its life'.[19] But they remain 'hints', and the lack of any precise dating for the prophecy means we can draw no safe conclusions on this score.

Joel's calls to drunkards, farmers and priests may contain more than meets the eye, in that both drunkards and farmers are mentioned explicitly by other prophets as likely to have been in cahoots with the priests in murky religious practices. A lot of drunkenness was associated with most forms of religious worship. Hosea, in a powerful passage on the theme 'like priest, like people', bluntly states that, because 'wine and new wine take away the understanding' (4:11), the nation has sunk into rank idolatry. Because priest and people have thus 'played the harlot', 'threshing floor and winevat shall not feed them, and the new wine shall fail them' (9:1–2).

Among the local mystery religions rife in Canaan, orgiastic drunkenness was a common way for a worshipper to achieve the goal of union with a particular deity. Wine and drink eased the trip to a state of ecstasy, in which you could step outside yourself and be lost in the deity's own world. Such ecstatic experience is not uncommon today, usually linked with drug-induced states, in similar forms of religious expression.

Furthermore, farmers in those days in that land were, perhaps more than anybody else in the community, susceptible to Canaanite fertility practices in honour of the Baal and the Asherah. They

---

[19] Hubbard, p. 29.

would have been severely tempted, like all dependent for their livelihood on the natural elements, to turn away from obedient trust in the LORD to any possible source of help, provision or protection, particularly in times of crisis. The fertility cults of Baal worship were heavily influential throughout the centuries following Israel's entry into the land under Joshua, in spite of the LORD's commandment through Moses to look to him in trust and obedience, in order to ensure his blessings on their land, their homes and their whole lives. From the outset the LORD had placed heavy sanctions against any dabbling with 'other gods . . . the gods of the people who are round about' (Dt. 6:14).

Such warnings (coupled with promises of blessing on obedience) were inscribed in the collective memory of the people. It is likely, therefore, that Joel effectively had no need to spell out the sins of the people. They knew all too well what had produced this catastrophe. Specific sin-calling was superfluous. The book's sevenfold mention of the phrase *your God* may indicate persistent idolatry and Joel's impassioned plea to them to return to the one true God; as his own name signifies, 'Yahweh is God'.[20]

But Joel is light years away from the kind of prophet who wades into the state of the nation from a personal stance which assumes the moral high ground. In the same breath as talking to the people about *your God*, he is speaking about *our God* (16) and indeed *my God* (13) in addressing the priests. Joel is at one with both the pain and the sinfulness of the people. He speaks for God from within the catastrophe. He himself knows the desolation (perhaps as one of the priests in the Jerusalem temple) of being deprived of 'the gladness of sitting at the same table with Lord'.[21]

It is, perhaps, difficult for us to enter fully into the depths of desolation which Joel is expressing. For us this profound and passionate interpenetration between daily life and worshipping life is not a common experience. New Testament theology also weans us off dependence on holy things in holy places with holy people. We like to think that our relationship with God is not so physically earthed or so externally demonstrated.

For us, in our tradition and culture, an equivalent desolation to that of Joel's time might be an endless inner experience of the absence of God – where prayer is meaningless, the Scriptures are dead, corporate worship is hollow and Christian fellowship has become intolerable. If these turn out to be our personal nightmare (and for many today it is), then a plague on a par with Joel's locusts may well be upon us.

[20] Hubbard, p. 30.
[21] A. Noordtzij, *Leviticus*, Bible Student's Commentary (Zondervan, 1982), p. 48.

5. The solution (1:14)

What then should we do? Joel says: *Cry to the LORD* (14). The Hebrew word carries the nuance of 'loudly and importunately'.[22] Through Hosea God had said of his people:

> They do not cry to me from the heart,
>   but they wail upon their beds;
> for grain and wine they gash themselves,
>   they rebel against me (Ho. 7:14).

Here is the nub of the matter: when we are facing bitter and utter desolation, it is not our immediate reaction to cry out to God. It is easier and more common to turn in on ourselves (to 'wail upon [our] beds') and to take it out on others, particularly those nearest to us. This kind of behaviour shows how rebellious towards God, or at the very least self-sufficient, we can become even at times when we know we most need him.

The kind of importunate crying Joel advocates is very different. It is close to the prayer endorsed by Jesus in his story of the insistent widow:

> In a certain city there was a judge who neither feared God nor regarded man; and there was a widow in that city who kept coming to him and saying, 'Vindicate me against my adversary.' For a while he refused; but afterward he said to himself, 'Though I neither fear God nor regard man, yet because this widow bothers me, I will vindicate her, or she will wear me out by her continual coming.' And the Lord said, 'Hear what the unrighteous judge says. And will not God vindicate his elect, who cry to him day and night? Will he delay long over them? I tell you, he will vindicate them speedily. Nevertheless, when the Son of man comes, will he find faith on earth?' (Lk. 18:2–8).

The fact is that trouble has the habit of devouring, rather than nurturing, faith in God. Joel's instruction, in effect, tells the people to jettison any vestige of pride, self-sufficiency, anger or rebelliousness and to cry out to God. Unlike the judge in the parable, God does not need to be badgered and he certainly does not feel importuned, let alone imposed upon, when we cry out to him. But he looks on the heart and he looks for our cry to come – and to keep on coming – from the heart. He can sniff out any residual self-sufficiency, let alone rebelliousness.

[22] Hubbard, p. 49.

When Jonah prophesied that disaster would soon hit the city of Nineveh, the king was the first to set the wheels in motion with a public decree: 'Let neither man nor beast, herd nor flock, taste anything; let them not feed, or drink water, but let man and beast be covered with sackcloth, and let them cry mightily to God' (Jon. 3:7–8). In his decree the pagan king of Nineveh parallels the instructions from Joel to the priests in Jerusalem as the nation's spiritual leaders; sackcloth and fasting were to express outwardly the inner seriousness of their hearts. Sackcloth on the animals adds a slightly comic, quasi-ecological touch.

This combination of external actions expressing the internal condition of our hearts is important. The one without the other is insufficient, especially in the context of a community and a nation *in extremis*. Oriental and middle-eastern cultures find such 'togetherness' easier to hold than western people, especially Anglo-Saxons and Northern Europeans. Those who feel the pain deep within but never allow it to come out remain isolated and imprisoned in their pain. But, equally, superficial public expressions of grief help nobody and do not fool God.

So Joel instructs the priests (not the civil authorities, it should be noted) to give a lead to the people, first by their own behaviour and then by calling on the nation (*all the inhabitants of the land*) to observe a fast, *a solemn assembly* (14). Everyone is to come together at the temple for this purpose. The indications are that this required cessation from all normal activities as well as from all food. *The elders* are specifically mentioned because of the influence they held in the community. There is at least a suggestion here, incidentally, that there are times of national crisis when spiritual leaders should take the initiative in calling on political and other leaders to cry out to God.

When Joel says *Sanctify a fast*, he sounds a note which he will take up again in greater detail later (2:12–17), when we shall look more fully at its significance. Here it serves to emphasize the need for everyone together in one place (*the house of the LORD*) to cry out to God. A day of fasting is probably envisaged, without the distractions of preparing, consuming and clearing away food and without the cares and responsibilities of work. Fasting, apart from anything else, sharpens spiritual sensitivity. Solemn assemblies were an integral part of the people's major festivals:[23] to call a solemn assembly on such an occasion, when the festivities were plainly impossible, indicated (to God and to everyone) that these were unique circumstances – we are here not to celebrate, but to cry out to God.

[23] *Cf.* Lv. 23:36; Nu. 29:35; Dt. 16:8.

The direction of the cries is crucial. In words from God through Zechariah a significant question is put to the people and to the priests: 'When you fasted and mourned in the fifth month and in the seventh, for these seventy years, was it for me that you fasted?' (Zc. 7:5). The sheer repetition of a day of fasting twice a year for seventy years could well have moved the focus away from crying out to God. Joel here is looking for just one day directed towards God.

Joel himself sets the example for his people: *Unto thee, O Lord, I cry* (19) – another way in which he demonstrates his qualities of leadership in the national crisis, never requiring of anyone (or everyone) else what he is not prepared to initiate himself. There is probably a barb in the tail of his comments, because his last word is: *Even the wild beasts cry to thee* (20). The suggestion, hardly veiled, is that irrational beasts know what to do in a catastrophe – and they also know where to direct their cries. But what about human beings? What about the people of God? Do we cry out to God? If not, why not? Joel's words give a whole new meaning to the roar of a hungry lion or the trumpeting of an elephant bereaved of her young.

6. The urgency (1:15)

Joel has one more crucial and determinative perspective to consider:

> *Alas for the day!*
> *For the day of the Lord is near,*
> *and as destruction from the Almighty it comes* (15).

The day of the Lord is Joel's main message. It is the hinge of the whole book; it is the hinge for each section of the book. Whatever else Joel has said or will say about the impact of the locust invasion, it is all in the perspective of this great day of the Lord. Although we shall return to this theme several times,[24] it is important to develop a basic understanding of its meaning and significance, both in the overall teaching of the Bible and in the specific content of Joel's message.

Joel's approach is summed up in his introductory word, *Alas!* It is a word reflecting the sound of a person being winded by a thumping blow to the stomach – that distinctive release of breath which expresses pain and astonishment: it causes extreme distress, not least because it takes us completely by surprise. When Joel introduces the day of the Lord with that little word *Alas!*, he knows that he is about to cause the people of God a combination of deep pain and great astonishment: *The day of the Lord is near – Alas!*

[24] See comments on 2:1–2, 11, 31; 3:14.

In contrast to what the people of God in Joel's time might have believed about this day of the LORD – that it would bring them nothing but victory and vindication – the prophet says that it is *a day of destruction from the Almighty*, destruction on themselves. They knew it would mean destruction for all the enemies of God: this suggestion was both astonishing and distressing in equal measure.

If Joel was an early prophet, he would have agreed with Amos, who used his usual trenchancy to declare:

> Woe to you who desire the day of the LORD!
>> Why would you have the day of the LORD?
> It is darkness, and not light;
>> as if a man fled from a lion,
>> and a bear met him;
> or went into a house and leaned with his hand against the wall,
>> and a serpent bit him.
> Is not the day of the LORD darkness, and not light,
>> and gloom with no brightness in it? (Am. 5:18–20).

If Joel was a late prophet, he would have endorsed similar words by Malachi (4:1).

Popular understanding saw the day of the LORD basically in terms of Almighty God celebrating his sovereignty by a complete eradication of all forces, nations and individuals opposed to him. This perception was probably rooted in a common notion that a commander worth the name could rout his enemy in a single day. Once the LORD decided to do that, his enemies would simply capitulate and vanish – veritably 'the day of the LORD'.

Within such an understanding, Joel's contemporaries would have seen the locust plague as the result of God's enemies having their day – but the LORD would act on behalf of his people to deliver them. This conviction may well have been seriously undermined as the impact of the catastrophe went on and on: but one day God would act ... No, says Joel, we are not *waiting* for the day of the LORD; this catastrophe is evidence that the day of the LORD is upon us. Nor is this the end. The worst is yet to come.

It is hard to appreciate how devastating such a message would have been to an already demoralized people. The day of the LORD comes, not as a day of deliverance, but as a day of destruction. The Hebrew text actually has a powerful play on words in the last phrase of verse 15; the word for destruction is *šōḏ* the word for Almighty is *šaddai*. Different attempts have been made to capture this wordplay in English, such as 'a mighty ruin from the Almighty', 'overpowering from the

Overpowerer', 'devastation from the Devastator', 'a shattering from Shaddai'.[25]

The people had, in effect, taken the day of the LORD and attempted to make it their own, interpreting its significance for their own benefit and ignoring its exact and only meaning, to wit, that the LORD's day is *his* day: 'He writes the script and he acts it out.'[26]

What then is the biblical script for the day of the LORD? Its origins are necessarily obscure, especially because it is so difficult to date the prophecy of Joel, which is steeped in this theme. 'The Day of the Lord was a traditional theme and various prophets used a set stock of phrases to describe it. If Joel preceded Isaiah, he could have coined the phraseology.'[27] The oldest datable reference is the passage from Amos (5:18–20) already mentioned (eighth century BC), by which time the concept was already so well established that Amos could introduce it without explanation: indeed, the people longed for it.[28]

It will be helpful to quote three passages in full at this point:

> Enter into the rock,
>   and hide in the dust
> from before the terror of the LORD,
>   and from the glory of his majesty.
> The haughty looks of man shall be brought low,
>   and the pride of men shall be humbled;
> and the LORD alone will be exalted in that day.

> For the LORD of hosts has a day
>   against all that is proud and lofty,
>   against all that is lifted up and high;
> against all the cedars of Lebanon,
>   lofty and lifted up;
>   and against all the oaks of Bashan;
> against all the high mountains,
>   and against all the lofty hills;
> against every high tower,
>   and against every fortified wall;
> against all the ships of Tarshish,
>   and against all the beautiful craft.
> And the haughtiness of man shall be humbled,

---

[25] Allen, p. 59; Bewer, quoted by Dillard; Dillard, p. 266; Patterson (*EBC*), p. 243.
[26] Hubbard, p. 37.   [27] Finley, pp. 35–36.
[28] There are twenty-eight references in Isaiah. The phrase is also found in Jeremiah (46:10), Ezekiel (7.5ff.; 30:2), Zephaniah (1:7–18), Obadiah (15), Zechariah (9:14; 14:1–7) and Malachi (3:2, 17; 4:1–5).

and the pride of men shall be brought low;
  and the LORD alone will be exalted in that day.
And the idols shall utterly pass away.
And men shall enter the caves of the rocks
  and the holes of the ground,
from before the terror of the LORD,
  and from the glory of his majesty
  when he rises to terrify the earth (Is. 2:10–19).

Wail, for the day of the LORD is near;
  as destruction from the Almighty it will come!
Therefore all hands will be feeble,
  and every man's heart will melt,
  and they will be dismayed.
Pangs and agony will seize them;
  they will be in anguish like a woman in travail.
They will look aghast at one another;
  their faces will be aflame.

Behold, the day of the LORD comes,
  cruel, with wrath and fierce anger,
to make the earth a desolation
  and to destroy its sinners from it.
For the stars of the heavens and their constellations
  will not give their light;
the sun will be dark at its rising
  and the moon will not shed its light.
I will punish the world for its evil,
  and the wicked for their iniquity;
I will put an end to the pride of the arrogant,
  and lay low the haughtiness of the ruthless.
I will make men more rare than fine gold,
  and mankind than the gold of Ophir.
Therefore I will make the heavens tremble,
  and the earth will be shaken out of its place,
at the wrath of the LORD of hosts
  in the day of his fierce anger.
And like a hunted gazelle,
  or like sheep with none to gather them,
every man will turn to his own people,
  and every man will flee to his own land.
Whoever is found will be thrust through,
  and whoever is caught will fall by the sword.
Their infants will be dashed in pieces
  before their eyes;

their houses will be plundered
and their wives ravished (Is. 13:6–16).

Thus says the LORD God: Disaster after disaster! Behold, it comes. An end has come, the end has come; it has awakened against you. Behold, it comes. Your doom has come to you, O inhabitant of the land; the time has come, the day is near, a day of tumult and not of joyful shouting upon the mountains. Now I will soon pour out my wrath upon you, and spend my anger against you, and judge you according to your ways; and I will punish you for all your abominations. And my eye will not spare, nor will I have pity; I will punish you according to your ways, while your abominations are in your midst. Then you will know that I am the Lord, who smite.

Behold, the day! Behold, it comes! Your doom has come, injustice has blossomed, pride has budded. Violence has grown up into a rod of wickedness; none of them shall remain, nor their abundance, nor their wealth; neither shall there be pre-eminence among them. The time has come, the day draws near. Let not the buyer rejoice, nor the seller mourn, for wrath is upon all their multitude. For the seller shall not return to what he has sold, while they live. For wrath is upon all their multitude; it shall not turn back; and because of his iniquity, none can maintain his life (Ezk. 7:5–13).

These particular passages exemplify the consistent message of the Old Testament prophets about the day of the LORD. Frequently there were false prophets,[29] who held out nothing but hope to the people of God, hope that the day of the LORD would be a day of light and joy. True, the glory of the LORD was also to be revealed on that day, but it was neither appropriate nor accurate to describe such a revelation as unalloyed joy and peace. Those who spoke the word of the LORD to the people invariably stressed that, whatever the day would bring for cities and nations opposed to him, it would be a day of reckoning for *all* sin – whoever had committed it. The LORD's face had, for all time, been set against human pride, arrogance and haughtiness. They might have their day now, whether in achievements or in abundance of material possessions; but God's day was coming and it would be a day 'against' every expression and every emblem of human pride.

Joel was in the vanguard of this prophetic movement. In the context of the locust plague he is forcing into the open a fundamental question: is this the hand of God? For any Israelite locked into only

---

[29] See Je. 14:13–18; 23:23–40; 27:8–22; Ezk. 13:1–23; Mi. 3:5–12.

one way of interpreting the terms of the covenant and contemporary events, such a thought was unthinkable, even blasphemous. But for Joel, the absence of grain, wine and oil from the community, and the absence of gladness, worship and praise from the sanctuary, together said only one thing: the day of the LORD is at hand – and it is going to get very dark indeed. We have not seen anything yet.

There could, then, be no more powerful incentive to cry out to God. This present disaster could be the harbinger of still worse disasters. It hardly bears thinking about, but, when the word of the LORD becomes a reality in such terms, 'who can but prophesy?' (Am. 3:8).

Before we move on to chapter 2 and further examination of Joel's understanding of the day of the LORD, there is one further question to be directly addressed: did God send the locusts? So far in this study we have stepped all round this challenge. The words in 2:25 are determinative for answering our key question. Yes, God did send the locusts: in that verse he describes them as *my great army, which I sent among you.* We still, of course, have to wrestle with the meaning of such a statement, both for Joel's time and for us today.[30]

Nevertheless, such a bald and shocking answer is consistent with a crucial cameo in Amos:

Thus the Lord GOD showed me: behold, he was forming locusts in the beginning of the shooting up of the latter growth; and lo, it was the latter growth after the king's mowings. When they had finished eating the grass of the land, I said,

'O Lord GOD, forgive, I beseech thee!
How can Jacob stand?
He is so small!'
The LORD repented concerning this;
'It shall not be,' said the LORD (Am. 7:1–3).

The word translated 'was forming' in this passage is vivid and seminal. The action of forming a locust swarm is 'something only God can do'.[31] Amos was a farmer himself, so his language is particularly interesting. Earlier in the book he used the same word in a creative sense:

---

[30] See also Am. 4:9:
'I smote you with blight and mildew;
I laid waste your gardens and your vineyards;
your fig-trees and your olive-trees the locust devoured;
yet you did not return to me,'
says the LORD.

[31] Finley, p. 282.

> For lo, he who forms the mountains, and creates the wind,
> and declares to man what is his thought . . .
> the LORD, the God of hosts, is his name! (Am. 4:13).

It is, also, the same word in the Genesis account of creation: 'Then the LORD God formed man of dust from the ground, and breathed into his nostrils the breath of life; and man became a living being' (Gn. 2:7).

To see and to worship the LORD God as this kind of sovereign, almighty creator is, perhaps, to fly in the face of much contemporary thinking; but it has the merit of rescuing particular passages, in both Old and New Testaments,[32] from the ruins of oblivion. Some stunning phrases from Isaiah come into this category:

> I am the LORD, and there is no other.
> I form light and create darkness,
> I make weal and create woe,
> I am the LORD, who do all these things (Is. 45:6–7).

The same chapter continues immediately with a challenge to mere mortals who dare to question God about 'the work of my hands': 'Does the clay say to him who fashions it, "What are you making?"' (Is. 45:9).

Joel urges his contemporaries to cry to the LORD. Cry from your helplessness. Cry with all your agony and desolation. Cry to the LORD who is the only God. Cry to the one who formed all things, including the locusts; who formed you out of the dust; who formed you for himself. Cry with a heart ready to listen rather than to argue or justify. Cry in humble admission that you have nowhere else to turn and that you are utterly dependent on the mercy of God.

That is the practical implication of living in relationship with the LORD God as the first cause of all that is and has been and will be. It is not that secondary causes are unknown to biblical writers such as Joel, but they force us back to God himself as sovereign Lord. That means that, when we meet circumstances like those facing the people of Joel's day, we turn to God and cry to him for mercy and help in our time of need.

[32] See Acts 2:23; Rev. 8:7ff.

Joel 2:1–17
2. Return to God

Crying to God is not the same as returning to God. In his determination to be a faithful, not a false, prophet to the people, Joel has issued the first call – the call to his contemporaries to follow his lead (and that of the wild beasts) and to cry out to the LORD. That is a necessary first step. In the first part of chapter 2 he moves from another startling description of the national catastrophe to a clear message from the LORD himself (12–13). In crying out to the LORD they needed to be listening to him. Now he speaks – and the message is: *return to me* (2:12). The LORD is looking for a people who will not only cry out to him, but who will return to him with all their heart.

1. The dark future (2:1–11)

In the first eleven verses we have a vivid narrative of events in the land (2b–11a), flanked on either side by descriptions of the day of the LORD (1–2a, 11b).[1] As the prophet looks out on all the devastation across the land, he is convinced that *the day of the LORD is coming, it is near* (1). As he watches swarms of locusts riding high on the wind and blotting out the sun (2: *Like blackness there is spread upon the mountains a great and powerful people*; NIV 'army'), he pronounces that the day of the LORD will be *a day of darkness and gloom, a day of clouds and thick darkness!* (2).

In other words and on a larger scale, Joel sees the day of the LORD as an occurrence in people's lives for which he provides many advance warnings and many substantial foretastes. God is at work in all kinds of ways, which not so much pre-empt as prefigure the day

---

[1] 'At this juncture in the text, commentators have a major choice to make. They can read 2:1–11 as an account of a military invasion of which the locusts in ch. 1 are precursors; or they can read it as a more dramatic semi-apocalyptic account which itself is a harbinger of the Day. A third option would be to read the entire work as a cluster of figurative descriptions of military incursion' (Hubbard, p. 53 note).

of the LORD. In this sense it is true to say that the day of the LORD, for Joel, applied to what was happening then, what was about to happen soon and what eventually would happen when God called the nations to account.

This triple perspective will become more apparent as we follow Joel's prophecy right through. It holds good, in fact, for the entire biblical account of the day of the LORD, New Testament as much as Old. Any way in which God significantly moves in our lives may properly be called the day of the LORD. There are, also, major events – perhaps more in the progress of cities, nations and empires than in the experience of individuals – which are defining moments of truth, in which God's verdict on a particular country, city or system is made plain. This, too, is the day of the LORD and it is invariably a time of judgment.

But there is one great day, a day which is fixed by God, and is known only to God, when the whole world will be summoned before his throne. He will then make the ultimate decisions about every person's eternal destiny, based on the primary choices each has made in relation to God and his Word. The Old Testament is eloquent and vivid in its description of this great assize, but the New Testament takes it much further, in particular by seeing it as revolving around the Lord Jesus Christ. 'The O.T. eschatological expression "the Day of the Lord" is appropriated by Paul and made Christological. It is still "the Day of the Lord", but the Lord is none other than Jesus Christ.'[2]

'The day of the Lord is any day God steps into history to do a special work, whether of judgement or deliverance.'[3] For Joel, the locust plague feels like an inexorable build-up to such a day for Israel. The first thing to do is to *sound the alarm*; *Blow the trumpet in Zion* (1).

Listening to the BBC World Service recently, I discovered that in the British Army there are thirty-two different trumpet and bugle calls (trumpets for the cavalry, bugles for the infantry). Each call is distinctive and sounds a different message, readily identified by the troops, from Reveille to the Last Post. It was not that different among the people of Israel. In earlier times the LORD had given instructions to Moses about 'two silver trumpets': 'You shall use them for summoning the congregation, and for breaking camp.' More specific instructions are given within these two broad categories, some to do with blowing one trumpet only and some to do with blowing an alarm. 'An alarm is to be blown whenever they

[2] Gordon Fee, *1 Corinthians*, The New International Commentary on the New Testament (Eerdmans, 1987), p. 43.

[3] R. L. Alden, 'Malachi', in *Expositor's Bible Commentary* 7, ed. Frank Gaebelein (Zondervan, 1985), p. 719.

are to set out': only certain calls were alarm calls and they were to do with getting on the move. For example, 'when you go to war in your land against the adversary who oppresses you, then you shall sound an alarm with the trumpets, that you may be remembered before the LORD your God, and you shall be saved from your enemies' (see Nu. 10:1–10). This is God's trumpet call, through Joel, sounding the alarm on Mount Zion. There is war in the land. The adversary has invaded and is on the rampage. All the people must be warned. God himself needs to be reminded to act to save his people.

But the shocking, though gradual, revelation in Joel 2 is that the people are fighting against God himself: *The LORD utters his voice before his army* (11). The trumpet is blown to bring their disastrous situation to God's notice and to invoke his saving power, but then God himself appears as commander of the forces wreaking havoc in the land. This is followed by another surprise: God speaks to the people in tones of reconciliation, pleading to them to return to him. This, in turn, moves Joel to issue a second trumpet call (15). This time it is not an alarm call, because the war situation has been averted by the peacemaking initiative of God just recorded. So this is a trumpet call for gathering the people together. The situation is desperate.

> *Like blackness there is spread upon the mountains*
> *a great and powerful people* [or 'army'];
> *their like has never been from of old,*
> *nor will be again after them*
> *through the years of all generations* (2).

If ever the alarm should be sounded, it was now. Nothing in previous years approached this invasion for sheer size and terror: this was 'the big one', the catastrophe to end all catastrophes.

Such a dark day – *a day of darkness and gloom, a day of clouds and thick darkness!* – demands a loud, long trumpet blast: *Let all the inhabitants of the land tremble* (2). Nobody will escape and therefore everybody must hear the alarm. Joel sees himself as a watchman on the city walls, standing as a prophet placed there by the LORD with clear instructions to warn the people of impending disaster. 'The prophet is the watchman of . . . the people of my God' (Ho. 9:8).

The church of God as a whole has the responsibility to act as this watchman to the nation. Particular individuals are to carry out that responsibility as Christians in their own sphere of influence – at work, at school, in the community, in the corridors of power. It is a difficult and often lonely calling. But, in the words of the former president of Zambia, Kenneth Kaunda: 'What a nation needs is not so much a Christian ruler on the throne, but a Christian prophet in the palace' – to be the ruler's watchman, to whom the ruler can go with the question put to the prophet Isaiah: 'Watchman, what of the night? Watchman, what of the night?' (Is. 21:11). And it certainly is a question worth asking again and again.

Such watchmen tend to have abbreviated careers and abrupt ends, like John the Baptist, Stephen and Jesus himself. It is a perilous task to blow the trumpet anywhere, to sound the alarm when a country, a city, a company, a community is heading for the abyss. In purely secular terms, whistleblowing has become a major concern – mainly because general standards of behaviour have degenerated to the point where integrity and trust have been seriously eroded. As I write, Parliament at Westminster is at the point of passing new legislation to protect those who blow the whistle on unethical practices, so that they are not penalized in any way. There is no such guarantee for Christian watchmen who blow the trumpet, but they take their orders from another King and will stand before a higher court – like Ezekiel, Zephaniah[4] and Joel.[5]

It is when we get to the book of the Revelation of John that the full eschatological significance of such trumpet calls is made plain. One specific passage has direct relevance to Joel's exegesis of the meaning of the locust plague. It also helps us understand his teaching about the day of the LORD and the way it coheres with the rest of biblical material on the theme.

And the fifth angel blew his trumpet, and I saw a star fallen from heaven to earth, and he was given the key of the shaft of the bottomless pit, and from the shaft rose smoke like the smoke of a great furnace, and the sun and the air were darkened with the smoke from the shaft. Then from the smoke came locusts from the earth, and they were given power like the power of scorpions of the earth; they were told not to harm the grass of the earth or any green growth or any tree, but only those of mankind who have not the seal of God upon their foreheads; they were allowed to torture them for five months, but not to kill them, and their torture was like the torture of a scorpion, when it stings a man. And in those days men will seek death and will not find it; they will long to die, and death will fly from them.

In appearance the locusts were like horses arrayed for battle; on their heads were what looked like crowns of gold; their faces were like human faces, their hair like women's hair, and their teeth like lion's teeth; they had scales like iron breastplates, and the

[4] See Zp. 1:7–18.
[5] For New Testament references to the trumpet call of God, leading to the day of judgment, see Mt. 10:14–15; 11:20–24; 24:30–31; 1 Cor. 15:51–52; 1 Thes. 4:16–17.

noise of their wings was like the noise of many chariots with horses rushing into battle. They have tails like scorpions, and stings, and their power of hurting men for five months lies in their tails. They have as king over them the angel of the bottomless pit; his name in Hebrew is Abaddon, and in Greek he is called Apollyon [or Destroyer] (Rev. 9:1–11).

The similarities to Joel's description are uncanny, remarkable, and not a little frightening. The effects of evil are profound, powerful and prolonged. They do not just run into the sand, but bring indescribable misery and agony. Behind all evil, moreover, is a presiding genius, who is orchestrating his forces for maximum destruction. There is, notwithstanding, both a greater authority and an ultimate terminus, when God himself will demonstrate that he has said, 'So far, and no further.' Evil is having its day, but the day of the LORD is the last day and the great day.

Joel, however, lives and speaks before the coming of Christ. He sees the day of the LORD as *very terrible* (11). He cannot see how anyone could possibly *endure* such a day, let alone look forward to it. To him it looks like an irretrievably appalling prospect, presaged by these insect agents who invade *like a thief* (9).

> *The earth quakes before them,*
> *the heavens tremble.*
> *The sun and moon are darkened,*
> *and the stars withdraw their shining* (10).

'The whole fabric of the universe trembles and nature clothes itself in mourning.'[6]

It is the voice of the LORD that is heard, giving commands to his troops:

> *The LORD utters his voice*
> *before his army,*
> *for his host is exceedingly great:*
> *he that executes his word is powerful* (11).

The locusts are executioners of the purposes and commands of God. The land is devastated. The people are devastated. The prophet is devastated. This is (all but) the day of the LORD: *who can endure it?* (11). Nobody will escape.

Or will they? Could anyone escape the day of the LORD? Could anyone endure the day of the LORD?

[6] Keil, p. 195.

> The LORD is the true God;
>> he is the living God and the everlasting King.
> At his wrath the earth quakes,
>> and the nations cannot endure his indignation (Je. 10:10).

2. A glimmer of hope (2:12–17)

It is difficult to conceive of any situation darker and more hopeless than the one facing Joel and his contemporaries. It is into this extreme disaster that the LORD speaks:

> *'Yet even now,' says the LORD,*
>> *'return to me with all your heart,*
> *with fasting, with weeping and with mourning;*
> *and rend your hearts and not your garments'* (2:12–13).

Yet even now . . . It is never too late or too dark for God to speak such a word into our situation, except, that is, when by definition it is too late because 'the last trumpet' has sounded. Here we find the same God who, as commander of the locust army ravaging the land, has issued marching orders for troops on a mission of destruction, now taking the initiative to issue an invitation to the people to turn back to him.

Unless God is held responsible for the destruction of the land, the people can have no assurance that turning to him can have any impact. If the whole scenario is seen to be haphazard, sheer 'bad luck', the utter meaninglessness at the heart of the universe is grimly accentuated. If God is not held responsible, it means that some other force or being is – whether fate or Mother Nature or Baal or some other deity. Praying to God then becomes an exercise in pious wishful thinking, based presumably on the hope that he is aware of the situation, concerned about it, willing to act and able to overcome the forces responsible. The evidence, if God is not held responsible for such events, is that God would not necessarily be in line for any of these four things.

But it is quite a different matter to turn to the one who is in charge of everything and is, therefore, responsible for what has happened, especially if we have good reason to believe that he is open to such an approach. In this situation facing Joel and his contemporaries, they have God's own invitation to return to him. The very word, *return*, reminds them that they have been down this route before and therefore they know what God is like. They also know what it is like to be close to him, rather than far away from him – as they clearly are now. Even more than that, they know what kind of God he is from previous experience – a fact which Joel is swift to impress upon them (13).[7]

God is not looking for specific acts of atonement, either in ritual sacrifices or in good deeds. He wants his people back with him, at his side, enjoying his presence, basking in his favour. Everything else will flow from that. He does not, at this stage, even want to enter into any discussion or to spell out a diagnosis of the problem. He wants them to come back to him.

This is the story, in New Testament terms, of the prodigal son – or, better, the prodigal Father.[8] This is the father-heart of God: 'In thee the orphan finds mercy' (Ho. 14:3). The LORD has never changed: from that evening in the garden of Eden when he called out to Adam, 'Where are you?' (Gn. 3:9), right through to the closing invitation of the book of Revelation, 'The Spirit and the Bride say, "Come"' (Rev. 22:17). The invitation is the same: *return to me.*

The LORD wants Joel and all the people to understand that such a return is to be *with all your heart* (12), because he will settle for nothing less than such a heart-to-heart relationship.[9] He will brook no rivals. The LORD is like a jealous husband. He has taken them to be his bride and he wants their hearts. He longs for them to return with *all* their hearts; but he also makes it clear to them that they must *rend* their *hearts* (13); he wants a whole heart and he wants a broken heart. These two qualities, wholeheartedness and brokenhearted-ness, in fact describe the heart of God for his people, for everyone indeed created in his image. He wants our heart to be as his heart, something he had found in David, 'a man after my own heart'.[10]

What, then, is the significance of the words *with fasting, with weep-ing, and with mourning* (12)? Do they contradict the instruction to *rend your hearts and not your garments* (13)? Is there a place for external acts of contrition? If there is, what is it? The short answer is that, where the heart is properly broken, outward acts are entirely appropriate. The problem comes when people can 'switch on' the rele-vant actions without a corresponding contrition of heart. This is the dilemma of all regular acts of worship, whether liturgical or non-liturgical. Any outward action can degenerate into routine or cere-monial, reflecting nothing internal and therefore anathema to God:

> I hate, I despise your feasts,
>   and I take no delight in your solemn assemblies (Am. 5:21).

---

[7] *Cf.* Ex. 34:5–7.   [8] Lk. 15:11–32.

[9] This is 'the great and first commandment', to 'love the Lord your God with all your heart . . . soul, and . . . mind' (Mt. 22:38).

[10] The condition of David's heart before God makes a fascinating study; see 1 Sa. 13:14; 16:7, followed by references in psalms attributed to David to the state of his heart before God: *e.g.* Pss. 9:1; 34:18; 51:10, 17; 86:12.

The outward actions enjoined by God – fasting, weeping and mourning – are all to do with dying and death. They describe actions normally associated with bereavement, threatened or actual.[11] As we have seen, God here is concerned with the death of a relationship, his heart-to-heart relationship with his people. It has died a death. He is heartbroken. He wants his people to recognize that this relationship is dead, to let the impact of this break their hearts, and to return to him. Fasting, weeping and mourning are entirely apt in such a situation, whereas merely to tear one's clothes in an external show of sorrow would be entirely inappropriate.

Part of the hesitation over outward demonstrations of repentance (and rejoicing, in fact) can often be attributed to our culture and upbringing, rather than to any spiritual or biblical sensitivities. Only a fairly buttoned-up person emotionally can be heartbroken, as God is heartbroken, about their dying or dead relationship with God, and give no outward indication that anything might be amiss. One of the surer signs of true repentance and the work of God's Spirit in the hearts of people, especially perhaps many Anglo-Saxon males, is genuine weeping.

This, then, is the word from God into Joel's situation. Only such a word can halt the devastation. Joel has heard what the LORD has to say to his people. His response is threefold.

a. Assurance by the prophet (2:13–14)

Joel picks up the LORD's appeal to the nation:

> Return to the LORD, your God,
>   for he is gracious and merciful,
> slow to anger, and abounding in steadfast love,
>   and repents of evil (13).

Joel knows that a person's word depends entirely on his or her character. The same appeal from a capricious, calculating deity would have been worthless, if not misleading and pernicious. The prophet thus points the people to the covenant-making and covenant-keeping God; *your* God specifically emphasizes the personal relationship between the LORD and his people.

In describing what God is like, Joel rehearses the characteristics which the LORD himself stressed to Moses on Mount Sinai after the people had turned against him in the idolatry of the golden calf:

---

[11] See, for example, the action of David immediately before the death of the child born to Bathsheba (2 Sa. 16 – 17) and at the death of Absalom (2 Sa. 18:31 – 19:4).

And the LORD descended in the cloud and stood with him there, and proclaimed the name of the LORD. The LORD passed before him, and proclaimed, 'The LORD, the LORD, a God merciful and gracious, slow to anger and abounding in steadfast love and faithfulness, keeping steadfast love for thousands, forgiving iniquity and transgression and sin, but who will by no means clear the guilty, visiting the iniquity of the fathers upon the children and the children's children, to the third and the fourth generation' (Ex. 34:5–7).

The people of Israel had taken less than forty days to break the covenant which God had initiated with them in giving them the Ten Commandments and committing himself to be their God and the God of their children for ever. Could the relationship be rescued? It was into this situation that God descended and spoke, affirming his 'name' or changeless character. From that point onwards it could never be doubted that God is not like human beings. They had been faithless to the covenant; but he remained faithful to the covenant. God does not change.

Instead of citing God's assertion to Moses that he 'will by no means clear the guilty', Joel adds a phrase to this description of God: *and repents of evil.* This is not a straightforward phrase, but its meaning is probably rooted in the events following the golden calf,[12] when Moses pleads with the LORD not to destroy all the people. As a result of his intercessory passion, the LORD relents and promises a future and a hope in a restored relationship, albeit with somewhat restricted expression. Moses thereby established the effectiveness of prayer in our relationship with God, particularly in terms of moving God to lean towards pardon when everything calls for punishment – 'in wrath remember mercy' (Hab. 3:2).

This is the basis of Joel's assurance to the people that *Yet even now* (12) it is timely to return to the LORD. When you know that you have consistently and completely alienated someone (a parent, a partner, a friend), it is difficult to believe that you will receive a favourable response when you finally decide to build bridges again. Joel says, *Return to the LORD, your God*; you can trust him, even if you know that you do not deserve his mercy. Joel assures them that there is nothing to lose, everything to gain. He is *your God* and he is moved with compassion for you.[13]

Joel, for his part, believes that God has a *blessing* for the people. But he cannot be absolutely sure: hence the intriguing phrase, *Who*

---

[12] Ex. 32:1–35.
[13] It is the moving impulse in much of the ministry of Jesus; *e.g.* Mt. 9:36; 14:14; 15:32.

knows...? (14). Two kings in the Old Testament used this evocative phrase, each when faced with a devastating blow. The king of the Assyrian city of Nineveh was so shaken by God's message through Jonah, that the city would be destroyed within forty days, that he ordered a time of national fasting and repentance: 'Who knows, God may yet repent and turn away from his fierce anger, so that we perish not?' (Jon. 3:9). David, king of Jerusalem, faced by Nathan's exposure of his sins of adultery with Bathsheba and of murdering Uriah, followed by a word through the prophet that Bathsheba's child by him would die, said: 'Who knows whether the LORD will be gracious to me, that the child may live?' (2 Sa. 12:22).

Who knows? reflects, therefore, a contrite, broken heart. The prayer which comes from such a heart, however convinced it is of the unchanging character of God, can never be overconfident about any particular request. Even repentance from a contrite heart cannot guarantee a positive response from God: we are still entirely dependent on his grace. One of the balancing acts in Christian prayer is to combine faith with humility, to ask with confidence but to refrain from insisting on what we want.

Joel seems to visualize the LORD's hand as now raised against the people, at the head of the invading hordes of his *army*. If the people return to him, perhaps *he will... turn and repent, and leave a blessing behind him*; that is, he will relent, turn back and (instead of leaving a further trail of destruction) leave a substantial blessing. This *blessing* would be in sharp contrast to the 'curses' now plaguing the land.[14]

The blessing, at first glance, looks trivial: *a cereal offering and a drink offering for the LORD, your God.* But, in fact, it is the essence of everything the people should have longed for – everything that has been withheld in the current judgment: the resources to restore a daily expression in the temple of their relationship with the LORD (1:9, 13).

This blessing of communion with God is the most important we can ever receive: this is true gladness. To be deprived of the ability to know God and to enjoy him is to be as good as dead. Joel's hope of blessing is, therefore, a masterly understatement; but it forces us to question what counts as a true blessing for us. Are we obsessed with material blessings, to the neglect or devaluation of true spiritual blessing? And do we see material blessings as further opportunity to get on with our daily service to God?

---

[14] The language is probably a reference to the chapter on blessings and curses in Dt. 28.

b. Assembly by the people (2:15–16)

Joel's second response to the LORD's words to the people is to call for the people to return, not one by one, but together. So Joel calls for the trumpet to be blown a second time – not, as before, to sound the alarm because an invader is in the land; but to gather all the people together at the temple, to summon the congregation.[15] Joel gives eight staccato commands in two verses. He may, like any true messenger of God, be humble or even hesitant before the LORD; but he is direct and definite before the people, including their leaders.

Gathering at the temple is the way for the people, in practice, to return to the LORD. Left to each individual to make an inward journey back to God, the return would have been half-hearted, unreliable, and unverifiable. For the people to return to the LORD with all their heart meant that all the people needed to go together to one place at one time. Western individualism tends to jib at such mass movements. Our assumption is that any collective action necessarily has an element of manipulation or hysteria or both.

Joel thus reiterates and expands his earlier instructions (1:14). This is to be a day of fasting and it is to be a solemn assembly. The *elders* must be there – but also *the children, even nursing infants*. Nobody can plead any more important business – not even newlyweds: *Let the bridegroom leave his room, and the bride her chamber.* One of the law's striking provisions entitled a man to exemption from military service for a year after his wedding.[16] This solemn assembly held precedence over both marriage bed and military duty.

This is the force, also, of the double use of *sanctify: sanctify a fast . . . Sanctify the congregation.* The time needs to be set apart and made distinct; the whole people need to be set apart and made distinct. This consecration of the nation, from the oldest to the youngest, underlines 'the corporate nature of the guilt'[17] which was lying on the people. Without knowing what particular sins were prevalent in Joel's day, we see again the contaminating impact of breaking God's laws. The infants at the breast, though obviously innocent of specific sins, were implicated in the sin of the nation in turning away from God.

The nub of the matter in such *a solemn assembly* lay not simply in its being required by God, however harsh and bitter the circumstances, but in the expectation that God would also be there. God was not necessarily present at such an assembly. They were prescribed in the law, granted, but if the people as a whole had forsaken the LORD, God's word was uncompromising: 'I cannot endure [the combination of] iniquity and solemn assembly' (Is.

---

[15] Cf. Nu. 10:2.   [16] Dt. 24:5.   [17] Hubbard, p. 181.

1:13); 'I hate, I despise your feasts, and I take no delight in your solemn assemblies' (Am. 5:21).

This solemn assembly was to be different. Sanctifying the people would sort out any such hypocrisy. The preparations for this assembly would act as a purgative.[18] God would be there and would delight to be there. The words he spoke through Amos literally mean, 'I do not like to smell' your solemn assemblies – referring to the multitude of animal sacrifices, along with cereal offerings and drink offerings, which played such a major part in these gatherings[19] and which were normally 'a sweet-smelling odour to the LORD'.

At Joel's solemn assembly these sacrifices, together with the cereal offerings and the drink offerings, would be unavailable, or scarcely and skimpily available. The locust plague had seen to that. The people were expected to gather for this special solemn assembly without most, if not all, of the ingredients normally central to its effectiveness. The people knew that. The prophet knew that. The priests knew that. It would have been so easy not to gather. In gathering under such circumstances and facing such bitter reality, the people were indicating a truly wholehearted and brokenhearted return to God. Is this where Joel's *Who knows . . .?* would be gloriously fulfilled? Would the LORD visit this solemn assembly and leave behind *a cereal offering and a drink offering?* What a blessing that would be!

It all amounted to the 'obedience of faith'.[20] God, through Joel, was saying, 'Assemble . . . and see what happens.' That is usually where God's people find themselves in any generation, particularly when the circumstances require them to come together to seek his face for mercy. We come because he calls us together. We come because we believe that he will be there also – either welcoming us as we gather, or coming among us once we are together. The important thing is to come with expectancy, setting ourselves apart from everyday and extra-special events in order to be together in one place as the people of God.

Today we find it easier to do that for times of praise than for times of penitence, for celebration rather than confession, to express gratitude for all the marvellous things God has done rather than grief for all the miserable things we have done. But if God requires it, we must do it.

---

[18] *Cf.* the LORD's instructions to Moses, before the giving of the law at the foot of Mount Sinai, about sanctifying the people of Israel (Ex. 19:7–15).
[19] See Nu. 29:35–38.   [20] See Rom. 1:5; 16:26; Heb. 11:8.

c. Action by the priests (2:17)

Joel's third response to the LORD's words to the people is to call the priests to act. Joel had previously instructed them to get out of their splendid vestments and 'pass the night in sackcloth' (1:13). Now he gives them equally specific instructions – where to stand, what to do, and how to pray. As spiritual leaders of the nations, the priests were not accustomed to being given orders as to how to behave and what to say in the temple. They were the professionals and they were the ones who normally gave the orders when it came to religious matters and events. But Joel has a word from God for the priests as well as the people. So he delivers it.

The indications are that, until Joel brought the word of the LORD, the priests were as depressed as anyone else in the country. They were certainly in mourning (1:9), and it needed Joel to jerk them into appropriate action prior to these instructions. The stuffing had been knocked out of their daily routine. Their vocation seemed an empty charade. Their book of words had nothing but gloom and doom to speak into the catastrophe that engulfed the land. Their own daily life-style, dependent as it was on regular supplies through the sacrificial system in the temple, had fallen apart. They were a broken group of religious leaders: a pathetic sight and a pitiable group of men.

When the spiritual leadership of a community or a nation reaches this level of despair and listlessness, only a prophet can break into the inevitable leadership vacuum – with the word of the LORD. In one sense, Joel could have done everything he now challenged the priests to do. He could have stood where they stood. He could have prayed the way they prayed. But that would have been to let the priests abdicate their God-given responsibilities to stand before God as spokesmen for the people (through intercession and offering the prescribed sacrifices),[21] and to stand before the people as spokesmen for God (providing general instruction and specific guidance).[22] They were, in brief, to be mediators; and they had ceased to be that. They were no longer living up to their name as *ministers of the LORD*. They were self-serving, not God-serving.

But, to give them their due, they had donned sackcloth for a night of lamentation and self-humbling before the LORD. Now they were to take up a specific position *between the vestibule and the altar*, which was 'essentially a mediatorial position, between the altar where sacrifice was made and the dwelling of God'.[23] The privilege and the calling of priests, as *ministers of the LORD*, was to 'approach the LORD to minister to him' (Ezk. 45:4). So, says Joel, get on with

[21] See Ex. 28:29–30; Lv. 16:1–34. See also Heb. 5:1–4.
[22] See Lv. 10:8–11; Dt. 17:9; 21:5.   [23] Dillard, p. 283.

it: if ever the people needed the mediating ministry of their intercessory prayer, it was now.

The specific location indicated by Joel, although it was the
obvious and natural place from which to lead the prayers of the
people, might well have had extra significance on this occasion. The
uncertainty of the dating of Joel means we cannot know whether he
preceded or followed a striking event in the history of the Jerusalem
temple.

This is the place where the prophet Zechariah had been stoned by
the people when he stood up to say to everyone, 'Why do you
transgress the commandments of the LORD, so that you cannot
prosper?' King Joash, who hitherto had a good track record for
doing what was right in the eyes of the LORD, could not stomach
such a direct challenge, and had the prophet struck down there and
then in the temple. This led, within the year, to invasion and execution of the leadership by a small Syrian army.[24]

This incident may have remained just another sad item in the
annals of Israel, but for the dramatic words of Jesus when
confronting the hypocrisy and culpable arrogance of the scribes and
Pharisees as spiritual leaders of the people. Jesus saw them as 'the
sons of those who murdered the prophets', and warned that upon
them would come 'all the righteous blood shed on earth, from the
blood of innocent Abel to the blood of Zechariah the son of
Barachiah, whom you murdered between the sanctuary and the
altar' (Mt. 23:31–35).

It is clear that Zechariah's murder, which has been paralleled in
recent decades by the murders of Archbishop Janani Luwum in
Uganda and of Bishop Oscar Romero in El Salvador, became a
powerful part of the story of both temple and nation down the
generations. If, as is likely, Joel's ministry came some time after
Zechariah's, the priests would have been very much aware of that
particular location's bloody history.

Joel expects the intercession of the priests to come from the heart
(*weep*), not to be by rote. If the priests had become anaesthetized by
the sheer length and depth of the nation's suffering, they are now
being resensitized. Prayers out of the book, recited in deadpan or
professional voices, will not be appropriate. Joel himself indicates
the kind of prayer which will count with God. He suggests to the
priests material taken from the same source as some of the psalms
now called 'communal complaints'.[25] The book of Lamentations
also contains passages in similar vein.[26]

Joel is not, then, throwing the liturgy of the temple out of the

[24] 2 Ch. 24:20–24.   [25] *E.g.* Pss. 44; 79; 80; 89.
[26] See La. 1:12–22; 2:13–17; 3:40–51; 5:1–22.

window. It was, after all, the fruit of inspired worship down the centuries, and articulated all the ups and downs of human experience in the history of God's people. He tells the priests to recognize the unique seriousness of this national catastrophe, to allow its savage suffering to break their hearts, to take up their rightful place as spiritual leaders – and to pray as they have never prayed before.

The nub of Joel's prayer, which he must surely have been praying himself for some time, is the mercy of God and the glory of God. Neither is explicitly mentioned, but both form the ground for the intercession to be led by the priests in the temple.

The prayer begins with a cry of unreserved dependence on the mercy of the LORD: *Spare thy people, O LORD* (17). This word 'has the central idea of showing pity or compassion and is a plea for the Lord's tender feelings'.[27] All mothers and fathers know the persuasive power of a child who appeals to their feelings of compassion. Some children can do it artlessly, others deliberately; but most are effective. The very presence of toddlers, or even young babies, in the gathered congregation in the temple on that special day of prayer and fasting would have increased the impact on a God full of compassion and mercy.

So the priests are instructed to pray, *Spare thy people, O LORD*. There is here an acknowledgment that God is already embarked on a course of destruction – and justly so – but that, in his mercy, he might forgive. There is no trace of the 'easy believism' encapsulated in the cynical comment of the French writer, Renan: 'Dieu pardonnera; c'est son metier', 'God will forgive; it's his business.' There is, rather, the mood of the prophet Zephaniah, when he urged the people ('shameless nation') to assemble:

> Seek the LORD, all you humble of the land,
>   who do his commands;
> seek righteousness, seek humility;
>   perhaps you may be hidden
> on the day of the wrath of the LORD (Zp. 2:1, 3).[28]

Having leaned, first and foremost, on the mercy of God, the priests are urged by Joel to concentrate on the glory of God, to focus on the way in which God has for generations vested his reputation and his credibility in the people of Israel. So the priests are to bring to God's notice that this is *thy people . . . thy heritage* (17). Just as the LORD is not just any God, but a God full of compassion and mercy, so the people are not just any people, but a people called by his name. The LORD's glory is tied up with the people's welfare.

[27] Finley, p. 57.   [28] *Cf.* Abraham interceding for Sodom (Gn. 18:22–33).

However many times (and they were legion) the people had deliberately ignored their distinctive vocation and identity, and however many times prophets had warned them not to depend upon this special place in the affections and purposes of God, this appeal to the glory of the LORD remained a potent plea in prayer to God. Many can readily identify with the shame and the disgrace brought on the family name by wayward children. God's own name, which he had been unashamed to attach to the sons and daughters of a 'worm'[29] such as Jacob ('the God of Jacob'), was in danger of becoming *a reproach, a byword among the nations* (17).

But could it really be possible that God had renounced the covenant which he had made with his people? Could it be true? If it were so, then the piercing taunt of their enemies would be all too pointed: *Where is their God?* Joel instructs the priests to put the question directly to God:

> *Why should they say among the peoples,*
> *'Where is their God?'* (17).

Joel has already spoken of 'my God' (1:13), 'your God' (1:13–14), and 'our God' (1:16), each designation carrying its own impact and significance in the national situation. But the sneer contained in the reference by surrounding nations to *their God* carries its own nuances. Is the God of Israel simply that – or is he the God of all the earth, the God of every nation? Has he jettisoned Israel in favour of some other nation? Has he been forced to succumb to the gods of Canaan, or Assyria, or Babylon? Has he simply died, or gone away, or found more absorbing business? Or perhaps he was always a figment of overactive Israelite imagination, a creation of fertile religious aspirations, just a crutch?

Joel is urging the priests to take all these unthinkable thoughts to God in public prayer, so that priests and people can together face the facts honestly in the presence of God himself – throwing themselves on the mercy of God, but in the same breath appealing to the desire of God to guard his own reputation and to get glory for himself.

Joel has therefore brought the whole nation together into the presence of God in prayer. The LORD has taken the initiative to bring this into being. The prophet has given assurance that it is indeed time to seek the LORD. The people have responded to the instructions to assemble. The priests have taken action, as spiritual leaders, to take up intercession as their primary task. It all adds up to a glimmer of hope. What will happen? *Who knows?*

[29] See Is. 41:14.

Joel 2:18–32
3. Rejoice in God

1. The turning-point (2:18)

From this point it is clear that the tide has turned. The rest of the book is looking to the future. The vocabulary is full of *I will . . .* and *You shall . . .*[1] as the LORD speaks to his people about what lies ahead; what he will do and what they will experience. The turning-point has come with the priests leading the assembled people in intercessory prayer to the LORD, throwing themselves on his heart of mercy and appealing to his concern for his own glory.

> *Then the LORD became jealous for his land,*
> *and had pity on his people* (18).

No mention is made of an actual response by priest and people to the prophet's call. But the change in mood and substance in the rest of the book is so complete that it is right to assume that Joel's instructions were carried out to the letter. And so, with the nation still gathered at the temple for prayer, the LORD makes his response to the intercession led by the priests: *The LORD answered and said to the people . . .* (19).

The LORD was moved with jealousy for his land and pity for his people. These are the precise attributes in God's character to which the priests had been urged by Joel to appeal in prayer (17). God's jealousy, which is stressed in the rider to the second commandment about having no graven images, is as much part of God's love as his pity. God shows his love in both jealous possessiveness and in deep compassion. Both equally lead him to take action on behalf of his land and his people. He *feels* the jealousy and he *feels* the compassion, because he loves with such a passionate love.

The people had returned to the LORD with all their heart. Now

---

[1] *E.g.* 2:19, 20, 25, 28, 29, 30 (*I will*) and 2:19, 26, 27, 28 (*You shall*).

they were beginning to see the answer to Joel's tentative but hopeful question, 'Who knows whether he will not turn and repent and leave a blessing . . .?' (14).

The rest of chapter 2 (19b–32) contains the substance of the LORD's response to the people – words of promise and of hope. Most are couched in the first person singular, as Joel speaks in the style of an oracle from God: *I will . . .* The language alters temporarily, as Joel speaks himself to the land, the beasts of the field and then the people (21–24) with *the word of the LORD*. Then (25) the first person singular is resumed.

Before we look in more detail at this latter half of chapter 2, we need to glance at chapter 3 as well, because any division of the section 2:18 – 3:21 is somewhat arbitrary. The whole section, in effect, closes the door on the locust catastrophe and contains the promises of God for future years. Again the major motif is *the day of the LORD* (2:31; 3:14), but the perspective is a double thrust – the restoration of the fortunes of God's people and the judgment of the nations. The day of the LORD will see the climax of both.

Between the activity of God in putting to bed the locust invasion, with its impact on the land and on the people (19–27), and his action on the final great day of reckoning (30–32), there will be another event of great significance and immense impact – a time when, God says, *I will pour out my spirit on all flesh* (28–29).

2. Time for rejoicing (2:19–27)

Bearing in mind these three stages – what will happen now in Joel's time, what will happen at some future time, and what will happen when the day of the LORD fully comes – we look at this passage. Joel had hoped for a blessing (14). The LORD promises many blessings. It is time to rejoice in God.

a. I am sending to you grain, wine, and oil (2:19, 24)

These three products of the land constituted the people's staple diet (1:10). They had not been available for a long time. The force of the word *Behold*, followed by the present continuous tense of the verb 'send', is to let the people know that God's great reversal is already under way. They do not have to wait. What was destroyed, what had failed and languished, was being supplied in abundant measure.

Abundance is the main feature of these blessings. Nothing is stinted. There is lavish giving from a generous God, in line with the prolific blessings promised in the Old Testament, if God's people are obedient to God's word.[2] The result is that *you will be satisfied* (19) – an assurance which is repeated: *You shall eat in plenty and be satisfied* (26). In God's economy abundance leads to satisfaction, not to luxury and waste. Enough is enough – neither too little nor too much. Nobody will feel neglected, deprived or undernourished.

The same promise is reiterated:

> *The threshing floors shall be full of grain,*
> *the vats shall overflow with wine and oil* (24).

For every inhabitant of the land to be satisfied, production needed to be at full tilt. The sources of supply will be full to overflowing, so that no-one will have less than enough, which is *plenty* (26). God as creator has provided in abundance for all; there is enough and more than enough (*plenty*) to meet our need, but not our greed.

b. I will no more make you a reproach among the nations (2:19, cf. 26–27)

This had been one specific thrust of the prayer enjoined on the priests by the prophet: 'Make not thy heritage a reproach, a byword among the nations' (17). Three times the LORD promises this will not happen – *no more, never again, never again.* This promise is as fulsome and as abundant as the previous one. *My people shall never again be put to shame* (26–27).

There is a double thrust to the promise: the people will no longer have to put up with taunts and mockery; God's name will not be brought into disgrace. The LORD has indeed been touched on the raw by the prayer brought to him by the priests. If the nations were brazenly challenging the people of Israel, 'Where is your God?', then it was time for him to act, for his own sake as well as for the sake of his people. They needed to have solid evidence that he was still around and that he was very much active among them.

By the end of chapter 3, God's sovereign authority over the nations will have been very firmly established. It will not merely be a matter of silencing the taunts and insults of neighbouring countries, but of gathering all nations for judgment on the basis of their treatment of Israel (3:2, 12).

c. I will remove the northerner far from you (2:20)

At first sight, *the northerner* seems like a reference to a military invader, perhaps from Assyria or Babylon, perhaps evocative of or

[2] See Dt. 28:1–14.

similar to Jeremiah's prophecy about a boiling pot facing away from the north and thus foretelling that 'Out of the north evil shall break forth upon all the inhabitants of the land' (Je. 1:13–14). The geography of Palestine, especially the vast northern expanse of the Arabian Desert on its eastern boundary, meant that military invasion invariably came from the north. So the phrase *the northerner* could have come into popular parlance as a vivid description of any national threat – in this case the locusts. Locusts normally invaded Palestine from the south or the east, although on this particular catastrophic occasion they might well have come from the north. Joel could be referring both to the locust invasion and to a military invasion, in which case the LORD is promising to remove either or both. The immediate context (especially 21–25) suggests that the reference again is to the locusts.

The northerner's destination in the eastern and western seas, from which *the stench and foul smell of him will rise*, ties in with known facts about the appalling odour let off by a mass of dead locusts, which often do end up in great piles by the seaside. This plague will end up *far from you* – as far away as possible, never to return.

This is total reversal. The same commander who gave them orders to cause destruction in the land (11) is now issuing orders for their destruction, consigning them to *a parched and desolate land* where they will have nothing to feed on, and driving a wedge between their forces, so that one half drowns in the Dead Sea and the other in the Mediterranean. God is in charge of every stage of the locusts' existence, just as he is in charge of any evil which is launched on his people today.

d. I will restore to you the years that the locusts have eaten (cf. 2:21–25)

The locusts have done *great things* (20), but there is no cause for further fear, *for the LORD has done great things* (21), more than outweighing the impact of the locusts. It is certainly time to *Be glad and rejoice*. Joel calls on the three victims of the catastrophe to join in the rejoicing: the land (21), the beasts of the field (22) and the people (23).

Again the atmosphere is one of abundance: *their full yield* (22), *abundant rain* (23), *full of grain* (24), *overflow* (24). God never does things by half measures. He is lavish and generous in his work of restoration. When we look at the world he has created, it seems extravagant – such variety, intricacy, grandeur, imagination and fantasy. It is as true, if not more so, in restoration and re-creation. There is no need to fear (21–22) when such a God is at work. Joel's way to deal with fear is to fix everyone's eyes on the LORD's activity:

> *... the pastures of the wilderness are green;*
> *the tree bears its fruit;*
> *the fig tree and vine give their full yield* (22).

But the greatest need after such a prolonged period of devastation and drought is rain, and lots of it. This is precisely what the LORD begins to give: *he has poured down for you abundant rain* (23).[3] The triple reference to rain (*the early rain ... abundant rain ... the early and the latter rain*) emphasizes God's rich provision of a basic necessity.

The LORD is restoring the annual cycle of rainfall *as before* (23) the locust invasion. This in itself would be a vindication of the people, because the absence of rain indicated God's withdrawing his blessing upon them. With the rain now falling, and falling not just in abundance, but regularly and steadily at the right time and in appropriate amounts, the people's place in the affections and purposes of God was firmly established once again. What is more, God's own righteousness was being again demonstrated; the rain proved that he could be trusted to keep his promise of restoration to a penitent people.[4]

This brings us to the explicit promise of restoration:

> *I will restore to you the years*
> *which the swarming locust has eaten,*
> *the hopper, the destroyer, and the cutter,*
> *my great army, which I sent among you* (25).

Here for the first time God gives straightforward expression to the truth which has gradually become more and more apparent under Joel's prophetic leadership. The locusts are – were – the army of God. God sent the locusts. Perhaps it is relevant that this shocking truth comes out into the open only at this point, when the sheer abundant goodness of God is being demonstrated. Perhaps such plain speaking has to be withheld while the suffering is intense. Perhaps we can hear its message only when the bruises have begun to heal and we have regained at least some of our peace and poise.

The locusts had brought devastation over a lengthy period (*years* probably means more than simply two). Those years had been utterly and completely negative – wasted years, lost time, nothing but misery and deprivation, erosion of potential. A natural human

---

[3] A variant reading (*yāreh*, teacher, rather than *môreh*, early rain) would give rise to the rendering 'he has given the teacher of righteousness' in place of *he has given the early rain for your vindication* (23).

[4] This is the thrust of the NIV translation, 'he has given you the autumn rains in righteousness' (23).

tendency, once they have finally been concluded, is to consign them to the past as a particularly bad memory: better not even to think about them, let alone speak about them.

But God says, *I will restore* those years. The meaning of the Hebrew word is 'repay', 'pay back', 'make up for'. It has legal connotations, meaning 'compensation'. God, in acknowledging all the damage done to the land and to the people, promises to provide ample compensation for all they have suffered.

We live at a time where legal compensation is a major issue, with individuals sometimes being awarded huge financial amounts, especially in lawcourts in the USA. At other times people with appalling injuries are awarded trivial damages. Often we read of people who have been compensated in large measure for, say, the death of a partner or a parent, yet say that no amount of money can bring back the loved one or make up for the pain and emptiness they still suffer.

That is probably how the people felt in Joel's time about the years devoured by the locusts. But God declares: 'They are not lost; they are not wasted; they are not irredeemably negative. I want to make them up to you. I was ultimately responsible for them in the first place and, if you can now accept the painful and perplexing truth in that – indeed, if you can see them, in retrospect, as my gift to you – then you are in the best place for me to restore them to you. If you choose to write them off and to wipe them out of your memory, then what I am going to do in restoration will probably pass you by. It will certainly not be the time of full re-creation which I have in mind for you.'

Because the historical origins of the word 'restore' or 'repay' are in the lawcourt, it is easy to think of God's relationship with his people in legalistic terms, and to interpret this verse accordingly. Indeed, the first use of the word is in a chapter dealing with making restitution for various injuries, insults and damages acquired in everyday life.[5] It is not in the LORD's nature to pay us back in a tit-for-tat fashion. He is just and righteous, certainly, but he does not treat us as we deserve. If for a moment he were to behave like that, we would be annihilated.

The steadfast love and compassion of our Father God drives him in all his dealings with his people. This is, at once, both within our comprehension (because we know such stirrings in our own human relationships) and beyond our comprehension (and therefore we oscillate in our reactions between awe at over-the-top magnificence and resignation at such inscrutable purposes, neither of which seems just or fair).

God has, then, declared what he is about to do by way of

[5] Ex. 22.

unrestrained blessing. Now (26–27) he spells out what this will mean for his people, and they will realize afresh that he *has dealt wondrously* with them. Such acts of grace will cause them once again to break out in hallelujahs (the root word in the Hebrew for 'praise' is *hll*), something not heard in the temple services for a long, long time. Plenty should always lead to praise, but often does not do so: we forget that we owe the plenty and the power to find it to the LORD himself; we forget to bring him the praise he deserves and desires. That is the slippery slope to being *put to shame* once again. There is a preventative for such a miserable condition: *You shall . . . praise the name of the LORD your God* (26).

The core of the people's praise is the restoration of the covenant relationship:

You shall know that I am in the midst of Israel,
and that I, the LORD, am your God and there is none else (27).

The three cardinal truths expressed in these words had all been undermined. They had come to believe that God was absent and far distant, that he no longer wished to be associated with them and be their God. They had probably begun to flirt, at least in their hearts and minds, with other gods, so desperate were they to find a way out of the catastrophe.

For Joel and his contemporaries the taunt of their enemies cut to the quick: 'Where is their God?' (17). Now they could reply with complete assurance: 'He is in the midst of us, and moreover there is no other god like him.' The covenant, initiated and expressed in the Ten Commandments, was back in place. That was restoration – and endless cause for the people to rejoice in God.

3. I will pour out my Spirit (2:28–32)

If the promises of God in Joel's generation can be summarized in the words 'I will pay back . . .', his promises for some later time can be expressed in the words *I will pour out . . .* (28–29). As we look at 2:28–32, we must beware of making too strong a division between these last five verses of chapter 2 and the whole of chapter 3. They are of a piece, as is indicated by the opening phrases of chapter 3: '. . . in those days and at that time . . .'

C. H. Dodd also makes an important general point about Joel 2 and 3. They 'played a significant part in moulding the language in which the early church set forth its convictions about what Christ had done and would yet do'.[6] In proportion to its length, the book

---

[6] C. H. Dodd, *According to the Scriptures* (Nisbet, 1952), pp. 63–64.

of Joel arguably had more impact on the writers of the New Testament than any other Old Testament book. And if Isaiah 53 is the key scripture for our understanding and experience of the cross of Christ, then Joel 2 is essential for our understanding, teaching and experience of the coming of God's Spirit.

Our first, foundational task is to ask the question (as always): what did these words mean to Joel and to his contemporaries? What did it mean to the people of Joel's day when the prophet mentioned God's Spirit? Here again we are somewhat limited by our ignorance about the dating of Joel's prophecy. This uncertainty means that we cannot take particular events and passages and state, with complete confidence, that these would have conditioned Joel's approach to the activity of God's Spirit.

There is, however, an overall theology of the Spirit in the Old Testament Scriptures, beginning with 'the Spirit of God ... moving over the face of the waters' in creative brooding (Gn. 1:2). Much of this theology is rooted in particular events in the history of Israel which did take place before Joel's time. The events and their record were part of Israel's identity and self-definition. They were also part and parcel of the temple services and the temple cult. The stories were passed down in each family from one generation to the next. This oral tradition was extremely strong and reliable, whatever the nature of the written records.

The majority of Old Testament references to the Spirit of God record the way certain individuals were empowered at specific times for particular tasks.[7] As a result, or because of their position, they were all leaders in the community. This empowerment was crucial to be effective in God's service and, until the time of David, it remained the mark of God's chosen person. One such leader, Elijah (perhaps due to the unusual end to his life, apparently bypassing death), was expected to return to the earth as an immediate prelude to the coming of the Messiah. Such an event is specifically prophesied by Malachi as part of the build-up to 'the great and terrible day of the LORD' (Mal. 4:5).

For Joel and his audience, therefore, there was an experience (even if only in their past history), but also an expectation, of the Spirit coming on individuals for some expression of leadership among the people of God. Two events may well provide an important background for Joel's words here. The first is in the time of Moses and the second in the time of Saul.

The first is described in Numbers 11 and 12. During the forty years' wandering in the wilderness, Moses reached a point where he had had enough of leading such a fractious people. A combination

---

[7] *E.g.* Bezalel (Ex. 35:30–31), Jephthah (Jdg. 11:29), Samson (Jdg. 14:6, 19; 15:14).

of factors made for a highly combustible situation: God's anger with the people, Moses' frustration and exhaustion, the people's expectations of Moses, Moses' expectation for himself, Moses' anger with God for expecting him to be a nanny for the people, his sense of failure and the apparent endlessness of it all. It is an accurate picture of the loneliness of leadership.

God tells Moses to gather seventy elders and officers at the tent of meeting: 'And I will come down and talk with you there; and I will take some of the spirit which is upon you and put it upon them; and they shall bear the burden of the people with you . . .' (Nu. 11:17). Moses followed the LORD's instructions and it all began to happen as God promised: 'the LORD . . . took some of the spirit that was upon [Moses] and put it on the seventy elders; and when the spirit rested upon them, they prophesied. But they did so no more' (11:25).

Two elders, Eldad and Medad, had not turned up at the tent of meeting, but they found the Spirit resting on them back in the camp, and they began to prophesy as well. Joshua, 'one of his chosen men' (11:28), wanted Moses to forbid these two mavericks from prophesying in the wrong place at the wrong time. We then have Moses' classic riposte: 'Are you jealous for my sake? Would that all the LORD's people were prophets, that the LORD would put his spirit on them!' (11:29). Moses had seen enough to want everyone to have the same experience. To see God putting his Spirit on seventy men alongside him in the tent of meeting was water to a thirsty soul. To hear that God had put the Spirit on two others as well, when he was not even present himself, was an added bonus. If this was burden-sharing and burden-bearing, Moses could not have too much of it. He recognized the jealousy in Joshua, who was being groomed for up-front leadership once Moses had gone; but here was the best lesson in spiritual leadership anyone could receive: seventy or seventy-two men were moving in the power of God's Spirit, not just in the 'holy place' but 'in the camp' as well.

Miriam and Aaron reveal their own jealousy of Moses' special relationship with God and position as God's spokesman: 'Has the LORD indeed spoken only through Moses? Has he not spoken though us also?' (12:2). Joshua, Miriam and Aaron each held recognized and important office under Moses. Whey they saw the Spirit moving on other less qualified and less authoritative individuals, they suspected both a very risky development and a subtle undermining of their own position.

The LORD then tells Miriam and Aaron that their brother, Moses, is indeed unique in the purposes of God: 'With him I speak mouth to mouth, clearly, and not in dark speech' (12:8). But, equally, 'if there is a prophet among you, I the LORD make myself known to him in a vision, I speak with him in a dream' (12:6). It is reasonable

71

to conclude that this was the way the elders prophesied. Their prophetic ministry took the form of visions and dreams – visual pictures of one kind or another, though not necessarily in any ecstatic fashion. Basically, others witnessed familiar people acting in an unfamiliar way, able to do something hitherto beyond their ability.

The other scenario involves Saul, son of Kish and first king in Israel. Samuel, who is 'often called the last of the judges and the first of the prophets',[8] having privately anointed Saul for his kingship, prophetically announced a number of events which would happen to him. One of these was that a band of prophets would meet him, the Spirit of the LORD would come upon him, and he would find himself prophesying. When it happened exactly as Samuel predicted, Saul was 'turned into another man' (1 Sa. 10:6), and 'all who knew him before said to one another: "What has come over the son of Kish? Is Saul also among the prophets?"' (1 Sa. 10:11).

This last phrase became a proverb among the people of Israel (1 Sa. 10:12; cf. 19:24). It would, therefore, have been in Joel's consciousness at one level or another, and in that of the people. For Joel and his generation, therefore, it was meaningful to think and to talk of God putting his Spirit on individuals in leadership or marked out for leadership. The thought might even have fostered the hope that God would take action in their day.

Turning now to the text of Joel, we notice that this activity of God's Spirit will take place *afterward* ('after this', 'after these things') – after the promises of restoration (2:19–27) have been substantially, if not entirely, fulfilled in the land. Likewise, the phrase *your sons and your daughters* (why not 'you'?) suggests the next generation, at least, or certainly some subsequent generation: much later, but undated and undatable.

The phrase *pour out* is very significant. In the immediate context it picks upon the earlier theme of rain: *rejoice in the LORD, your God . . . for he has poured down for you abundant rain* (23). Just as rain to a thirsty land, so is God's Spirit to a thirsty soul and a thirsty people. God promises that the time will come when he will pour out his Spirit.

The picture and the reality of God pouring out his Spirit, as distinct from putting his Spirit on individuals, are altogether more dynamic. The prophet portrays something lavish, exuberant, almost wasteful. There is nothing stinted, nor is there anything for anyone to do to enjoy it except to be there when the Spirit is poured out. It is not a drizzle, but a downpour. It is the way the activity of the

---

[8] R. F. Youngblood, '1, 2 Samuel', *The Expositor's Bible Commentary* 3, ed. Frank Gaebelein (Zondervan, 1992), p. 620.

Spirit is anticipated by other prophets, such as Isaiah, Ezekiel and Zechariah.[9]

This outpouring of the Spirit of God will fall on *all flesh*. Biblically this phrase can refer to every living creature, human or not. Here, it is clearly referring to human beings – although, in the light of the LORD's opening the mouth of Balaam's ass and enabling it to speak like a human being,[10] we should not be adamant about this. There is debate as to whether, for Joel and his contemporaries, *all flesh* meant all the people of Israel or all the people in the world. It may, in fact, have remained ambiguous to both prophet and people.

This outpouring of the Spirit will clearly have a dramatic impact on the community life of the people of God. As each individual person is affected, so social and other distinctions will become muted and less determinative. There will be no discrimination, as far as the activity of the Spirit is concerned, in terms of age, sex or status.

Older people have always enjoyed respect in Israel. In this passage there may be an indication of a levelling-out of the age-gaps in this regard, as young men feel the impact and show the evidence of God's Spirit in their lives. There will also be a significant change in the positions enjoyed by men and women as a result of the Spirit's activity, which are here presented as equivalent. Although the Old Testament is not uniformly loaded in favour of men, it is essentially portraying a male-dominated society.

But it is notably in the way that the Spirit is given to *the menservants and maidservants* that the old order is to be turned upside down. 'Slaves and slave-girls' would be on the receiving end as much as anyone else. Although Israelites were sometimes sold as slaves among their own people (usually because of temporary adversity and then as children in order to give their parents some leeway and hope of recovery), servants were normally foreigners acquired on their travels or after military campaigns. Even if they were assimilated into the community, accepting and adopting its customs and practices, they were still outsiders. 'It is important that the modern reader does not miss the radical character of what Joel announces . . . Joel envisages a sociological overhaul . . . This statement from Joel must be contrasted with the ancient daybreak prayer of the Jewish male, "I thank you, God, that I was not born a Gentile, a slave or a woman." '[11]

The impact of this outpouring on all and sundry will be that

---

[9] Is. 44:3; Ezk. 39:29; Zc. 12:10. [10] Nu. 22:28.

[11] Dillard, p. 295. Note that this prayer is not in the Old Testament, and can be found only many years after the writing of the canonical Scriptures.

> *your sons and your daughters shall prophesy,*
> *your old men shall dream dreams,*
> *and your young men shall see visions.*

What did it mean then to prophesy? What did it mean to dream dreams? What did it mean to see visions? The fulfilment of the promise, whenever it might happen down the track, need not be limited to the current understanding and expectations of Joel. But the answers still need to be identified, before we proceed to later events.

What did it mean, in Joel's time, to prophesy? The Hebrew verb, *nāḇa'*, occurs as a verb 115 times in the Old Testament, although only once in the Pentateuch: in the key chapter of Numbers 11, describing the experience of Moses with the elders. The prophets were individuals who spoke the words that God gave them. (They were normally men, but at least three prophetesses are mentioned: Miriam, Deborah and Huldah.)[12] This is described in a number of common phrases, such as 'Thus says the LORD' and 'The word of the LORD came to . . .' (literally 'was to' or 'became a reality to'). Some wrote books. Others were counsellors to kings, but there was usually an uneasy relationship, certainly a complex one, between prophets and rulers. We hardly ever hear of a prophet living at court: they are normally on the move, taking the word of God to the people.

God is said to have spoken his word to most of the prophets, but to some of them he gave dreams and visions. What did it mean to dream dreams and to see visions? Dreams are commonplace in the Old Testament. They are important in the lives of people like Abraham, Jacob, Joseph, Gideon, Solomon and Daniel.[13] Dreams are significant, also, in the lives of individuals in nations other than Israel.[14] Whether among them or in Israel, dreams invariably needed interpretation.

The biblical record is ambivalent in its attitude to dreams and dreamers. In earlier times this way of receiving a message from God was apparently regarded with less suspicion than in the days of people like, say, Jeremiah, who regarded messages purporting to come from God through dreams as being virtually equivalent to false prophecy.[15]

So dreams and visions can be *bona fide* communication from God, but require interpretation. There is another, more direct way of inspiration by the Spirit – hearing and speaking the word of the

---

[12] Ex. 15:20ff.; Jdg. 4:4; 2 Ki. 22:14.
[13] Gn. 20:1–18; 28:10–17; 31:1–16; 37:5–11; Jdg. 7:9–18; 1 Ki. 3:3–15; Dn. 7:1–28.
[14] For examples see *TDOT* 4, pp. 421–426.   [15] Je. 23:25–32.

LORD. It is this genre which was probably more respected by Joel's time. His prophecy here, while not giving *carte blanche* to a prophetic ministry involving a more pictorial approach, certainly endorsed it and would have been heard in that way by his listeners. Visions, equally, had a respectable pedigree in Israel's past. They were akin to dreams, but were normally received while awake, not asleep. They were closely associated with people called 'seers' (*ḥōzeh*, seer; *ḥāzôn*, vision), and they were almost 'a technical term for divine revelation'.[16] There was not the same scepticism or hostility towards those who had visions as there was for those who dreamed dreams. The earlier chapters of Zechariah contain examples of such visions, introduced by phrases such as 'I saw in the night, and behold, a man riding upon a red horse!', 'I lifted my eyes and saw ...' and 'He said to me, "What do you see?"'[17]

It is an open question whether Joel's prophecy about old men dreaming dreams and young men seeing visions has distinctive implications; for instance, did old men normally see visions and young men dream dreams? It is also an open question to what extent ecstatic manifestations would have been expected in prophetic activity in Joel's day.[18] Historical precedent certainly included such experiences, but they were not necessary or important in receiving a message from God. Indeed, the more unusual manifestations were more frequent in pagan prophecy, often resulting from deliberate trances or artificially stimulated experiences. The ministry of a genuine prophet in Israel is normally contrasted with similar roles played in other nations by diviners, astrologers, soothsayers, sorcerers or even 'the prophets of Baal' (1 Ki. 18).

Joel's prophetic words about God's Spirit must have had a big impact on a nation just beginning to emerge from a long, dark tunnel. In the deep darkness of their desolation, they must have wondered if they would ever again know the presence of the LORD in their midst. Now here is Joel bringing them a glorious message from the LORD that *all flesh* would receive a dramatic outpouring of the Spirit – a message made doubly sure by its repetition of the phrase, *I will pour out my spirit*.

This promise of the Spirit is, however, placed uncompromisingly in the context of *the great and terrible day of the LORD* (31). There has been so much unrelieved blessing in the previous paragraphs that it comes as a bit of a shock to be confronted by the dramatic imagery of apocalyptic language: *And I will give portents in the heavens and*

---

[16] See D. E. Aune in *The International Standard Bible Encyclopedia* 4, ed. G. W. Bromiley (Eerdmans, 1988), pp. 993–994.   [17] Zc. 1:8, 18; 2:1; 5:9; 6:1; 4:2; 5:2.
[18] For comments on and references to the ecstatic element in Old Testament prophetic activity, see R. F. Youngblood in *The Expositor's Bible Commentary* 3, ed. Frank Gaebelein (Zondervan, 1992), pp. 624–626.

on the earth, blood and fire and columns of smoke. The sun shall be turned to darkness, and the moon to blood, before the great and terrible day of the LORD *comes* (30–31).

What is signified by these *portents? Blood, fire* and *smoke* all have their counterparts in the exodus narrative. The blood of the Passover lamb secured for the Israelites safety and protection from the LORD's holy judgment on the Egyptians.[19] A pillar of fire led the people by night through the wilderness.[20] The mountain was wrapped in smoke as the LORD descended at Sinai to speak with Moses.[21] All three portents expressed the overwhelming reality of a holy God present with his people, protecting, preserving, providing, proclaiming, and thereby calling them to attention and the watching world to account.

Before the great and terrible day of the LORD comes, there will be another such demonstration of God's all-consuming holiness: *The sun shall be turned to darkness, and the moon to blood* (31). Jesus himself spoke about similar realities when describing 'the coming of the Son of man'.[22] Inklings of these penultimate events were also given in the earthquake and midday darkness that accompanied the dying of Jesus.[23] The book of Revelation picks up the apocalyptic language of Joel and Jesus.[24] In each case the supreme reality is the dread inspired by events which unveil the fearful majesty of almighty God, expressed in the terrifying paradox of 'the wrath of the Lamb'.[25]

So the people of Joel's day are dragged back to confront the day of the LORD. The locust plague is on the way out, but Joel has already emphasized three times that the locusts were harbingers of an even greater disaster. So restoration from the locusts, followed by the whole people experiencing the Spirit of God being poured out upon them, signified divine intervention in readiness for the great day of judgment.

The gift of the Spirit was not to be for personal satisfaction, or even for national recovery and stability. It was to strengthen the people of God to take up a position of prophetic leadership[26] among the nations in a world heading for an apocalyptic day of final reckoning. If individual prophets had the task of taking God's word to a nation at risk of God's judgment, a prophetically inspired people would have the task of taking God's word to a world on the brink of ultimate judgment.

Joel's perspective includes the warning that to live *in Mount Zion*

---

[19] See Ex. 11:1 – 12:32.   [20] See Ex. 13:21–22.   [21] See Ex. 19:16–18.
[22] See Mt. 24:27–31.   [23] See Mt. 27:45–54.
[24] See Rev. 6:12–17; 8:1–13; 16:1–9; 20:11–15.   [25] Rev. 6:16.
[26] Note that the legacy passed on to Joel's generation spoke of God's Spirit equipping for *leadership*.

and in Jerusalem will be no guarantee of surviving that day of judgment. It will be *terrible* (inspiring utter dread and deep fear) for everyone, Israel and the nations alike. The thrust of the day is judgment, and so the only issue that is of any significance is: will anyone escape? Will there be any *survivors*? Yes, says the LORD through Joel, *there shall be those who escape* (32).

These survivors are defined in two parallel phrases: *All who call upon the name of the LORD* and *those whom the LORD calls* (32). This looks like the two sides of a coin, reflecting the initiative of God in making his call clear, and the responsibility of the hearers to respond by calling on the name of the LORD.

This, then, is the scenario which Joel foresees will *come to pass afterward*, after the locust plague has been removed and the land and its people have been restored. We are now in a position to consider how and why Peter took this passage to explain what happened to the followers of Jesus in Jerusalem on the day of Pentecost several centuries later.

It is notable that the LORD's promise through Joel about the outpouring of his Spirit on *all flesh* had no known fulfilment for so many years. Depending on where we date the book of Joel, the promise took at least 400 years and as long as 900 years to be fulfilled. This, in itself, teaches us an important but virtually indigestible truth about the purposes and the activity of God. He does not seem to be in nearly as much of a hurry as we are, nor does he share our opinion that our generation is when it all must happen.

Peter, however, was clear that nine o'clock in the morning on a particular feast of Pentecost, which fell on the third day of the third month in the year, was the time when God fulfilled his promise through Joel. He had, in the preceding hour or so, been witness and subject to a remarkable experience of spiritual power. He had neither the time nor the theology to put together a plausible explanation for such staggering events, which had not happened in a corner but were fully in the public domain. But he was sure that 'this is what was spoken by the prophet Joel' (Acts 2:16).

God's choice of Pentecost as the time to pour out his Spirit through Jesus on the 120 disciples holds intriguing significance. That particular Jewish festival was to begin seven weeks from the time the sickle was put to the standing grain[27] – parallel to seven weeks since Jesus was crucified. It was the day of the firstfruits of the harvest, brought by the people to the temple, given to God but enjoyed by the priests. Under the new covenant in the blood of Jesus, the 'royal priesthood'[28] of all believers in Jesus enjoy God's gift of the Spirit to his people as the firstfruits of their full inheritance.[29]

[27] Dt. 16:9.　　[28] 1 Pet. 2:9.　　[29] See Je. 1:18; 1 Cor. 15:20, 23; Rev. 14:4.

There are several more or less significant alterations in the text from Joel to Peter. The switch from *afterward* to 'in the last days' is arguably the most significant. It alters the thrust of the passage from being a historically linear statement to being expressly eschato-logical: instead of God's promise to pour out his Spirit being applied to some future time, it becomes an event inextricably bound up with the wind-down of history and the fulfilment of God's eternal purposes.

The pouring out of God's Spirit at Pentecost indicated that the final chapter of God's history of the world had begun with the birth, life, death, burial, resurrection and ascension of Jesus of Nazareth. As Peter told the assembled crowds in Jerusalem: 'Being . . . exalted at the right hand of God, and having received from the Father the promise of the Holy Spirit, he has poured out this which you see and hear' (Acts 2:33).

Peter's last alteration holds great significance – his omission of Joel's final section: *for in Mount Zion and in Jerusalem there shall be those who escape, as the LORD has said, and among the survivors shall be those whom the LORD calls*. It is strange, at first glance, that Peter should exclude mention of Jerusalem when he is speaking in that city explicitly to 'all who dwell in Jerusalem' (Acts 2:14).

It appears that the Holy Spirit himself may have cut Peter short in his quotation, because the sentiments in Joel 2:32 actually do appear a few minutes later in Peter's words to the people. After speaking to them in direct, if not blunt, terms about the true identity of 'this Jesus' whom 'you crucified' (Acts 2:23), he finds the people so cut to the heart that they ask him what they must do. Peter says: 'Repent, and be baptized every one of you in the name of Jesus Christ for the forgiveness of your sins; and you shall receive the gift of the Holy Spirit. For the promise is to you and to your children and to all that are far off, every one whom the Lord our God calls to him' (Acts 2:37–39).

Having previously omitted reference to those in Mount Zion and in Jerusalem, Peter here adds the dramatic phrase 'all that are far off', qualifying its apparent lack of any discrimination with Joel's phrase (or something rather like it): 'every one whom the Lord calls to him'. The promise, says Peter, is also for future generations ('your children'), but in addition it is for those far away. Neither time nor space need exclude anyone from receiving the outpouring of the Spirit. What did Peter mean, or think he might mean, by the phrase 'all that are far off'? The Peter of the day of Pentecost might have answered rather differently from the Peter who had met Cornelius,[30] and even more differently from the Peter who had to face the

---

[30] Acts 10.

opposition of Paul about full fellowship in Christ between Jewish and Gentile believers.[31] Paul found it easier than did Peter to grasp who 'those afar off' were and what their inclusion among God's people signified.[32]

When Peter had had more time to think, to listen, to pray and to watch God at work in different parts of the world, he came to know very well what he meant when he 'forgot' Joel's last few words, and 'invented' those powerful few words of universal invitation. His letter to disciples of Christ, Jewish and Gentile, scattered around the Middle East, written thirty years or so later, beautifully encapsulates the truth he articulated on that Pentecost morning in Jerusalem: 'You are a chosen race, a royal priesthood, a holy nation, God's own people, that you may declare the wonderful deeds of him who called you out of darkness into his marvellous light. Once you were no people but now you are God's people; once you had not received mercy but now you have received mercy' (1 Pet. 2:9–10).

Each phrase in these two verses provides a perfect commentary on the prophecy of Joel, the coming of the Spirit at Pentecost, Peter's creative use of Joel's words, and the impact of those events and that preaching both on those who were present and on future generations and other cultures. God continued, through Jesus at work in his church, to pour out his Spirit on all flesh.

The promise, by its very nature and because of its Author, was never going to be a once-and-for-all happening, one sudden torrential tropical rainstorm of the Spirit. God has continued to pour out his Spirit on all flesh. We, today, are not expected to go and jump in the lake caused by the activity of God in Jerusalem at Pentecost. We are invited to rejoice in a God who is still pouring out his Spirit on those who, in glad and humble response to his call, turn to him to be saved – from the grip of sin and the powers of death, but supremely from the day of judgment: 'Save yourselves from this crooked generation' (Acts 2:40). They then become part of the people of God, a 'remnant' called and equipped to speak his word to their own generation and, by such ministry, to provide godly leadership in society at every level.

---

[31] Gal. 2 and Acts 15.   [32] Eph. 2:13–14.

Joel 3:1–21
4. Fear God

In the final chapter, Joel's words concentrate on what will happen as the day of the LORD finally approaches. We can see here how that day will be both a day of destruction and a day of deliverance: but it is also a day of decision – not by human beings, but by God. As this great day is portrayed, Joel for the first time becomes specific about places and nations. Hitherto, he has mentioned only Jerusalem and Mount Zion (2:1, 15, 23, 32). In this chapter he refers to Tyre and Sidon and all the regions of Philistia (4), the Greeks (6), the Sabeans (8), the valley of Shittim (18), Egypt and Edom (19). Judah is mentioned six times, Israel twice, Jerusalem four times and Zion three times.

In a book which still frustrates those who want to settle on a date for its composition and context, this specific focus is striking. Joel understands the day of the LORD to have an impact that is worldwide, comprehensive and decisive. *All the nations* (2) are to be involved, even if Joel's own horizon is necessarily limited to *all you nations round about* (11), and to particular nations of which he has heard.

More than that, Joel's perspective is the way surrounding nations have treated Israel. The decisions taken by God on the day of the LORD relate to the decisions taken by nations through the centuries concerning their treatment of Israel. That much is plain from the text of the chapter, and in view of the references made to specific nations and places, it is difficult to sustain the argument that this will not literally be fulfilled: on the day of the LORD nations will be judged for their treatment of Israel.

It is more debatable, however, whether this will be the essence, let alone the exclusive thrust, of that great day. Joel, it would seem, gives one perspective and one ingredient of the day of the LORD. Even within the teaching of his book as a whole, there are wider perspectives and other ingredients, however allusive and implicit. For example, at the end of chapter 2 it is clearly stated that, among the inhabitants of Jerusalem, there will be 'survivors', those who call on the name of the LORD; not everyone in the city will be delivered. The entire thrust of Joel's prophecy points in the same direction: the day of the LORD is a time of judgment for Israel as well as for the nations.[1]

Chapter 3 is couched mainly in the form of direct speech from the LORD, addressed sometimes to Israel and at other times to the nations. The middle section (9–16) contains one statement in the first person singular (12) and one statement where the LORD is directly addressed (11). In spite of this quirk in the middle of the passage, it seems best to take the whole chapter as a clear message from God, through Joel, to any who will listen: a message, as we have indicated, about a day of decision, destruction and deliverance; a day bringing a verdict, vengeance and vindication. The three themes interweave throughout the chapter.

1. Decision (3:1–8)

The chapter opens with an apparently clear time-link between what is about to be described and what has just been promised: *For behold, in those days and at that time* ... The first phrase repeats the statement (2:29) about the time when God pours out his Spirit on all flesh. The second phrase is less specific, but in a general way seems to refer to the time when the Spirit's abundant activity merges with apocalyptic events heralding the imminence of the day of the LORD.

If this is correct, the next phrase, *when I restore the fortunes of Judah and Jerusalem* (1), is not harking back to the work of God in restoring land and people after the locust devastation. That restoration took place, in both Joel's prophecy and in actual fulfilment, before the outpouring of the Spirit. So God's activity in restoring (or repaying the people for) the years which the locust has eaten (2:25) was completely distinct from his activity in restoring the fortunes of Judah and Jerusalem. That is of a different order and in a different time frame.

This is underlined by the meaning of the phrase translated *restore the fortunes of*, which is different from the word in 2:25. It is, in fact, a key phrase in Old Testament interpretation and comes several times to describe events of central importance in Israel's history. The Hebrew word has two essential meanings, either of which is possible in this context: 'restore the fortunes of'

---

[1] Other insights into what matters on the day of the LORD are given in Is. 24:1–27:13; Zc. 14:1–7; Mal. 3:16–4:6; Mt. 12:36; Acts 17:30–31; 1 Cor. 3:13; 4:5; 15:52; 2 Cor. 5:10; 1 Thes. 3:13; 2 Thes. 1:8.

or 'turn the captivity of'. It appears eighteen times and 'constitutes a much debated crux in Old Testament study'.[2] The first rendering speaks of a change which is not necessarily time-specific; the second seems to have a more narrow application, for instance to a period of actual captivity. Examples of the latter meaning[3] apply to Judah's return from captivity and exile in Babylon. A more general reversal of national fortunes is indicated elsewhere.[4] In the absence of any reference to Babylon (instead, we have Tyre and Sidon mentioned, 4), it is reasonable to assume that the Joel usage is speaking of a wider restoration, that is, the impact on God's people of the Spirit's outpouring, leading on to deliverance from destruction for survivors in Jerusalem as the day of the LORD draws near.

While that is going on, the LORD will also be at work among the nations, calling them to account for the way they have treated Israel: *I will gather all nations and bring them down to the valley of Jehoshaphat, and I will enter into judgment with them there, on account of my people and my heritage Israel* (2).

The name *Jehoshaphat* means 'God judges', and it is probable that Joel is not referring to any valley actually known by that name, but underlining the reality of judgment by God. The valley is called *the valley of decision* (or, the verdict) (14): another wordplay on the theme of God sitting as judge and handing down his verdict on each nation before his tribunal.[5] A modern parallel to this usage is our way of referring to the 'killing-fields' of, say, Vietnam or Uganda, Bosnia or Rwanda.

The initiative, on this day of reckoning for all the nations, lies entirely with God: *I will gather* and *bring them down*. Both verbs are words of sovereign action. The nations may feel safe, miles away in the fastnesses of their own territory. Each nation may keep very much to itself, have little or no dealings with any other nation, and be entirely self-sufficient economically, commercially and militarily; but God says, *I will gather* them. They may be immensely powerful and prosperous, world leaders with world-class cities and a boom economy – but God says, *I will . . . bring them down* (the word 'may mean to "prostrate", "topple", or "humiliate"').[6]

God will be concerned, as 'the Judge of all the earth' (Gn. 18:25), for one issue: *I will enter into judgment . . . on account of my people and my heritage Israel* (2). God is not a disinterested third party; he is not an impartial judge: he is concerned for his people and his own

---

[2] Dillard, p. 300.   [3] Je. 29:14; 30:18; 32:44; Zp. 3:20.   [4] Ho. 6:11; Ezk. 16:53.
[5] For other biblical valleys taken as locations for similar scenarios, see Je. 7:31ff.; 19:7; Is. 22:10, Ezk. 39:11; Zc. 14:4–5.
[6] Hubbard, p. 74.

heritage. They belong to him and nobody else; no other nation has the right to do what they like with his own possession.

There are three charges which the LORD will bring against the nations; three matters for which each nation will have to render account:

a. The first charge: they have scattered them among the nations (3:2)

The first charge is rooted in all that God has done to gather his people together into one nation in the promised land. He had expended infinite resources in order to achieve this great purpose, starting with Abraham's call to leave Ur of the Chaldees. Then came the sagas of the patriarchs and the appalling time (400 years or more) in harsh bondage in Egypt, broken at last by God's own 'mighty hand and outstretched arm' as he led them out of captivity under Moses; forty years of patient leadership provided to a fractious, motley multitude with little sense of identity and even less of unity; and finally, under Joshua, entry into and capture of major cities, eventually culminating in conquest of the whole land. And that had been just the beginning.

Century after century, prophet after prophet, king after king, crisis after crisis: all the time God had treated them like the apple of his eye,[7] gathering, gathering, gathering – from captivity, from wandering, from exile, from idolatry. In the light of such age-long commitment to gathering his people, God was not going to let the nations, any nation, get away with scattering them. A day of reckoning was coming: each nation in any sense responsible for scattering, not gathering, the people of God will be in the dock. It is important to keep the beginning of chapter 3 firmly in the context of what 2:28–32 describes: God's pouring out the Spirit and ushering in the great and terrible day of the LORD. We can then see that this day of reckoning will essentially focus on the way nations have treated the church of Christ, God's people under the new covenant, the Israel of God.[8]

To what extent, if any, that includes a modern nation's policy and practice towards the present nation-state of Israel is a moot question. Successive Presidents of the United States, for example, have felt the heat of (mainly Christian) lobbyists, who are sure that their nation's prosperity significantly depends on providing full-blooded support for modern Israel's survival and success. Active endorsement for gathering Jews in their land may turn out to be substantially different from enthusiastic approval of policies pursued by a secular (and largely atheistic) government.

[7] Dt. 32:10; Zc. 2:8.   [8] See Gal. 6:16.

b. The second charge: they have divided up my land (3:2)

The second charge that God will bring against the nations is in connection with the land, which in Joel's time had suffered such devastation through the army of locusts: *they ... have divided up my land*. In any culture and country, ownership of land is of fundamental importance. In East Africa, for example, one of the reasons for very different attitudes today towards *muzungus*, or foreigners (especially white people), in Uganda as distinct from Kenya is the question of land. Uganda, a protectorate in the days of the British Empire, was a country where *muzungus* generally owned no land; it remained in the hands of Ugandans. Kenya, on the other hand, was a colony, and Europeans owned virtually all the best land. The residue of each historical reality is plain today: in general, Ugandans welcome Europeans, but Kenyans are more suspicious and often hostile.

From the beginning in Canaan, the LORD made it clear that the whole land belonged to him. It was his – as indeed is the whole earth – and entirely within his discretion to give to the people he chose. He chose to give it to the people of Israel.[9] He promised it to Abraham centuries before Joshua led the descendants of Abraham across the Jordan to take possession of it.[10]

Solomon, at the dedication of the temple in Jerusalem, gladly acknowledged in prayer to God that it was 'the land, which thou hast given to thy people as an inheritance' (2 Ch. 6:27). When the people forgot, as they frequently did, to whom the land truly belonged, along came a prophet to remind them:

> I brought you into a plentiful land
>   to enjoy its fruits and its good things.
> But when you came in you defiled my land,
>   and made my heritage an abomination (Je. 2:7; *cf.* 16:18).

We shall see later (19) that the nation of Edom, in particular, was guilty of this charge of parcelling out the land which the LORD had called *my land*. In fact, only God was entitled to divide out the land, and had done so: each tribe had its portion. But the Israelites themselves had been given strict instructions not to treat the land like any normal 'real estate': 'The land shall not be sold in perpetuity, for the land is mine; for you are strangers and sojourners with me. And in all the country you possess, you shall grant a redemption of the land' (Lv. 25:23–24).

This commandment, as much as anything else, emphasizes that

---

[9] Jos. 1:1–6.   [10] Gn. 13:14–17.

not even an Israelite could lay claim to even a part of the land. They were pilgrims, not property-owners. Even less, then, did non-Israelites have the right to treat the land in the way they treated land in their own country. Nations will be called to account for that kind of behaviour in the only part of the world which can be called 'God's own country'.

c. The third charge: they have cast lots for my people (3:3)

The third charge accuses the nations of effectively treating human beings like chattels, and particularly of dealing with the people of God in the same cavalier and callous way that slaves were put up for sale in the marketplace. This was a national lottery to end all national lotteries – God's holy people apportioned as prizes. 'The scene is that of dividing plunder after battle';[11] all too reminiscent of battlefield brutality today.

The specific war crimes mentioned by Joel have their counterparts today. Take this report about Rwanda:

At least half a million people were slaughtered between April and June 1994. A third or more of those who died were children. In some of the largest mass graves, up to 45% of the victims were children. UNICEF estimates that up to one million child survivors have been touched by the genocide. In a survey conducted by the fund near Kigali, 56% of children had seen children taking part in the massacres, usually following the commands of adults, while 47% had seen children killing other children. Two thirds of all children witnessed massacres. One in five witnessed rape and sexual abuse. More than half of those questioned had seen family members being killed.[12]

Yet even such horrors fall short of Hitler's 'ultimate solution' with the extermination of six million Jewish men, women and children in the Holocaust.

The LORD, through Joel, is not merely expressing his loathing of the atrocities of war, especially when directed against his own people. He is also registering his hatred of inhuman cruelty towards the most defenceless and vulnerable in society – children, boys and girls: *they . . . have given a boy for a harlot, and have sold a girl for wine, and have drunk it.* In Jewish society extra care and consideration are shown to children, and 'there is a sense in which any society can be measured by the treatment accorded to children'.[13]

[11] Dillard, p. 301.   [12] *The Independent*, 23 December 1995.
[13] Dillard, p. 301.

A nation does not have to be at war for such appalling behaviour to be a common occurrence and to render that country liable to God's judgment. One wonders what the LORD will have to say on that day to modern nations, not least in the West, who are abusing (or allowing people to abuse) their young people in a plethora of different ways – from abortion, through sexual and physical violence, to child prostitution, drug-pushing and sheer abandonment.

Shall we all be asked questions about the way we may have *scattered* God's people in different ways? Will his scrutiny be directed at the way we deal with property and possessions, especially when we treat them as belonging to us and not to God? Shall we be tackled about any dehumanizing, arrogant or callous behaviour towards those whom Jesus called 'the least of these my brethren' (Mt. 25:40), and who are, therefore, God's own children?

d. Examples: Phoenicia and Philistia (3:4–8)

The scene now changes, somewhat abruptly, to a specific example of the general theme of God gathering the nations for judgment: Tyre, Sidon and Philistia (4–8). The behaviour for which these nations are called to account will have its recompense in a further historical event, not at the end of time. This perspective is consistent with the rest of Scripture: God has fixed a day on which he will judge the world in righteousness (the day of the LORD). But his righteous judgment is at work all the time – in the self-destructive nature of evil,[14] in the outworking of the 'sowing and reaping' principle,[15] in the rise and fall of nations, and in the frightening implications of Paul's striking phrase, 'God gave them up.'[16]

It is dangerous, morally and spiritually, to develop an understanding of divine judgment which effectively puts it all off until a final day of judgment. It is far more healthy, and biblical, to live each day in the light of eternity: to hold ourselves accountable before God today for today. This whole chapter is a lesson in accountability. There can be few matters more crucial to our generation and our culture.

Tyre, Sidon and Philistia were some of Israel's traditional foes. The Philistines (chiefly through David and Goliath,[17] followed by Samson and Delilah)[18] have found their way into the English language as a byword for uncouth and uncivilized behaviour. For several centuries they were immensely powerful, particularly in the wealth, violence and arrogance in their five cities, Gaza, Ashdod, Ashkelon, Gath and Ekron.

[14] Ps. 7:12–16. [15] Gal. 6:7–8. [16] Rom. 1:24, 26, 28. [17] 1 Sa. 17.
[18] Jdg. 16.

Ezekiel summarizes the cruelty of the Philistines with characteristic vividness: they 'acted revengefully and took vengeance with malice of heart to destroy in never-ending enmity' (Ezk. 25:15). Through the prophet Zechariah God promises:

> I will make an end of the pride of Philistia.
> I will take away its blood from its mouth,
>   and its abominations from between its teeth (Zc. 9:6–7).

The Phoenicians, whose main ports were Tyre and Sidon, were probably (through the years covered by the Old Testament) the major seafaring nation of the Mediterranean world. Tyre was the chief trading seaport: 'Tyre ... dwells at the entrance to the sea, merchant of the peoples on many coastlands' (Ezk. 27:3). It became the marketplace of the world. Its immense wealth is described in the rest of Ezekiel 27, and its worldwide reputation in those days makes it sound like New York, London and Tokyo rolled into one. Every other nation traded with the Phoenicians, because the Tyre cartel controlled both markets and prices:

> When your wares came from the seas,
>   you satisfied many peoples;
> with your abundant wealth and merchandise
>   you enriched the kings of the earth (Ezk. 27:33).

With Tyre's vast commercial success went brazen arrogance, even to the point of declaring itself a god (Ezk. 28:2), leading to this word from the LORD, again through Ezekiel:

> ... by your great wisdom in trade
>   you have increased your wealth,
>   and your heart has become proud in your wealth ...
> In the abundance of your trade
>   you were filled with violence, and you sinned ...
> By the multitude of your iniquities,
>   in the unrighteousness of your trade
>   you profaned your sanctuaries (Ezk. 28:5, 16, 18).

Phoenician arrogance and Philistine violence were, therefore, well known far and wide, not just in Israel. Each has a timeless expression and a very modern ring. The sheer pride of those who control the markets, even of those who play them rather than run them, in today's capital cities is at times breathtaking – living as though there is no tomorrow, no ethical sanction, no need for accountability, no day of reckoning. The collapse of Barings Bank in the City of

London is one fairly recent example, but there are many others around the world. Philistine-type violence is endemic among the drug cartels of Latin America and Mafia-controlled operations in North America and Europe (and Mafia-like thugs in Russia).

When Joel directly addresses the Phoenicians and Philistines, in the name of God, he puts the situation in terms of somewhat sarcastic enquiry: *What are you to me, O Tyre and Sidon, and all the regions of Philistia? Are you paying me back for something?* (4). The first question is dismissive; the second is almost one of bewilderment. God is about to deal with them in the way he might flick an insect off his arm. In his second question the LORD expresses some surprise that the two nations should persistently target Judah and Jerusalem. They appear to be working off a grudge of some sort against God. Such anger against God is often vented on those who represent God (such as priests, church leaders, active believers, even church buildings). The word *pay back* is the same as that used when God promised to pay back the people of the land for all the devastation caused by the locusts (2:25). That was positive repayment. Here the LORD promises repayment of a different kind – retribution, in fact: *If you are paying me back, I will requite your deed upon your own head swiftly and speedily* (16).

The LORD's charges against these two nations are that *you have taken my silver and my gold, and have carried my rich treasures into your temples* (5) and *You have sold the people of Jerusalem and Judah to the Greeks, removing them from their own border* (6).

The first charge gives a specific, historical example of the general indictment levelled against the nations, when the LORD had spoken about *my people... my heritage... my land* (2–3). Here he speaks about *my silver... my gold... my rich treasures.* The LORD so identifies with Judah and Jerusalem that he regards every person and thing as belonging to him. To attack, despise, destroy or remove anyone or anything is to target God himself: 'he who touches you touches the apple of his eye' (Zc. 2:8). This principle is reiterated in the New Testament, when the early church's vicious persecutor, Saul of Tarsus, is struck to the ground and blinded. When he asks, 'Who are you, Lord?', the reply is clear: 'I am Jesus, whom you are persecuting' (Acts 9:5).

There is, apparently, no historical record of such plundering by either the Philistines or the Phoenicians. It is likely that their motive was a mixture of opportunism and sheer greed: 'Tyre said concerning Jerusalem, "Aha, the gate of the peoples is broken, it has swung open to me; I shall be replenished, now that she is laid waste"' (Ezk. 26:2).

Empire builders have always been the same: if the door is open for trade and wealth, then the commercial and patriotic thing to do is to go through it. Any ethical or theological questions can be left to later generations or religious specialists. It is no matter if the country or the city in question is on its knees or incapable of striking an agreement which will lead to just and equitable sharing in years to come. History is littered with Tyrian plunderings of this kind, as nations are looted and raped in the name of progress and for the sake of profit.

The Phoenicians hit God's people when they were down, seizing their prized possessions (particularly those in the temple of Jerusalem) and carrying them off to fill their own state buildings (the word translated *temples* could also be 'palaces').

But there was more to their treatment of God's people than mere pillage: *You have sold the people* (6) into slavery. There is solid historical evidence for this slave trade between these Mediterranean cities and the Greeks: 'Contact between these Ionians [*i.e.* Greeks] and the Assyrian empire as early as the eighth century BC is well documented.'[19] Amos also refers to the way Tyre was involved in the wholesale removal of an entire people into slavery.[20] It was widespread, common, appalling and culpable.

Not only were the Phoenicians happy to sell people, including Israelites, into slavery to fill their own coffers; they were equally happy to take people to be their own slaves in payment for their rich variety of goods: 'Javan [*i.e.* Greece], Tubal, and Meshech traded with you; they exchanged the persons of men and vessels of bronze for your merchandise' (Ezk. 27:13).

The slave trade was centred on the seaports (Tyre, Sidon, Ashkelon), as it was in London, Bristol and Liverpool in the days of the slave trade between Africa and America. That trade was targeted by William Wilberforce when he became Member of Parliament in the 1790s, and he lived to see it firmly on its way to abolition by the time of his death thirty years later.

Such trafficking in human souls and bodies has always been anathema to God. The people of Israel themselves did not have a clean sheet: Amos denounces them in virtually the same breath as the city of Tyre, 'because they sell the righteous for silver, and the needy for a pair of shoes' (Am. 2:6).

Buying people's gifts, time, loyalty and expertise is a respectable modern form of slavery. In major cities today, employers, especially major conglomerates and multinationals, virtually buy a person body and soul by giving a reasonable salary but adding powerful incentives, which can be realized only by maintaining a schedule and a commitment that amount to chaining the individual to his or her computer screen morning, noon and night, seven days a week. That is a subtle way to turn people into slaves, but it works.

[19] Hubbard, p. 76.   [20] Am. 1:9.

Slave labour of a not so subtle kind is rife, also, in the way men are moved by plane halfway across the world from their home countries, confined to a job and a compound in an alien culture (especially, but not only, in the Middle East), with protracted hours and a wage that is derisory in local terms (though much more productive than back home), and allowed to return to their families for two weeks every Christmas. Often the women receive similar treatment as domestic servants in wealthy homes in cities like London and New York; they are given bed and board, plus a wage well below the going rate and against the law. Such migratory labour practices were one of the most loathed realities of apartheid in the old South Africa.

Removing people – any people but particularly God's people – *far from their own border* (6), from their homeland (NIV), arouses God's righteous judgment – *I will requite your deed upon your own head* (7). The punishment is entirely appropriate: *I will sell your sons and your daughters into the hand of the sons of Judah, and they will sell them to the Sabeans, to a nation far off* (8). They will become slaves themselves, these proud Phoenicians and Philistines. Their victims will be the agents of this particular transaction – not, let it be noted, to enjoy the experience of owning slaves, but to sell them on.

The Phoenicians and Philistines had sold Israelites on to the Greeks, miles away across what, to the Israelites, was the dreaded sea – exactly as African slaves felt about the Atlantic Ocean. Israelites would sell them across the deserts of Africa to the people of Sheba, great traders themselves.[21] The Phoenicians had not stopped to think about the terror that Israelites felt with regard to the sea; now these intrepid seafarers would taste the barrenness and the brutal heat of the desert.

To achieve his purposes God says, *I will stir them up from the place to which you have sold them* (7): God will arouse them from the lethargy and anomie inevitably brought about by forcible removal from their homeland, terrifying journeys across the ocean, and the demoralizing indignities of slavery. This was action with which God was very familiar on behalf of his people. He had galvanized and gloriously redeemed them out of slavery in Egypt. He is going to do the same with those sold into the ownership of the Ionian Greeks: he would bring them home. Such stirrings among God's own people have happened again in an intensified and worldwide way in the last fifty years. When God decides to *stir them up*, anything can happen.[22]

[21] *E.g.* the Queen of Sheba in 2 Ch. 9:1–12 and the Ethiopian 'Chancellor of the Exchequer' in Acts 8:26–39.

[22] The phrase 'stir up', is often used of the LORD's activity in and with different people and nations, *e.g.* Is. 13:7; 19:2; 41:2, 25; 45:13; Je. 50:9; 51:1; Ezk. 23:22–23.

The truth is as clear as it is both simple and profound: God is in charge of events in every nation and his hand is on any nation's leaders, at any time moulding their decisions and arousing them to the activity which will serve his purposes. In the final phrase of this section in Joel about the Phoenicians and the Philistines, the absolute reliability of this perspective on world affairs is given maximum emphasis: *for the LORD has spoken* (8) – 'a formula of divine certification to endorse its authority'.[23]

As far as the promised fate of Tyre is concerned, none other than Alexander the Great was God's chosen and aroused instrument of judgment. In 332 BC he besieged and captured the city, selling into slavery 30,000 people, including women and children.

The Phoenicians and the Philistines were in no sense Israel's most dominant or destructive enemies. Joel's focus on them in this chapter has the twin effect of opening eyes to the very specific and accurate nature of divine judgment in the course of history, and of reassuring faint hearts that 'there is a judgment' (Jb. 19:29) which will be full, fair and final. If there is a sharp note of vengeance or retribution here, we need to remind ourselves that, in such an attitude, God is not a human being, and we should not therefore project our kind of vindictiveness on to him. His vengeance is as pure as his jealousy (Joel 2:18). Both Old and New Testaments bear the same testimony: 'Vengeance is mine, I will repay, says the Lord' (Rom. 12:19, quoting Dt. 32:35).

2. Destruction (3:9–16a)

Joel now returns in his mind's eye to the valley of Jehoshaphat (12). As he gazes at the scene, he finds himself describing a battlefield – not the killing-fields he has previously had to recall, where God's own people had been treated as the spoils of war, including mere boys and girls; but the scene of a holy war.

This is the significance of the phrase rather tamely translated, *Prepare war* (9). It is the same word used earlier in the book, where the prophet instructed a people plagued by locusts to 'sanctify a fast' (1:14; 2:15) and 'sanctify the congregation' (2:16). The fast and the congregation were to be holy. And so here, 'sanctify war' means that the war was to be holy. This is a war, for sure, but it is very different from any other – set apart from the normal conduct and activities of war, set apart for God to conduct his own strategy and to pursue the activities he will choose. These are all linked with his one intention: *there I will sit to judge all the nations round about* (12).

Because there is going to be such a war, and because the LORD

---

[23] Hubbard, p. 77.

himself is going to be the sole person on one side of the conflict, it is striking – if not rather strange – to see him sitting down to fight. Sitting is done once everything has been accomplished. We then realize that this holy war involves no actual combat, only decisions or verdicts and their execution. The valley is called *the valley of decision* or the valley of the verdict (14).

There is, however, an expected confrontation – between *all the men of war* among the nations (9) and the warriors of God (11). The phrase *mighty men* (9) is actually used of both armies, the mighty men of the nations and the mighty men of the LORD: warriors all.

Joel envisages 'total mobilization'[24] of every human being to be present in the valley of decision: *all the men of war* (9; those who have made a career out of soldiering), those whose only weapons were *ploughshares* and *pruning hooks* (10; those who spend their days on the land, the majority in any nation from Joel's perspective),[25] and *the weak* who think they are too feeble for either instruments or weapons (10; the very young, the very old, the halt, the lame and the blind, anyone normally too feeble to work or too scared to fight). '*I, too, am a warrior*' (or 'a mighty man'), they will all say (10).

Everyone from all the nations is to be there:

> *Hasten and come,*
> *all you nations round about,*
> *gather yourselves there* (11).

This is the time to rouse yourselves, just as every member of the nation had to be gathered for the day of fasting in the temple (1:14; 2:16), young and old alike. There is no time to waste. This is Almighty God calling. Joel sees *Multitudes, multitudes, in the valley of decision* (14). The word translated *multitudes* has the connotation of panic and hubbub; it is a very noisy and confused gathering, with perhaps a hint of the din caused by billions of locusts. There are too many to be counted – *all the nations* (four times the nations are mentioned in four verses). This is the word for 'Gentiles'; the people of Israel are there already, because Joel sees this holy war as taking place in the holy land within the hearing of the holy people in the holy city (16).

It is into this packed valley that the prophet prays to God to bring down his mighty ones: *Bring down thy warriors, O LORD* (11). This

[24] Hubbard, p. 77.

[25] In identical passages (Is. 2:4 and Mic. 4:3) a future time is envisaged when the opposite happens: men hammer their swords into ploughshares and their spears into pruning hooks. The saying is likely to have been a popular phrase for learning to make peace, not war. If so, Joel is saying here that the day of the LORD is a time for war.

prayer almost seems like a sudden response to the prophet's realiza-
tion that the battle lines are being drawn in very unequal numbers –
all the multitudes of the nations against the LORD and his people. Joel
seems to be saying, 'We need your angels, O LORD God of hosts' (the
'hosts' in that title refer to angelic beings in battle array).

There may also be a subliminal reminder of the locusts, which
God had clearly called 'my great army' (2:25):

> The LORD utters his voice
> before his army,
> for his host is exceedingly great (2:11).

Joel's conviction is that an army of angels, on a par (numerically at
least) with God's locust army, will be needed in this great showdown
with the nations. There is a hint, also, of Elisha's prayer for his
young servant when huge Syrian forces had surrounded the people
of Samaria: 'O LORD . . . open his eyes that he may see' that 'those
who are with us are more than those who are with them'. The LORD
then opened the young man's eyes and he saw that 'the mountain
was full of horses and chariots of fire round about Elisha' (2 Ki.
6.15–17).

What, then, will happen in the valley of decision, with all the
multitudes of the nations gathered for this holy war and the LORD
himself on his judgment seat? The atmosphere is electric: in 3:9–13
there are fifteen imperatives, 'giving vivid expression to the frantic
tenor of the passage'.[26] The voice of supreme authority rings from
the throne of judgment:

> *Put in the sickle,*
> *for the harvest is ripe.*
> *Go in, tread,*
> *for the wine press is full.*
> *The vats overflow,*
> *for their wickedness is great* (13).[27]

These commands are presumably directed to the angels, God's
warriors. They are sounded out in a voice like thunder: *the Lord
roars from Zion, and utters his voice from Jerusalem* (16). The
prophet sees the valley of decision as being close to Jerusalem, in a
similar vein to Zechariah's description of the LORD, in judgment with
his holy ones, straddling a huge valley caused by a massive split in
the Mount of Olives – and in that valley are gathered 'all the nations'
(Zc. 14:1–5). From such a vantage point, the LORD's resounding voice

---

[26] Dillard, p. 306. [27] For the winepress imagery see Is. 63:3–6.

shakes *the heavens and the earth* (16) with its sheer volume, but even more with its pronouncement that *their wickedness is great* (13).

This pronouncement by God in the valley of the verdict makes it clear once for all that we indeed live in a universe where the ultimate questions are moral and spiritual. When God sits in judgment, the issue is human wickedness. No longer will wickedness triumph. No longer will it be covered up, or seem fascinating or attractive, or be confused with goodness. No longer will it be exalted, admired, envied, ignored, glamorized or trivialized. When God looks at wickedness, to him it is never anything less than *great* – large, widespread and loathsome.

The language of harvesting grain and wine again evokes the locust devastation. God's army had then chomped the fields bare and stripped the vines of their grapes (1:10–12). This destruction had been reversed by the goodness of the LORD (2:22–24). Now the harvest was ripe again – for judgment, not joy. The vats were again overflowing (2:24; 3:13) – with wickedness, not wine.

If there is one single feature of fallen humanity's wickedness which sticks in God's gullet, it is violence. This has already become apparent in the charges God brings against the nations in this chapter.[28] There may well be a deliberate angle to the instruction about ploughshares and pruning hooks (10): 'When the nations were assembled in the valley, fully equipped for battle, they would receive a shock; they would find there the Judge of all the nations and in their hands they would be holding the incriminating evidence of their own history of violence.'[29]

Joel for the third time asserts that *the day of the LORD is near* (14).[30] We actually get the strong impression that, in the valley of decision, that day has already dawned. It is certainly too late for any decisions to be taken by the nations or by individuals: they have already taken the decisions that matter – to follow wickedness, to reject God and to attack his people. The only decision to be taken (or perhaps announced) on that day in that valley is the verdict of God. John's vision in Revelation 14 describes the scene:

> Then I looked, and, lo, a white cloud, and seated on the cloud one like a son of man, with a golden crown on his head, and a sharp sickle in his hand. And another angel came out of the temple, calling with a loud voice to him who sat upon the cloud, 'Put in your sickle and reap, for the hour to reap has come, for the harvest of the earth is fully ripe'. So he who sat upon the cloud swung his sickle on the earth, and the earth was reaped.

[28] Reflected elsewhere in the prophets (*e.g.* Is. 59:6; Je. 6:7; Ezk. 7:23; Ho. 12:1; Am. 3:10; Mi. 6:12), notably in the major theme of Habakkuk (1:2, 3, 9; 2:8, 17).
[29] Craigie, 1, p. 116.   [30] *Cf.* 1:15; 2:1.

And another angel came out of the temple in heaven, and he too had a sharp sickle. Then another angel came out from the altar, the angel who has power over fire, and he called with a loud voice to him who had the sickle, 'Put in your sickle, and gather the clusters of the vine of the earth, for its grapes are ripe.' So the angel swung his sickle on the earth and gathered the vintage of the earth, and threw it into the great wine press of the wrath of God; and the wine press was trodden outside the city, and blood flowed from the wine press, as high as a horse's bridle, for one thousand six hundred stadia [about 200 miles] (Rev. 14:14–20).

This appalling scene of destruction, to bring an end to all destruction and violence, is to be accompanied, says Joel, by portents in the heavens and on earth: *The sun and the moon are darkened, and the stars withdraw their shining* (15) – a repetition word for word of the locust scenario (2:10). A neighbour in our village in the foothills of the Pyrenees has told us that this was precisely the experience when a locust horde invaded the area during the Second World War. It aggravated the total destruction brought on the maize crops by the locusts and the destructive presence of German troops, including the Gestapo, in the region.

3. Deliverance (3:16b–21)

On that day, familiar, well-worn truths will be manifest: *the LORD is a refuge to his people, and a stronghold to the people of Israel* (16).[31] Simply in the generation living in Joel's time the people had proved this to be true. When their world was being dramatically shaken, they had discovered that there is a place of safety in the LORD himself. When there was nowhere else to run, because the locusts got everywhere, they ran to the LORD and found refuge. On the great day of the LORD's judgment on all nations, there would again be only one place to hide. But it would not be of any avail to seek the LORD then if they did not seek the LORD now. There is no new truth to discover on that day; only the confirmation of truth already revealed and received. The difference is that the stakes are much higher. This will be the last time, because this will be the time when *the heavens and the earth shake* (16) in one final spasm of destruction.

It is only when our comfortable surroundings are being shaken to the core that we truly experience the relevance of old, familiar truths. This statement about the LORD (16) is a classic example. If our world seems safe and sure, who needs a refuge? If we have our lives well

[31] See over thirty psalms, familiar to Joel in the liturgy of the temple: *e.g.* Pss. 18; 31; 46; 57; 62; 71; 91; 118; 142.

organized with plenty of material, social, religious and human resources to surround us, we hardly need a stronghold elsewhere to run into. Many self-sufficient, competent and adjusted people genuinely see no point in having faith in God; he is superfluous – only for wimps and other losers.

The sad and serious aspect of such complacency, of course, is that even that kind of respectable atheism (practical, usually, not intellectual) tends to be shaken at one time or another. That produces an internal conflict which can be worse than the adversity that causes it. Having effectively dismissed faith in God as a crutch for emotional cripples, they find that the same quiet pride in which they sailed on in their serenity now paralyses them in their agony.

It is of prime importance for the messengers of God in every generation to communicate not a God of the gaps or of the gullible, but a sovereign Lord of heaven and earth who, in Christ, has called for every knee to bow before him. Although the hurt, the damaged and the broken-hearted will be more ready to bow the knee before him, the missing link is humility, not hopelessness.

The last five verses of Joel (17–21) are topped and tailed with what, for the prophet and his people, was plain and fundamental, but had become a matter for serious doubt during the locust devastation: *the LORD dwells in Zion* (21, *cf*.17, *I am the LORD your God, who dwell in Zion*). Two astonishing events – the restoration of God's land and people after the locusts (2:27) and the deliverance of God's people on the day of judgment (17) – will have a similar impact: *So you shall know that I am the LORD your God.*

This 'recognition formula'[32] is often to be found in the Old Testament, underlining the fact that God 'acts to accredit himself'. What he promises to do, he then does – with his people and with the nations. And the result of his actions is to demonstrate yet again what has never failed to be true – that he lives among his people. Nothing in the course of history or in the day of judgment can alter that fact. 'Fear not, for I am with you':[33] this promise remains for ever God's statement of intent.

When (and whenever) God's people live in the assurance of God's presence, then they know that he truly is the Lord and that he is their God. Their life together takes on three characteristics: they are holy (17), they are satisfied (18); and they are different (19–20). The first is the determinative one: we can be satisfied without being holy, and we can be different without being holy; but when God is dynamically in our midst, we cannot but be holy – and that is what brings the satisfaction and makes the difference.

[32] Dillard, p. 292; the formula ('then you will know that I am the LORD') comes in, *e.g.*, Ex. 6:7; 1 Ki. 20:13, 28; Is. 43:10; Ezk. 39:6.
[33] Is. 41:10, but the promise, in one form or another, comes several times.

a. God's holy people (3:17)

Jerusalem shall be holy (17). The LORD has just called Zion *my holy mountain* (17), and this is the first time holiness has been mentioned by Joel – a tacit admission, perhaps, that the city was anything but holy at the time. Things will change in those days, as another prophet declared: 'Thus says the LORD: I will return to Zion, and will dwell in the midst of Jerusalem, and Jerusalem shall be called the faithful city [or 'the city of truth'], and the mountain of the LORD of hosts, the holy mountain' (Zc. 8:3). Zechariah also sees this holiness permeating the whole city, down to the basic implements and appurtenances of daily living: 'And on that day there shall be inscribed on the bells of the horses, "Holy to the LORD." And the pots in the house of the LORD shall be as the bowls before the altar; and every pot in Jerusalem and Judah shall be sacred to the LORD of hosts' (Zc. 14:20–21).

In biblical perspective, nothing and nobody is holy unless everyday life and everyday things (like pots and pans) are holy. There used to be a message above the kitchen sinks in some Christian homes: 'Divine service is performed here three times daily.' That is the spirit of this passage in Zechariah and it is the spirit of the kingdom of God, already ushered in by the Messiah, but to be consummated as a result of the day of the Lord: *Jerusalem shall be holy* (17).

In the book of the Revelation John, too, has a vision of the new Jerusalem in similar vein:

> Then I saw a new heaven and a new earth; for the first heaven and the first earth had passed away, and the sea was no more. And I saw the holy city, new Jerusalem, coming down out of heaven from God, prepared as a bride adorned for her husband; and I heard a loud voice from the throne saying, 'Behold, the dwelling of God is with men. He will dwell with them, and they shall be his people, and God himself will be with them' (Rev. 21:1–3).

Holiness is the result of the presence of God. God makes Jerusalem 'the holy city' because he dwells there with his people. There is no other way to holiness, no other kind of holiness. A holy people, a holy life, a holy place, a holy city come from the presence of a holy God.

Joel foresees another aspect of this holiness: *strangers shall never again pass through it* (17). *Strangers*, or 'foreigners', refer to invading armies and anyone with designs on the city. The history of Jerusalem has been a constant saga of foreign invasion, occupation, appropriation and devastation. Jesus himself foretold both the fall of Jerusalem in the lifespan of his own contemporaries (which happened in AD 70), and the fact that Jerusalem would be 'trodden down by the Gentiles, until the times of the Gentiles are fulfilled' (Lk. 21:24).

This is not an Israelite form of xenophobia, because 'sojourners' (also translated 'strangers', but in fact a different word in the Hebrew) were not only welcomed in Israel, but given special rights (in memory of Israel's sojourn in Egypt).[34] The concern is to keep out anyone who will despise or, by their very presence, destroy the holiness of the city. Isaiah captured the mood:

> Awake, awake,
> put on your strength, O Zion;
> put on your beautiful garments,
>   O Jerusalem, the holy city;
> for there shall no more come into you
>   the uncircumcised and the unclean (Is. 52:1)

– or, in the words of John, 'nothing unclean shall enter it, nor any one who practises abomination or falsehood, but only those whose names are written in the Lamb's book of life' (Rev. 21:27). Holiness is gloriously positive – nothing less than the nature of God – but it also excludes anything or anyone unholy.

b. God's satisfied people (3:18)

Joel's second characteristic in the new Jerusalem is satisfaction:

> ... in that day
> the mountains shall drip sweet wine,
>   and the hills shall flow with milk,
> and all the stream beds of Judah
>   shall flow with water;
> and a fountain shall come forth from the house of the LORD
>   and water the valley of Shittim (18).

Holiness leads to a deep satisfaction, here expressed in the abundant provision of wine, milk and water. The wine will be sweet, not bitter, and it will simply ooze out of the grapes, as though the mountain-slopes with their vineyards were dripping, making viniculture unnecessary, winepresses an anachronism, and vats superfluous. The cattle will be in such fine fettle that the milk will positively flow from their udders: no need for them to be milked. Instead of rain running from the hills, they will seem to flow with

---

[34] See Ex. 23:9; Lv. 19:33–34.

milk. Water will rush down the river beds and, if that is not enough, a spring will emerge to bring water to the valleys.

This picture of superabundance surpasses the years of blessing following the restorative work of God after the locust plague (2:22–24). Nothing anyone has experienced, even in the most halcyon days of God's blessing, can begin to compare with what will be available to the people of God on that day. The promised land had originally been 'a land flowing with milk and honey' (Jos. 5:6). Now, after all the vicissitudes of famine, war, locusts and other plagues, its fertility was to be assured. This superabundance would also indicate that the curse, pronounced on the land by God after the disobedience of Adam and Eve ('thorns and thistles it shall bring forth to you', Gn. 3:18), had at long last been lifted.

The true source of all this superabundance is made very plain: *A fountain shall come forth from the house of the LORD and water the valley of Shittim* (18).[35] This spring of water is seen to be a supernatural provision, coming from the worshipping life of the people of God. As their holiness is renewed and deepened by the presence of God in their midst, so this profound satisfaction will become a reality as a fruit of their life with God.

c. God's different people (3:19–21)

The third characteristic of the people of God on that day is that, by the holiness that the presence of God provides, they will be utterly different from everyone else, here typified by Egypt and Edom (19). As the Phoenicians and Philistines were selected as an example earlier in the chapter (4–8), so the Egyptians and the Edomites are singled out *for the violence done to the people of Judah, because they have shed innocent blood in their land. Innocent* here means, not without sin or even some guilt before God, but 'not deserving' the treatment meted out to them by the Egyptians and the Edomites. Our own use of the term 'innocent sufferers' needs similar care.

Violence again is the charge, violence against Israel in Israel. Both nations had a long history of hostility towards Israel. Both will be destroyed, devastated and depopulated: *Egypt shall become a desolation and Edom a desolate wilderness* (19). Unlike the time-specific prediction of judgment on the Phoenicians and the Philistines (7–8), there is only a general pronouncement here. The context would suggest that this judgment is one that falls on the day of the LORD. It is wise, therefore, to see Egypt and Edom from

---

[35] 'Shittim' could be translated 'acacia trees' (*šiṭṭim*). Finley (p. 101) writes of 'evergreens with yellow flowers and useful wood that grow mainly in the valleys around the Dead Sea'.

that eschatological perspective. Egypt stands for worldly powers in their attempts to exterminate the people of God, while Edom represents the incessant hostility and hatred between the world and the people of God.

The difference between Egypt and Edom on the one hand, and Judah and Jerusalem on the other, is that the first will be desolate while the second will be inhabited – *for ever . . . to all generations* (20). The desolation of Egypt is particularly striking, because of the massive fertility of the Nile valley.

This, again, is the decision of the LORD. It is possible to trace specific occasions in the history of both nations when they acted violently towards Israel and Judah. The Egyptians, for example, had Josiah put to death at Megiddo in 609 BC; the text says bluntly that 'Pharaoh Neco slew him at Megiddo, when he saw him' (2 Ki. 23:28–30).

The Edomites, descendants of Jacob's twin brother Esau, particularly attracted the attention of Obadiah as spokesman for God. When Nebuchadnezzar, king of Babylon, eventually captured and destroyed Jerusalem in 586 BC, the Edomites took advantage of their neighbour's (and brother's) misery with 'vicious opportunism:[36]

> On the day that you stood aloof,
>   on the day that strangers carried off his wealth,
> and foreigners entered his gates
>   and cast lots for Jerusalem,
>   you were like one of them.
> But you should not have gloated over the day of your brother,
>   in the day of his misfortune;
> you should not have rejoiced over the people of Judah
>   in the day of their ruin;
> you should not have boasted
>   in the day of distress.
> You should not have entered the gate of my people
>   in the day of his calamity;
> you should not have gloated over his disaster
>   in the day of his calamity;
> you should not have looted his goods
>   in the day of his calamity.
> You should not have stood at the parting of the ways
>   to cut off his fugitives;
> you should not have delivered up his survivors
>   in the day of distress (Ob. 11–14).

[36] Hubbard, p. 83.

Obadiah, in fact, states the moral principle at work in 'the day of the LORD' as far as nations such as Egypt and Edom are concerned:

> As you have done, it shall be done to you:
> your deeds shall return on your own head (Ob. 15).

God's verdict is summarized in the final verse of Joel, where the best rendering of a confused manuscript is probably: 'I will avenge their blood which I have not avenged' (21, NASV).

With such a concluding – and conclusive – declaration, God makes it absolutely plain that, however long it takes, he will see to it that nations are punished for their acts of violence, especially to his people. Behind such a specific assertion would be another more general promise, to the effect that nobody, but nobody, gets away with anything in this world. God sees it all, knows it all and will judge it all.

This important factor in God's judgment of the world should strongly dissuade us either from taking things into our own hands, or from giving up faith in a just God and (therefore) a moral basis to the universe. The Egyptians and the Edomites no doubt thought that, with the passing of the years and the occurrence of other acts of violence, their own record would pass into the mists of time and be forgotten. Joel disabuses them of any such vain hopes.

God's memory and attention to detail do not chop and change like our contemporary media, according to the latest disaster or genocide. He has both books[37] and a bottle,[38] which together are more accurate and permanent than the world's most up-to-date computer with the latest software. These have limitless capacity. They contain everything that anyone has ever thought, said or done. In one particular book are written the names of those on the citizen-roll of the new Jerusalem.[39] In the bottle are stored all the tears and the tossings of God's people.

The day will come – the day of the Lord – when he 'will bring to light the things now hidden in darkness and will disclose the purposes of the heart' (1 Cor. 4:5), all from his complete records. His verdict will then be made public. This verdict will make clear to everyone the radical and eternal difference which God makes between those who are God's people and those who are not.

No doubt there will be many surprises, but there will be no more discussions or decisions. Of his own people God says: 'They shall be mine ... my special possession on the day when I act, and I will spare them as a man spares his son who serves him. Then once more

---

[37] Rev. 20:12. [38] Ps. 56:8. [39] Rev. 20:15.

you shall distinguish between the righteous and the wicked, between the one who serves God and one who does not serve him' (Mal. 3:17–18).

It cannot escape our attention that, at the end of a book that has spoken eloquently of both the wrath and grace of God, God's final statement of intent is one of vengeance: *I will avenge their blood* (21). This is the same God who says, 'I will pour out my spirit on all flesh' (2:8). Locusts . . . rain . . . his Spirit . . . his judgment: these are the themes of this book, which came to Joel as *the word of the LORD*. Each theme is presented as something overwhelming and abundant. Each theme is couched in the perspective of the day of the LORD.

It is, then, absolutely right to fear God in the light of the message of Joel – not the faithless fear which Joel has directly addressed (2:21), but the fear of the LORD, which is 'clean' (Ps. 19:9) and which is 'the beginning of wisdom' (Ps. 111:10). Joel bids us cry to God (chapter 1), return to God (2:1–17), rejoice in God (2:18–32) – but then to fear God (chapter 3).

> Come, O sons, listen to me,
> I will teach you the fear of the LORD (Ps. 34:11).

If, in the poignant word in Malachi, we are going to be spared on that day when God finally acts,[40] we surely need to pray the prayer of Habakkuk:

> O LORD, I have heard the report of thee,
> and thy work, O LORD, do I fear.
> In the midst of the years renew it;
> in the midst of the years make it known;
> in wrath remember mercy (Hab. 3:2).

That is to be our response to Joel's message today: 'Lord, renew and make public (for all to see) the work of your Spirit. Lord, in the day of your righteous judgment, remember mercy.'

[40] Mal. 3:17.

Introduction to Micah

Unlike the prophecy of Joel, for which we can establish no firm date or specific historical situation, the book of Micah describes a definite, if prolonged, context in the latter part of the eighth century BC. The opening lines of the book locate Micah's ministry *in the days of Jotham, Ahaz and Hezekiah, kings of Judah*, that is, between 742 and 686. These are the first and last dates possible, and Micah probably operated for a rather shorter period within this span of fifty-six years.

Micah himself would have grown and matured in his prophetic calling and as a person during these years. The circumstances around him were constantly changing in fairly dramatic ways, as we shall see; and the impact of his faith was inevitably altering him personally. In this sense, it is a distillation of what must have been a costly, demanding and (at least in certain circles of power in the land) extremely unpopular ministry.

Like most of the prophets, Micah seems to have exercised his ministry mainly by preaching ('Hear' . . . 'Hear this' . . .).[1] But the sections we have in the book, which are too succinct to have been his full text for preaching, are perhaps his 'sermon notes', the result either of preparation for preaching or of careful compilation afterwards to be preserved for later generations.

The text itself is full of contrasts in both content and feel. Messages of divergent significance stand side by side in the book. This is readily understandable when we consider that the upheaval, in both national and international events during this period of forty or fifty years, would have elicited far from a monochrome or static response from a person so demonstrably passionate for his God and his country.

Let us take a closer look at the situation, the prophet and the book itself.

[1] See Mi. 1:2; 3:1, 9; 6:1.

1. The situation

The second half of the eighth century witnessed the most affluent period in the kingdoms of Israel and Judah since the break-up of the single nation after the death of Solomon in approximately 922 BC – a split summarized by the Chronicler in these words: 'So Israel has been in rebellion against the house of David to this day' (2 Ch. 10:19). Both capitals – Samaria in the north, Jerusalem in the south – had begun to enjoy immense material prosperity. In the face of this wealth and the godlessness which walked with it, prophets of boldness and incisiveness spoke 'the word of the LORD' to both parts of the divided nation: Amos and Hosea in the north, Isaiah and Micah in the south. These four men represent the essence of Hebrew prophecy.

'Micah deals with the Judaean version of the development of a commercial and "secular" culture.'[2] We have seen the emergence of such a phenomenon in the countries of Western Europe and other westernized countries at the end of the twentieth century. There is a similar, though distinctive, story in the USA. In Micah's time, as in our own, this development led (seemingly inexorably) to a few rich people getting richer, not simply at the same time as the poor becoming poorer, but at the expense of the poor. It has been, and will continue to be, a major political and economic debate whether increasing affluence necessarily produces these disparities. For Micah there was no debate, only denunciation. His book, in common with most Old Testament prophets, makes it plain that in both Judah and Israel the fabric and foundation of national life were being systematically threatened.

The divided kingdoms were, of course, inheritors of an unique pattern of socio-economic life. Essential to it was a promised land, designated for them by God[3] and allotted to the twelve tribes in a careful and specific manner.[4] Not the least of God's commands for the land, which belonged to him and was entrusted to the people only in stewardship,[5] was a set of instructions concerning the 'jubilee'[6] and clear provisions for the helpless – the poor, the widow, the orphan and the sojourner (or resident alien).[7] By these provisions, all land returned to its original owner every fiftieth year, and those who owned land were mandated to take special care of the less fortunate.[8]

In Micah's day, increasing affluence led to increasing callousness (2:1–2) and eventually (inevitably?) to blatant disregard of these foundational laws from God (6:10–12). Those responsible for administering justice in accordance with these laws became involved

---

[2] Marsh, p. 80.   [3] See *e.g.* Nu. 33:50–56.   [4] See Jos. 13 – 19, esp. 14:1–5.
[5] See Lv. 25:23.   [6] See Lv. 25:1–55.   [7] See Dt. 14:28–29; 15:7–11.
[8] Ex. 22:21–24; 25:1–55; Lv. 19:9–10, 33–34.

in conspiracy, bribery and other forms of corruption (3:1–3, 9–11; 7:3). This venality became endemic, even in a purported theocracy, when both priest and prophet bought into the same network of injustice (3:11). Few things are more calculated to arouse the ire of true patriots like Micah.

All this took place under the veneer of continuing religious performances (3:11), to which the wealthy minority regularly subscribed and which they would have indignantly denied to be in any sense a veneer. They had managed to perfect the perennial heresy of compartmentalizing their religious beliefs and practices from their daily occupations and business.

The pernicious impact of the 'enemy within' the nation was accentuated by the huge upheavals happening all around them in the Middle East. The second part of the eighth century saw the emergence and domination of the Assyrians, one of the most bloodthirsty, manipulative and arrogant of history's evil empires. Micah's ministry spans the reign of four Assyrian kings, each of whom made devastating inroads into the Holy Land.

Tiglath-Pileser III (744–727) launched Assyria on its ambitious policy of imperial expansion. Philistia, Damascus, Galilee and Trans-jordan all succumbed to his armies. His successor, Shalmaneser V (726–722), attacked Samaria, the northern capital of Israel, although the city fell only to Sargon II (722–705). 'The once-proud kingdom of the north now became an Assyrian province called Samaria.'[9]

The shockwaves of Samaria's demise, as one would expect, reached Judah and Jerusalem, but met with a mixture of fear and complacency. Hezekiah, when he came to the throne in Jerusalem in 715, set about reforming the apostasy and idolatry of his predecessors.[10] Under Sargon II the Assyrians frequently infiltrated the land without actually taking it. When Sargon II died, Hezekiah thought it politically and strategically appropriate to ally himself with a coalition of other states, including Egypt and Babylon, to take a stand against Assyrian imperialism.[11] He reckoned without the prophets Micah and Isaiah and without the emergence of the most vicious Assyrian king of them all, Sennacherib (704–681). Sennacherib waited for about three years and then in 701 moved in great strength to attack the cities of the coastal plain and of the Shephelah. He captured forty-six towns and cities, including the nine mentioned in Micah 1:10–15, and sent his representative, the Rabshakeh, to convince king Hezekiah of the wisdom of surrender.[12]

Micah and Isaiah both urged Hezekiah to repent of his alliances with Egypt, Babylon and the rest, in order to avert the same fate as

---

[9] Waltke, p. 591. [10]See 2 Ch. 29:1 –31:21. [11]See 2 Ki. 18:21; Is. 39:1–8.
[12] See Is. 36:1ff.

had befallen Samaria and the northern kingdom. The biblical record indicates that God intervened dramatically to send Sennacherib's army in disarray from Jerusalem; Isaiah, together with the writers of 2 Kings and 2 Chronicles, attributes the death of nearly 200,000 Assyrian soldiers to the 'angel of the LORD'.[13] The Greek historian Herodotus implies that the cause was a bubonic plague carried by rats.[14] However God chose to act, Jerusalem was spared and the country did not fall totally into the hands of the Assyrians.

This dramatic turn of events, and its resulting spell of relief for Jerusalem and Judah, did not succeed, however, in turning the nation's leadership back to God. 'The city only staggered from crisis to crisis for one more century',[15] when the Babylonian supplanters of Assyria completely destroyed Jerusalem under Nebuchadnezzar's armies, and removed virtually the whole population into exile in Babylon.

We can only guess at the scale of politicking in Jerusalem's corridors of power while all this international mayhem was happening around them – within their borders as well as in neighbouring territories, even up to the city gates. Of one thing we can be sure: Micah's voice was heard loud and clear in the royal palace and among the king's advisers, judges and religious leaders.

2. The prophet

He is known as 'Micah of Moresheth' (1:1). Moresheth-gath (to give it its full name, as in 1:14) was one of the thriving country towns of the Shephelah, 'an undulating coastal plain ... dotted with fortified cities, located about twenty-one miles southwest of Jerusalem'.[16] Because Micah was known by this description, it is likely that he grew up in an agricultural community, but went at the calling of God to the capital to declare the word of God to the city.

Adam Smith has a somewhat idealized description of the region around Moresheth-gath:

> The home of Micah is fair and fertile. The irregular chalk hills are separated by broad glens, in which the soil is alluvial and red, with room for cornfields on either side of the perennial or almost perennial streams. The olive groves on the braes are finer than either those of the plain below or of the Judaean tableland above. There is herbage for cattle. Bees murmur everywhere, larks are singing, and although today you may wander in the maze of hills for hours without meeting a man or seeing a house, you are never

---

[13] Is. 37:36–37; 2 Ki. 19:35–36; 2 Ch. 32:22–23.   [14] Herodotus, *Histories* II.141.
[15] Marsh, p. 81.   [16] Waltke, p. 594.

out of sight of the traces of ancient habitation and seldom beyond the sound of the human voice – shepherds and ploughmen calling to their flocks and to each other across the glens . . .

. . . The Shephelah is sufficiently detached from the capital and body of the land to beget in her sons an independence of mind and feeling, but so much upon the edge of the open world as to endue them with that sense of the responsibilities of warfare, which the national statesmen, aloof and at ease in Zion, could hardly have shared.[17]

However romanticized, the description evokes well the contrast between, on the one hand, a life spent with the seasons and the elements, the crops and the vines, the birds of the air and the beasts of the field and of the forest, and on the other the business, the bartering and the brutality of the marketplace, the temple, the palace and the courts. Micah knew both well, and knew how to function in both places. But his instinctive empathies were with the farmers, shepherds and smallholders of the Shephelah. He had, like Amos, 'the simple heart of the countryman. He was not lured away by the glittering façade of the new culture – fine houses, advanced fashions, get-rich-quickly businesses – but kept a firm grip on the moral realities that make for true national greatness.'[18]

Micah has, therefore, been called the 'conscience of Israel'.[19] We know very little of the man himself – only, in fact, what we glean by studying this selection of his messages delivered over a period of forty to fifty years. There is much that we can infer, little that we can assert. We know, for example, that a hundred years later his prophetic message and status were still being affirmed in Jerusalem in the days of Jeremiah, when the city was on the brink of destruction by the Babylonians. On that occasion Jeremiah's life was under threat because of his fearless proclamation of God's judgment on a rebellious nation. But

. . . certain of the elders of the land arose and spoke to all the assembled people, saying, 'Micah of Moresheth prophesied in the days of Hezekiah king of Judah, and said to all the people of Judah: "Thus says the LORD of hosts,

    Zion shall be ploughed as a field;
      Jerusalem shall become a heap of ruins,
        and the mountain of the house a wooded height."

Did Hezekiah king of Judah and all Judah put him to death? Did he not fear the LORD and entreat the favour of the LORD, and did

---

[17] G. A. Smith, pp. 402–403.   [18] Marsh, p. 81.
[19] A phrase borrowed by Craigie, p. 4.

not the LORD repent of the evil which he had pronounced against them? But we are about to bring great evil upon ourselves' (Je. 26:18–19).

So Micah' ministry was not simply remembered. His message was still being asserted and respected a century later. Micah clearly got his message home to a rebellious, dissolute and rapacious leadership. In his own lifetime he saw limited success and acceptance, although it was from king Hezekiah himself. It is a mark of the indelible impact of God's word through his servants that Micah continued to speak with effective force long after his death – and continues to speak today.

3. The book

There is a notable measure of agreement among scholars and commentators about the structure of the book. Inevitably, ongoing research fosters re-examination of accepted conclusions; but the basic, simple structure remains convincing. This sees the book as containing three cycles, each containing warnings or threats of judgment and a promise, and each beginning with a call to 'hear' or 'listen.'[20] This structure is as follows.

First cycle (1:2 – 2:13). Israel is threatened with exile on account of their sin (1:2 – 2:11); but the LORD will gather his chosen 'remnant' into Jerusalem; they will survive the siege and the LORD will become their king (2:12–13).

Second cycle (3:1 – 5:15). Because the city's leadership is thoroughly corrupted, the LORD threatens to dismantle Jerusalem (3:1–12); but the LORD promises to lift up Jerusalem high above the nations (4:1–5), to gather the 'remnant' within its walls (4:6–8), and to send a ruler as Messiah for this purified people, who will lead them to victory (5:1–15).

Third cycle (6:1 – 7:20). The fabric of the nation has become irretrievably threadbare (6:1–16) and is unravelling (7:1–7); but the chosen remnant of God's people will be forgiven and saved by God (7:8–20).

'The hope oracles, all of which pertain in part to the remnant, match the topics of doom and so resolve the crises.'[21] These messages of hope (the three 'but' statements above) each bring the promise of light at the end of a dark tunnel. The light of God's revelation through Micah exposes the darkness in the city and the nation, but then points out the way back to God and forward into all that he has planned for his people.

[20] *Cf.* 1:2; 3:1; 6:1.
[21] Waltke (p. 594), whose outline of contents is here summarized.

Micah 1:1
Preface

The superscription of the book (1:1) is precise and specific, not only about the historical context of the prophecy (*in the days of Jotham, Ahaz, and Hezekiah, kings of Judah*), but also about its content. This is described in two familiar but important phrases: *The word of the LORD that came to Micah . . . which he saw . . .*

The first phrase occurs at the beginning of Joel,[1] the second at the beginning of Habakkuk. The phrase 'the word of the LORD' occurs 242 times in the Old Testament, of which 225 are a technical term for prophetic revelation. Of particular interest is the use of these words as a collective description of the entire book, and in this sense it stands as a definition of Micah's whole ministry throughout the period covered by the three kings: Micah's message came from the LORD God himself. Through his servant, Micah, God communicated what he wanted the people of Samaria and Jerusalem to hear. That is still the solemn significance of both absorbing and announcing God's word in any context or generation. The word *came* (more literally 'was' or 'happened') points to the living experience which Micah had of God impressing his word on him.

This experiencing of the word of the LORD is further unfolded in the phrase *which he saw*. As we shall note in commenting on the same word at the beginning of Habakkuk, something more than either hearing God's voice or grasping God's mind and heart is indicated in this distinctive word. Today we refer to some people thinking and speaking pictorially rather than conceptually. It is likely, in fact, that far more people are thus inclined, and that concepts are the stock-in-trade of a relative minority who read (and write) books.

Micah, along with most Old Testament prophets, *saw* with clarity

[1] See also Ho. 1:1; Zp. 1:1; Jon. 1:1; 3:1; Hg. 1:1, 3; 2:1, 10, 20; Zc. 1:1, 7; 4:8; 6:9; 7:1, 8; 8:1, 18.

and with insight. The vivid pictorial content of his messages indicates that he might well have been describing, in prophetic form and language, what he either grasped with his mind or saw with his eyes – or a combination of both.[2] However the process operated for Micah, God gifted him both in seeing into and speaking about such realities: 'Micah had the gift of seeing and revealing hidden things which the common man could not see.'[3]

The text specifically mentions three kings on the throne of the southern kingdom, ruling in Jerusalem, but in significant silence makes no reference to kings during the same period in the north and its capital, Samaria. This omission, as with other prophets of the eighth century such as Isaiah and Hosea, might have been deliberate: Micah would not lend even minimal respectability to those who had 'usurped the Lord's throne through assassinations; they set themselves up, but not by divine prophetic designation'.[4]

Micah is clear, however, that his prophetic message concerns both Samaria and Jerusalem. Although explicit reference is made to Samaria only once (1:5–7), and even then the focus is on Jerusalem, the thrust of the whole book is God's word to Jerusalem in its capacity as the centre of the divine purposes for the united country and for the whole world. On a number of occasions, instead of the name 'Judah', the designation 'Israel', which historically and politically in Micah's time referred to the northern kingdom, is used in respect of the whole nation under its original Davidic monarchy.[5] This is Micah's way of declaring God's original and ultimate intention that there should be one people in one nation under one government – his own.

[2] See, for example, the vivid language of 1:3–4, 6–7, 8, 16.   [3] R. L. Smith, p. 14.
[4] Waltke, p. 614.   [5] *E.g.* 1:13, 14, 15; 2:12; 3:1, 8, 9; 5:1–3; 6:12.

The first cycle

Micah 1:2 – 2:13
Pervasive evil and a promised king

Micah announces God's forthcoming judgment on the whole nation: on Samaria (1:5–7), on the towns and cities of the fertile Shephelah (1:10–16) and on Jerusalem (2:1–5). Although such a message is highly unpalatable and meets scornful rejection, Micah insists on a hearing (2:6–11). He ends with the promise of a new day, beyond the darkness of sin and judgment, when the LORD himself will rule as king (2:12–13).

Micah 1:2–16
1. Micah's message to the world

1. A message for the nations (1:2–5)

The double command to *hear* and to listen, issued with such peremptory suddenness at the beginning of Micah's prophecy, is directed to *you peoples* and addressed to the *earth, and all that is in it* (2). Everyone and everything in the entire world is required to pay attention to these words. They may be concerned with one small area at one specific point in time, but they contain crucial lessons for all people at any time.[1]

---

[1] See Dt. 32:1–3; Ps. 49:1–2; Is. 1:2ff., and particularly the whole of Ps. 50.

The peoples of the whole earth are to listen carefully,[2] because they must *let the* LORD *God be a witness against you* (2).[3] The atmosphere is that of a lawcourt (as later in the book), with the nations in the dock along with, and as much as, Israel herself. What God intends to do to Samaria and Jerusalem will act as testimony in the LORD God's case against them all. Israel was in a special covenant relationship with the LORD, but had violated the terms of the covenant, and judgment was inevitable without appropriate penitence and reformation.

If God intended to act thus against his own people, other peoples could be under no illusions but that he would act in judgment on their persistent and impenitent defiance of his requirements. The principle is endorsed by Peter in the New Testament: 'the time has come for judgment to begin with the household of God; and if it begins with us, what will be the end of those who do not obey the gospel of God?' (1 Pet. 4:17).

There is, therefore, a timeless principle at work in these verses: what happens to the covenant people of God is a clarion call to everyone, in every nation at any period of history, to understand that God is a righteous king and judge, to whom everyone must give account and before whom everyone is liable to judgment. Micah saw this in a way hidden from his contemporaries. 'When he heard the daily news and observed the events taking place in his and neighbouring nations, he saw what the unaided eye cannot see by itself.'[4]

The sovereignty of God is underlined in the vivid picture of his striding forth *out of his place* (3) (that is, *his holy temple*,[5] 2) and coming down from his throne in heaven to *tread upon the high places of the earth* (3). The earth's high places signify both the pre-eminence of sheer height, and the places where pagan power was concentrated and celebrated. In many cities, towns and villages in our own cultures the highest location has been chosen for centres of worship. Similarly, in the areas in and around the Promised Land, high places had been set aside for worship of Baal and other deities. The people of Israel had from the beginning been instructed to destroy such high places and not to use them for their own worship.[6]

This reference to God treading on the high places of the earth contains, therefore, both a military and political dimension, and a spiritual and religious dimension. In the politically volatile and militarily active period into which Micah was speaking, his words

---

[2] The Hebrew for 'hearken' is different from 'hear' and has a more intense meaning.
[3] *Cf.* 6:1–5 for a similar lawcourt atmosphere.   [4] Craigie, 2, p. 10.
[5] High above the earth the LORD watches, scrutinizes and makes his decisions; *cf.* Ps. 11:4–7; 2 Ch. 16:9.
[6] See e.g. 1 Sa. 9:14; 10:5; 1 Ki. 11:7; 2 Ki. 17:9, 29; 23:13. Destroying such high places was the key element in Hezekiah's response to Micah's words; *cf.* 2 Ki. 18:1–6.

spoke of the LORD God's sovereign control of the movement of armies and of empires. In the religiously competitive and combative climate in which Israel operated, Micah's message was of the LORD as God of gods who was tolerating – but was coming to establish his supremacy over – all other claimants to human worship.

Such activity by the LORD would be accompanied by dramatic natural phenomena:

> ... *the mountains will melt under him*
> *and the valleys will be cleft,*
> *like wax before the fire,*
> *like waters poured down a steep place* (4).

When God decides to act, he is irresistible and awesome. The scene combines the power of a volcanic eruption with the force of a huge torrent in a raging thunderstorm: the devastation is total and terrifying. Micah's scenario could be literal, or descriptive of the Assyrian armies on the march, or symbolic of human impotence in the face of divine judgment on the move: or it could be a mixture of all three.

These devastating events have a specific reason:

> *All this is for the transgression of Jacob*
> *and for the sins of the house of Israel* (5).

It is notoriously difficult to interpret natural disasters or international conflicts in terms of the judgment of God. And yet Micah's pronouncement is unequivocal: 'Micah saw behind the Assyrian juggernaut the invincible march of God.'[7] God's people had broken his laws and walked all over his commandments. The word *transgression* underlines their wilfulness in deliberate rebellion against God; the word *sins* refers more to their waywardness as they miss their way by failing to hit the targets God set for them. They had gone over the top and they had gone their own way. Their entire behaviour was out of order – not just inappropriate, but cynical, ungrateful, 'in your face' defiance. The modern aggression of the head-butt comes to mind.

This behaviour was in deliberate disobedience to the covenant relationship between the LORD and his people. The language of these verses underlines the personal nature of this covenant. God and Israel are linked, not by a contract or by a series of contracts ('which are essentially based on distrust'), but on a covenant which 'is based on an I-Thou commitment to one another, which is conceived in love and brought forth through faith'.[8]

[7] Waltke, p. 619.   [8] *Ibid.*

God's response to such deliberate and sustained behaviour was, eventually and ultimately, one of judgment. Israel needed to know that. The nations needed to know that: 'The wages of sin is death' (Rom. 6:23). To look for flagrant examples of Israel's transgression and *sins*, they needed to travel no further than the two capitals:

> *What is the transgression of Jacob?*[9]
> *Is it not Samaria?*
> *And what is the sin of the house of Judah?*
> [What is Judah's high place? NIV]
> *Is it not Jerusalem?* (5).

Dwellers in major modern cities will not be surprised at this condemnation of a nation's capital, which seems inevitably to encapsulate a nation's degeneration. But it would have come as a devastating diagnosis to the inhabitants of Jerusalem, city of peace and God's special dwelling-place, to be designated a 'high place'. Set on Mount Zion it may have been, with the temple taking pride of place; but to be called a pagan shrine and lambasted as the focal point of national transgression would have been horrifying.

The appalling state of idolatry at the heart of the nation and its capital takes on particular significance when we appreciate what normally took place in these pagan high places. 'A high place had an "asherah", perhaps a pole, symbolising the fertility-goddess, and a "masseba", one or more stone pillars, symbolising the male fertility-god. A stone altar was either separate from the holy place or was part of it. The high place also contained a tent or room where the cultic vessels were stored and where sacrificial meals were eaten.'[10]

There was no way in which such practices and beliefs could sit side by side with the worship of the LORD God Almighty. Yet that is what had infiltrated and been tolerated, first in Samaria and then in Jerusalem. Not just Israel, but the nations of the earth needed to understand that such practices are anathema to the one true God. They still need to understand today, not least those who practise Freemasonry, with its explicit rituals invoking 'Jahbulon', a composite deity incorporating Yahweh, Baal and Osiris. No less offensive to God are attempts to place him in the same bracket as the gods worshipped in other religions, let alone the modern practice of multi-faith services.

---

[9] *Jacob* is used here as a title for northern Israel.
[10] Waltke, p. 619. For further explanation of these pagan practices, see the comments on 1:7 below.

2. A message for Samaria (1:6–9)

Eighth-century Samaria was a byword for prosperity and luxury. It had also become irretrievably pagan and corrupt to the core. It was doomed. 'What Micah saw, and his audience did not, was that Samaria's fall would be God's doing: the Assyrian armies would merely be God's instrument.'[11]

So the LORD declares, through Micah, *I will make Samaria a heap in the open country, a place for planting vineyards* (6).[12] The same fate will eventually overtake Jerusalem (3:12). To catch the breathtaking force of such a pronouncement, we need to imagine ourselves on a vantage point in, say, the City of London or Manhattan. It is virtually impossible to imagine that such bastions of success and prosperity could ever be reduced to *a heap* – the odd building-site perhaps, but not the whole city turned into fields fit for planting vines.

The process of divine judgment is described in terms of Samaria's most characteristic features: *her stones, her foundations, her images, her hires, her idols* (6–7). Each of these will be smitten in an appropriate way.

Many years earlier, in the days of the prophet Elijah, Omri and Ahab had built the northern capital of 'exquisitely dressed stones – a style of masonry dressing which was not equalled in Palestine, or indeed anywhere else in the Near East'.[13] The founding of Samaria is simply described in the following terms: '[Omri] bought the hill of Samaria from Shemer for two talents of silver; and he fortified the hill, and called the name of the city which he built, Samaria, after the name of Shemer, the owner of the hill' (1 Ki. 16:24). Ahab's later contribution, including the palace he built and inlaid with ivory, led to stinging words of woe by Amos about 'those who feel secure on the mountain of Samaria . . . who lie upon beds of ivory, and stretch themselves upon their couches' (Am. 6:1, 4; *cf.* 3:15).

No expense and no effort had been spared by Omri and Ahab in making Samaria a splendid capital city – an achievement maintained and extended down the years by successive rulers, so that by Micah's time *her stones* and her foundations were rock solid both in appearance and in substance. All that solid splendour would be reduced to *a heap*, in spite of its historical stability and in spite of its imposing magnificence. The sheer shame of such an experience for the people, especially the leading citizens of Samaria, may well be hinted at in

[11] Craigie, 2, p. 11.
[12] This is a direct fulfilment of God's word through Moses to his people: Dt. 13:16 (12–18). See also 1 Ki. 9:8; Is. 17:1; 25:2; Je. 9:11; 51:37.
[13] Kenyon, quoted by Waltke, p. 620.

the word *uncover* (6) or 'lay bare'; Samaria's destruction will be publicly paraded for all to see.[14]

As the walls and foundations of Samaria are thus dismantled, so will the shrines and symbols of her pagan practices be destroyed. These shrines, with their images and idols, were expensively decorated in gold and silver. When the Assyrians sacked Samaria, they were to strip the shrines of this wealth and turn it over to supporting their own cult practices. At the heart of both Samaritan and Assyrian religion was cult prostitution, both male and female. To obtain the favour and blessing of a particular deity, a client paid for the services of a temple prostitute with money, food or clothing.[15] The bulk of these fees went towards titivating the temple and providing for the priesthood.

The reference to prostitutes, whether in Samaria or Assyria, also highlights the fundamental faithlessness of God's people. Although betrothed to Yahweh and committed to faithfulness towards him, they had long since run off after other gods. This spiritual adultery was reflected in physical immorality under the guise of religion. 'Cultic prostitution finds its basis in the idea that the forces of life in nature, especially at the spring season, were revived through the union of a god and a goddess . . . and that this divine union, ensuring fertility of the crops and of the wombs, was effected through sympathetic magic and celebration involving the enactment of sexual intercourse' with a temple prostitute.[16]

Much New Age belief and practice is nothing more or less than a replica of these ancient superstitions. In ancient Egypt, Assyria and Babylon, devotion was given to female–male combinations (such as Isis and Osiris, Ishtar and Tammuz, Astarte and Adonis). Today, the focus is on the feminine forces of 'Mother Nature', often with less than subtle references to Artemis or Aphrodite and more sophisticated talk of ying and yang or Gaia. Ultimately, in terms of Micah's diagnosis of Samaria, they all turn out to be another recycling of pagan beliefs which place no moral obligations or boundaries on their adherents, pander to our naturally self-centred desires, and constitute a direct rejection of our creator God. The result of such refusal to bow the knee to the Lord is classically summarized by Paul: 'although they knew God they did not honour him as God or give thanks to him, but they . . . exchanged the glory of the immortal God for images resembling mortal man or birds or animals or reptiles' (Rom. 1:21–23).

These are the images (in eighth-century Samaria) which God, through the invading Assyrians, was about to reduce to fragments

---

[14] For this connotation, see Ezk. 13:14; Hab. 3:13.   [15] See Ho. 2:8–9.

[16] Waltke, p. 621.

and lay waste, leaving the victors to use the spoils of conquest to feed their own paganism: *for from the hire of a harlot she gathered them, and to the hire of a harlot they shall return* (7). Spiritual adultery by the people of God will surely be punished, but its essence will never be eradicated until this rebellious world is no more. The discipleship implications are spelt out by John: 'Do not love the world or the things in the world. If any one loves the world, love for the Father is not in him. For all that is in the world, the lust of the flesh and the lust of the eyes and the pride of life, is not of the Father but is of the world. And the world passes away, and the lust of it; but he who does the will of God abides for ever' (1 Jn. 2:15–17). Whatever may be the allure and the impact of New Age beliefs, there are much wider and deeper influences at work in our generation: 'mammon, prurient sex and drugs'.[17]

As Micah contemplates the inevitable destruction of Samaria, he reveals a heart broken with grief and shame:

> *For this I will lament and wail;*
> *I will go stripped and naked;*
> *I will make lamentation like the jackals,*
> *and mourning like the ostriches* (8).

Micah's vivid and visceral actions point to the uncomplicated involvement of the prophet in the people's present and future situation. Not for him any detached analysis or lofty denunciation. As he hears the words of God, he feels with the heart of God. He knows that Samaria's *wound is incurable* (9),[18] that the judgment must fall. And so he determines to go very public with his grief, for everyone to hear and see.

Micah likens his lamentations to the cries of jackals and ostriches. 'The jackal and the ostrich embody wildness and desolation. Jackals are scavengers that live in packs near human settlements . . . They move about at night, howling and evoking feelings of desolation and fear. The ostrich, on the other hand, is a two-toed flightless runner . . . It exhibits both cruelty and uncleanness. It is easily frightened and stupid.'[19] Micah's unflattering description of himself in such terms indicates something of the depths of his agony on behalf of the people of Samaria, who effectively were not his own people – another pointer to the prophet's resonance with the heart of God.

[17] Waltke, p. 620.
[18] The word 'incurable' is used in Scripture only of conditions which God himself has brought about and which he asserts he will not reverse, except on his own terms and in his own time; *cf.* 2 Ch. 21:18; Jb. 34:6; Is. 17:11; Je. 15:18 and particularly Je. 30:12–17.
[19] Kaiser, p. 34.

But Samaria's wound is not only festering in its incurable impact;
it is spreading:

> ... *it has come to Judah,*
> *it has reached to the gate of my people,*
> *to Jerusalem* (9).

It is difficult to feel another people's suffering until and unless it
impacts our own people. The disease which caused such trauma in
Samaria was contagious. It could not be contained. What had started
in Samaria had spread to Jerusalem. This is the nature of the disease
called sin. Nobody has a monopoly on sin, or a remedy for it.
Nobody can contain its ravages.

This is what turns Micah into a jackal and an ostrich, after the
manner of the psalmist:

> My heart is smitten like grass, and withered;
> I forget to eat my bread.
> Because of my loud groaning
> my bones cleave to my flesh.
> I am like a vulture of the wilderness,
> like an owl of the waste places;
> I lie awake,
> I am like a lonely bird on the housetop (Ps. 102:4–7).

The difference between the psalmist and the prophet is that the
former's lament is mainly for himself, while the latter's is for the
people. Perhaps that is the hallmark of a true prophet.

3. A message for Judah and Jerusalem (1:10–16)

Micah here anticipates the arrival of the Assyrians in the Shephelah,
the hill country around Jerusalem from which he himself had
emerged into the prophetic limelight in the capital. The nine towns
he mentions 'comprise a circle of nine miles in radius around Micah's
hometown of Moresheth-gath (14) and are visible from there'.[20] The
message is blunt, the prospect is appalling and the future of
Jerusalem as a capital is bleak: 'Without its satellites Jerusalem would
no longer be a capital.'[21]

The wordplay used by Micah is intricate. The Hebrew name of
each town is turned into a prophetic message in a variety of ways:
'For some towns he uses a pun, for others a play on the sound of the
town's name, for yet others he draws out the meaning implicit in the

---

[20] Waltke, p. 626.   [21] Craigie, 2, p. 15.

name as such.'[22] Craigie attempts to bring home the force of Micah's message by using the names of towns in his native Scotland: 'Crieff will know grief. Forfar will forfeit. Craill will be frail. Wick will be burned. Stornoway will be blown away. Edinburgh will be no Eden. For Tain there will only be pain.'[23]

In the event, it was in 701 BC that Sennacherib advanced on the Shephelah, capturing forty-six towns and cities, including those mentioned in this passage. But the impact of Micah's catalogue must have been chilling: town after town in the prosperous heartland of Judah would fall to the invader. No wonder the prophet felt the pain so profoundly. And yet there is something still more devastating in this tragic list, indicated by the first and the last names, Gath and Adullam. Evocative even today, these names recalled two of the lowest points in the life of David, the great king of Israel from whom Micah's contemporaries proudly traced their history. 'Though he is never directly mentioned, the figure of David appears hauntingly in the tapestry of destruction – not a David standing tall in triumph, but a David bowed down by humiliation.'[24]

The phrase *Tell it not in Gath* (10), with which Micah begins his catalogue of disaster, is a direct quotation from David's lament over the deaths of Saul and Jonathan at the battle of Mount Gilboa (2 Sa. 1:20), when the Philistines were victorious over Israel (Gath being the Philistine stronghold). As David did not intend the Philistines to gloat over the decimation of Israel in his day, so Micah declares to their enemies (the Assyrians in particular) that they are not to gloat over their success. Why? Because 'When Israel – God's light to the nations – is itself darkened, the nations are left without light and salvation.'[25]

Equally, the last phrase, *the glory of Israel shall come to Adullam* (15), refers to the time when David was on the run from Saul and took refuge in the cave of Adullam. We are told that a motley band of about four hundred men joined him there: 'every one who was in distress, and every one who was in debt, and every one who was discontented, gathered to him; and he became captain over them' (1 Sa. 22:2). Such a collection of no-hopers and no-gooders hardly reflected much credit on David. Yet this was precisely the future that Micah predicts for *the glory of Israel*[26] – the leading citizens of Jerusalem and Judah. As Saul harassed and hounded David, so Sennacherib would hound his descendants: 'Many of Israel's military leaders and officials had David's blood in their veins.'[27]

---

[22] *Ibid.*, p. 14.   [23] *Ibid.*   [24] McComiskey, p. 408.   [25] Waltke, p. 627.
[26] In David's lament over Saul and Jonathan, he begins with the words: 'Thy glory, O Israel, is slain upon thy high places' (2 Sa. 1:19).
[27] Waltke, p. 632.

There may be rather more than this poignant historical allusion in Micah's topping and tailing his Assyrian hit-list with places so redolent of major low points in David's life. He may well be making oblique reference, both to the way a band of no-hopers eventually grew to be the builders of the Davidic empire, and to the ultimate end of David's dynastic line and, by implication, to the emergence of 'great David's greater Son'.[28]

Whatever the details, implicit or explicit, of Micah's message to Judah and Jerusalem in these verses, the prophet clearly envisages and presages the end of an era, if not of a nation. Such a disaster, brought about by the hand of God himself, is no occasion for God's enemies to rejoice. Rather, it is a time for the inhabitants of each town and city to awake to its coming doom. This Micah highlights as he plays with each name.[29]

Beth-le-aphrah (10) means 'the house characterized by dust', a significance Micah applies to its inhabitants, who will roll in the dust as they are humiliated in defeat at the hands of Sennacherib. *Shaphir* (11), or 'beauty town', will be depopulated and its people will be forced to go into exile: *Pass on your way . . . in nakedness and shame.* To be stripped naked and to be made to parade through the streets by the Assyrians was the ultimate in shame and disgrace[30] – a punishment to which the Son of God was himself subjected in atonement for our sins.

In this utter shame the people of Shaphir might have expected some support from their neighbours in *Zaanan* (11), which suggests the verb 'go forth'. But no such help would be forthcoming: *The inhabitants of Zaanan do not come forth.* Likewise the people of *Bethezel* (11) – meaning perhaps 'the house of the taking away' – will be completely unable to provide any alternative place to stand firm against the invader: *the wailing of Bethezel shall take away from you its standing place.*

As the invasion gathers momentum and town after town is captured, those still to be attacked would have understandably looked for some relief to come from the capital, some strong reinforcements to confront the enemy and turn the tide. That was the hope of the inhabitants of *Maroth* (12) or 'bitter town'. Events had indeed turned sour, and it is not surprising that they *wait anxiously for good* (or, in this context, 'sweetness').

[28] See 5:2–4. The phrase is taken from the hymn 'Hail to the Lord's Anointed' by James Montgomery.
[29] Many of the place names in this section, together with Micah's playing on words, are uncertain in meaning; these comments will reflect that uncertainty.
[30] For a parallel to the fate awaiting these first two towns, see God's judgment on Babylon in Is. 47:1–3.

Micah's riposte to the people of Maroth encapsulates the shattering anomaly of what is to happen. The Assyrians are the all too visible agents of this appalling catastrophe, but in fact *evil has come down from the LORD* (12). *Evil* here means 'disaster'[31] or 'calamity', and of such an irresistible intensity as to reach *the gate of Jerusalem*. Jerusalem, so far from sending reinforcements, was about to be overrun itself.

So far there had been little or no explanation for this march to the scaffold for the inhabitants of the Shephelah. Then a clue is given:

> *Harness the steeds to the chariots,*
> *   inhabitants of Lachish;*
> *you were the beginning of sin*
> *   to the daughter of Zion,*
> *for in you were found*
> *   the transgressions of Israel* (13).

The two words *steeds* and *Lachish* sound similar in Hebrew, giving the sense that the people of the city are being instructed to evacuate their stronghold in the swiftest possible way. This command would have sent more shivers down their spines, because Lachish was a very important city and militarily the strongest place in the region. 'It was a town only some four miles from Micah's home. Doubtless there was much talk at Lachish of a "chariot brigade" involving the introduction of a horse, the "new weapon" of great mobility and power.'[32] The Egyptians were the first to use horses in battle. Harnessed to chariots, the charging animals presented fearsome and almost invincible opposition. That, in its turn, would probably have produced arrogance in an army able to mobilize cavalry and chariotry in large numbers; defeat was virtually out of the question. 'Lachish was a garrison town with a single mission: to fortify the western hills in the event of attack. Thus the technology of its defences must have been the very best that any kingdom could devise . . . Lachish was a formidable city that had to be negotiated whenever an Assyrian or a Babylonian army considered conquest of the region.'[33]

Lachish had become the headquarters of such military might in Judah. But Lachish was about to fall to the Assyrians. Lachish had become *the beginning of sin to the daughter of Zion*. Instead of humbly relying on the LORD himself, they had come to rely on the latest technology – hence Micah's conclusion: *in you were found the transgressions of Israel*. At the bottom of every act of revolt against

---

[31] *Cf.* Is. 45:7.   [32] Marsh, p. 92.
[33] G. M. Burge, in *NIDOTTE*, 4, pp. 862–863.

God, every *transgression*, is pride – the conviction that God's will and God's word are optional and that I have a right to choose what I want to do; indeed, that I am perfectly capable of running my own life and running it successfully.[34]

Such an attitude leads inexorably to any number of specific *transgressions*: self-reliance, self-assertion, self-glorification, self-sufficiency. The latest technology, whether it be horses and chariots in the eighth century BC or horsepower and computers nearly three millennia later, can be a snare and a delusion. It gnaws away at 'simple faith' and makes possible, by human means and with human-built machines, what would have boggled the imaginations even of our grandparents. We easily slip into a 'can do' mentality, which soon sidelines and ultimately excludes God from everything but the bits we cannot control or comprehend – and those are disappearing fast. We, as much as Micah's people, need the reminder that 'technology will prove worthless in the time of God's judgment against sin'.[35]

The meaning of the name of Micah's home town, *Moresheth-gath*, is uncertain, but might possibly suggest 'one who is betrothed', or more generally 'a possession'. The reference to *parting gifts* (14) could then be to a dowry, that is to paying tribute to the Assyrian conqueror as he takes the town's inhabitants off to his own home as his 'bride'. Alternatively, Micah may be making a more generalized remark about the town being on the point of saying goodbye to its possessions.

Achzib (14) means 'deception town', and was an important manufacturing centre, whose workshops provided a very lucrative business for several leaders in the region. These businessmen would have come to rely on the income received from Achzib. But the Assyrian invasion would turn their prosperity into an empty illusion, with the result that the boom years enjoyed by successive kings of Israel would suddenly be no more – not just a recession but utter destruction. This is what happens when God moves in judgment on a nation.

The *inhabitants of Mareshah* (15; a phrase that sounds again like the word for 'one who takes possession' and thus *a conqueror*) will have a complete role reversal. Instead of being conquerors, they will find a conqueror coming up against them; the possessor will be possessed. As at Adullam, the net result of this conquest of the Shephelah will be the survival of a remnant – and a not very prepossessing remnant at that. Anyone taking a look at David's motley

---

[34] See the powerful words of Micah's contemporary, Isaiah, in Is. 30:15–17, where a similar reliance on 'horses' and 'swift steeds' is dismissed.
[35] Waltke, p. 630.

crew in that cave of Adullam, when he was at his lowest ebb, would not have held out hopes of any recovery. Similarly, anyone seeing what was left in Judah and Jerusalem once the invading armies had departed would not have expected a future and a hope for the survivors. We have to wait to the end of this section (2:13–14) before we read an explicit promise to that effect.

So Micah's closing remarks come as no surprise: *Make yourselves bald and cut off your hair . . . make yourselves as bald as the eagle* (16). However trendy total baldness may be with certain folk today, in Micah's day baldness denoted disgrace and misery for the unutterable calamity threatening Judah and Jerusalem.[36]

As in any such conflict, the most tragic and appalling aspect is the fate of the children: *The children of your delight . . . shall go from you into exile* (16). What we bequeath to our children, in whom we often profess to take delight, is the acid test of how seriously we are prepared to take the word of God. By their rebellious pride, Micah's contemporaries were on the point of leaving their children a legacy of war, devastation and exile – realities which can be our legacy in spiritual terms as much as physically. We might well ask ourselves to what extent the conflicts, barrenness and rootlessness of so many children today are the result of parental transgression of God's laws.

When God decides to move in judgment, whole communities, towns, cities and nations are faced with the seriousness in his sight of their sins and transgressions – and feel the impact of his holy anger. The events described in these verses, however allusively and cryptically (to us at any rate), are the direct action of the LORD (12, *evil has come down from the LORD*; 15, *I will . . . bring*). At such times God turns familiar places and settled situations upside down. It is imperative, now as then, that the people of God sit up, pay heed and take appropriate action.

[36] *Cf.* Is. 3:24; 15:2; 22:12.

Micah 2:1–13
2. The preacher for this people

1. The kind of preaching Micah provides (2:1–5)

Micah now moves from generalities to specifics. Twice in chapter 1 he has referred to the people's sins and transgressions (1:5, 13). These are powerful biblical descriptions of human waywardness and wilfulness; but they remain just words without explicit examples, particularly in the ears of people hardened to religious language and secure in their self-sufficient prosperity. It is easy to become the kind of person who is hardened to religious language and secure in self-sufficiency, with the result that such talk is automatically applied to someone else. Micah's hearers could well have been like that.

Micah goes for the jugular:

> *Woe to those who devise wickedness*
> *and work evil upon their beds!*
> *When the morning dawns, they perform it,*
> *because it is in the power of their hand.*
> *They covet fields, and seize them;*
> *and houses, and take them away;*
> *they oppress a man and his house,*
> *a man and his inheritance* (1–2).

Sins and transgressions have now become *wickedness* and *evil*. Micah has, in these four words, summarized the impact of all human behaviour that is contrary to the will of God. It affects our relationship with God and with one another. The focus has now shifted from general trends to treatment of fellow human beings. *Wickedness*, in particular, turns the attention on the way those responsible treat other people. The overriding meaning is of 'deception actively practised by evildoers with the purpose of hurting others'.[1]

---

[1] Bernhardt, in *TDOT* 1, p. 142.

The wickedness was being practised by powerful landowners and men of property. Their victims were ordinary people with *fields* and *houses*, probably just one field and a single dwelling, all a man might own to pass on to his children – *a man and his inheritance*. In essence, says the preacher, wealthy city slickers are fleecing ordinary people under the guise of doing business efficiently and profitably. Land and property were being concentrated in the hands of a tiny, wealthy, arrogant minority. Such monopolies in ownership of farming land are still with us, with similar dangers for our society. But today's 'instruments of production are not just land but factories, raw materials and capital. The concentration of these instruments of production, distribution and communication in the hands of a few may threaten our society.'[2]

In today's marketplace, with its 'urge to merge' and apparently endless moves towards conglomeration, ruthlessness seems to have settled in. Banks are needlessly foreclosing, building societies are unfeelingly repossessing, employers are radically downsizing in order to maximize profits, manipulators of the markets and of its technology virtually 'create' money by playing on the inefficiency of internal banking systems. On the global scale, richer nations hold poor countries to ransom for money which they should never have loaned out in the first place.

One's perspective and one's view of such a situation depend – and always have depended – on where one lives and works. 'In the city of Jerusalem it may have seemed simply to be the operation of big business: wealthy men were increasing their land-holdings. But in Moresheth and the country-towns it was oppression, not business. The small landowner, who could provide for himself and his family, was suddenly destitute. Where once he was self-sufficient, he was now dependent on others, his livelihood lost to the unscrupulous dealers in real estate.'[3]

Micah's dual residence, in the country and in the city, gave him a distinctive insight into the impact of such unscrupulous business practices. He knew people back in Moresheth whose lives had been wrecked by property sharks, who probably had never met the individuals, let alone the families, whom they had fleeced in doing a good deal; they were just names on a contract or a bill of sale, clients or customers but certainly not fellow human beings.

Not all property deals, of course, need be unscrupulous and bordering on the fraudulent. But Micah leaves his hearers in no doubt that these deals were conceived in wickedness and executed in oppression – *because it is in the power of their hand* (1). They lie awake at night plotting new deals, regardless of the ethics involved,

[2] R. L. Smith, p. 24.   [3] Craigie, 2, p. 18.

and *when the morning dawns* they carry out their nocturnal schemes. That phrase, *because it is in the power of their hand*, is the give-away line. Wealthy and successful people usually reach a point in their lives when there is nothing they reckon they cannot achieve or acquire. They have the resources; all they need is the opportunity. And they become accustomed to using their resources to create their opportunities; the means and the morals are irrelevant. The bottom line is, 'I want it and I'm going to get it' – or, in Micah's words, *They covet fields, and seize them; and houses, and take them away* (2).

Greed is the central driving force of such people's lifestyles, the kind of greed that is never satisfied, scarcely recognized, rarely admitted and often rationalized. Most people involved in business would be horrified to be told, especially by preachers like Micah, that their transactions amounted to fraud and plundering the poor. The word *oppress* (2) speaks of violence, and violence is not confined to physical assault: 'It may be dishonest scales, extortion, outright show of force, or through the court system.'[4] It could, in Micah's day, be by making loans and then foreclosing on them. There were and are many forms of intimidation to deprive people of what is rightfully theirs and should remain theirs.

Because, in an agrarian economy, there was little alternative to working the land for a living for oneself and one's family, it spelt complete ruin to lose one's field or fields. As the rich few became richer in Micah's day, so many were becoming impoverished because of these oppressive practices, and a whole sector of 'new poor' had emerged. For Micah this was not a matter of political or economic doctrine, but of justice. The behaviour of the few amounted to *evil* (1).

As we would expect, Micah's denunciation (*Woe to those who . . .*, 1) is couched in language which would have jerked its hearers back into the cold air of God's covenant commandments. The single word *covet* (2) unmistakably recalled the tenth commandment, the one which eventually pinned down Saul of Tarsus[5] and many another wealthy, smug achiever. More than that, Micah's whole approach is a coded reminder that the whole land belonged to God and had been distributed carefully throughout the twelve tribes of Israel, with appropriate warnings and promises attached: not least the provision, indeed the instruction, that all land should revert to its original owner every fiftieth year, 'the year of jubilee'.[6]

So 'the covenant . . . instructed Israel about property rights',[7] and these wealthy land barons were in flagrant contempt of the covenant.

---

[4] Waltke, p. 637.   [5] Ex. 20:17; Rom. 7:7.   [6] Lv. 25:8–12.
[7] Waltke, p. 635.

The fact that they spent the night hours planning yet more acquisitions showed the inexorable grip of greed on their souls. There is not a little prophetic awesomeness in Micah's implication that he – and the LORD God – are fully aware of what is going on in the privacy of their homes, in the darkness of the night, in the secrecy of their hearts and in the daily business of their offices.

Whole families and futures were at stake. If the unrestrained scheming of the affluent minority was not halted, the national fabric and its social glue would perish. But it could not be halted by political change, economic reform or a new business ethic. That much is clear from Micah's diagnosis of greed in the human heart as the fundamental cause of such a situation. It cannot be halted even by the piercing words of preachers like Micah, let alone by acts of religious piety. Nothing less than the intervention of God himself can tackle the greed and pride which lie at the root of fraud and corruption in the business world.

When God begins to speak directly, it is the pride of the wealthy landowners and property barons that he addresses: *you shall not walk haughtily* (3). We have already noted the pride which would have produced in the people of Lachish (1:13) the 'beginning of sin' for the people of Judah and Jerusalem. That pride at work in Jerusalem had found a more blatant expression in unrestrained acquisition of land and property by a wealthy minority in the city. 'God resists the proud',[8] and these men would now experience the meaning of such resistance.

These acts of fraud and oppression provoke from the LORD a fearsome response:

> *Therefore thus says the LORD,*
> *Behold, against this family I am devising evil,*
> *from which you cannot remove your necks;*
> *and you shall not walk haughtily,*
> *for it will be an evil time* (3).

God's response echoes Micah's description (1–2) in three ways: first, the *evil* these wealthy landowners plot will be met with *evil* from the LORD and will lead to *an evil time*; secondly, they may *devise* all kinds of activity against the hapless poor, but God is *devising evil* against them; thirdly (and rather strangely) they *oppress a man and his house*, but the LORD is targeting *this family*. All three echoes are significant.

Micah has already expressed the gist of God's devising evil in the phrase about Maroth's fate in 1:12: 'because evil has come down

---

[8] Pr. 3:34; 1 Pet. 5:5.

from the LORD to the gate of Jerusalem'. There it has the connotation of 'calamity' or 'disaster', and the NIV uses both English words here: 'I am planning disaster against this people ... It will be a time of calamity.' The sense would seem to be that, when people behave toward God in a way that he regards as evil, God's response is to behave towards them in a way that they regard as evil. The point is that rebellious humanity and God have entirely different definitions of what is evil and offensive. We deem evil anything which impairs our convenience and comforts; God deems evil anything which ignores his commandments and character.

The second echo underlines that God's response to persistently haughty human evil is not haphazard, visceral or out of control: *I am devising evil.*[9] He takes his time, issues his warnings and plans his actions. The punishment he is planning fits the crime: as they attacked the property and the persons of others, so he will target their persons and their property. The difference is that their targets were innocent victims, which is the last thing that could be said about these oppressors of the poor. The disaster God is planning will force them to bow their necks, now held so proudly erect in their marketplace, under the yoke of slavery. They have been enslaving poorer people under their dominating influence; they will be forced to do what the Assyrian invaders demand. Thus will human pride be brought low – heads bowed, necks yoked.

The third echo introduces what, to the individualistic mentality of most westerners, sounds alien if not offensive. These corrupt landowners have reduced *a man and his house, a man and his inheritance*, to poverty and virtual slavery. So God will act against *this family*, that is, the nation as a whole. A proper perspective comes with the biblical doctrine of corporate solidarity. God sees Judah and Jerusalem, not as a multitude of individuals, but as a family. Indeed, it is likely that he sees all human beings in such terms, if we accept the significance of his words to Israel through Amos:

> You only have I known
>   of all the families of the earth;
> therefore I will punish you
>   for all your iniquities (Am. 3:2)

– words spoken 'against the whole family which I brought up out of the land of Egypt' (Am. 3:1).[10]

A significant aspect, therefore, of the seriousness of an individual's sin is that not only does it affect the lives of others in that person's family, fellowship and society, but it also involves them to a degree

---

[9] *Cf.* Je. 18:11.   [10] *Cf.* Je. 8:3.

in its 'wages' – what it inevitably reaps by way of divine judgment. Both perpetrator and victim of the crimes mentioned (1–2) will be on the receiving end of the evil which God is devising.

We need to say, however, that God is well able to draw distinctions in his dispensation of justice. Not least, he holds individuals ultimately accountable for their own sins, not for anybody else's.[11] He also knows how to rescue the godly[12] from all kinds of trouble and to lift up the downtrodden.[13] Nevertheless, when a *family* (a nation or a city) persistently tramples over his laws, his judgment is apparently and traumatically indiscriminate: the innocent suffer along with the guilty – a fact which has created angst in sensitive souls from time immemorial.[14]

Micah's contemporaries are staring into *an evil time* for the whole nation and for the entire city. But those particularly guilty will be particularly on the receiving end:

> *In that day they shall take up a taunt song against you,*
> *and wail with bitter lamentation,*
> *and say, 'We are utterly ruined' (4).*

When the Assyrians execute God's judgment on the land and on the city, these property magnates will see their whole world fall apart as they face utter ruination. What they will fail to recognize is that their experience will entirely reflect the experience of the small landowners and householders whom they had fleeced in earlier years.

This is expressed in the words of the *taunt song* put in their mouths by Micah:

> *he changes the portion of my people;*
> *how he removes it from me!*
> *Among our captors he divides our fields (4).*

Just as they had changed the portions of their victims, removing their property and their land from them, so everything will be redistributed by the Assyrians among themselves. There is a particular irony in the reference to *our fields*, the very fields coveted and seized in previous years – not truly their fields at all.

The climax of God's judgment is now stated:

> *Therefore you will have none to cast the line by lot*
> *in the assembly of the LORD (5).*

---

[11] See Ezk. 18:1–32. [12] See 2 Pet. 2:9. [13] See Pss. 145:14; 146:8; 147:6.
[14] See Gn. 18:22–33 (Abraham); Nu. 16:22 (Moses); 2 Sa. 15:17 (David).

These words look ahead to life beyond invasion, destruction and exile, to the time when the people are restored to the land and have their original possessions redistributed.[15] These wealthy criminals will not even get a mention; they will have no place in *the assembly of the LORD*, when plots of the land, promised in perpetuity to Abraham, will again be allocated. In effect, this punishment was a sentence to exclusion from the life of the people of God. They would be banned from the land, and thus from the life of God, for ever.

We can see how direct and pointed Micah's message was. It was certainly not calculated to win friends among the wealthy and the powerful. There was a cost to be paid for such boldness, and it seems that Micah was not afraid to pay the cost.

2. The kind of preaching Micah renounces (2:6–11)

The wealthy businessmen of the city did not mind listening to a preacher. What they wanted, however, was a preacher who would endorse their way of living and trading. In this paragraph we have the prophet in dialogue with false prophets about the activities of these businessmen. They object to Micah's message, but that simply provokes him to more denunciation of their behaviour. The paragraph ends with a prophetic call to abandon such an arena, coupled with a wry comment about the kind of preacher who would go down well in the city.

Micah returns to the work of false prophets in the next chapter (3:5–8). Here he represents them as hand-in-glove with the corrupt landowners he has just been accusing. Those in power are seldom averse to the legitimization provided by the patronage of religious figures. Indeed, the reverse is also true: religious people like the patronage of the rich and the powerful, as Micah's words indicate. The powerful attempted to have Micah silenced, because he was not prepared to go along with such collusion.

The word translated *preach* literally means 'fall drop by drop', referring to the steady impact of a person's words on the hearers. The instruction, *'Do not preach'*, is in the second person plural, showing that the false teachers were aiming their message at anyone who presumed, like Micah, to operate on their patch and, still worse, to bring a message calculated to raise the hackles of their patrons (and paymasters?).

The strictures of these prophets revolved around the direct confrontation between Micah and these leading property moguls: *'one should not preach of such things'* (6). They reckoned that

---

[15] *Cast the line by lot* is a reference to the original distribution of the land to the twelve tribes, carried out by the priest (Nu. 26:55–56; Jos. 19:51).

preaching should not tackle issues of daily behaviour and business ethics. Preachers should concentrate on spiritual matters and not interfere in marketplace issues. They should talk about worship, prayer and a personal relationship with God, not fraud and corruption. Still worse was Micah's language about imminent disaster – *Disgrace will not overtake us.* It was arrogant, insensitive and farcical to talk about divine judgment on legitimate business activity. The way they chose to operate in the marketplace was their own affair, not the prophet's. What did he know, let alone understand, about property and finance?

Micah's response is curt and unequivocal: *Should this be said, O house of Jacob?* (7). The reaction of these false teachers to clear words from God is out of order. If there is sin to be addressed, then a true prophet will speak accordingly, not take refuge in generalities and smooth talk. If *such things* (fraud, corruption and oppression) are in fact commonplace, they are certainly not the LORD's *doings*.[16] But the LORD's patience is sorely tried by such wickedness and nobody can say that *the Spirit of the LORD* has been *impatient* in his attitude towards it. Such behaviour has been going on for decades, with a number of reprimands from faithful prophets. If God has now chosen to call it a day and announce imminent judgment, it would be crass folly not to pay heed and make a few changes in such perverse business practices.

God's rhetorical question, through Micah, is eloquent: *Do not my words do good to him who walks uprightly?* (7). Nobody in the entire land would dare to deny the truth of this challenge. So, clearly, a lot more uprightness was called for, and far less bent and crooked behaviour. In case the corrupt magnates had failed to get the message, Micah proceeds to spell out other results of their dealings:

> . . . *you rise against my people as an enemy;*
> *you strip the robe from the peaceful,*
> *from those who pass by trustingly*
> *with no thought of war* (8).

These people were so bent on making ever greater profits and gaining ever larger possessions, that they had become their generation's equivalent of corporate raiders and asset strippers. Instead of seeing their compatriots as friends and allies, they treated everyone in the same way as an enemy would treat them, mounting attacks on people quietly getting on with their own lives and turning peaceful scenarios into battlefields. They were always spoiling for another aggressive takeover, without the slightest consideration for

---

[16] This phrase picks up 'such things' (6) – 'Does God do such things?'

the less robust and the more vulnerable: *The women of my people . . . and their young children* (9). Family life is always the major casualty when wage-earners and breadwinners are driven out of their jobs. Yet little or no attention is given to these hidden costs of fraud and corruption in high places. Wives have to leave *their pleasant houses* and young children's lives are deprived of what should be basic and non-negotiable: stability and security, an inheritance which God vividly describes as *my glory.*

When things reach such an appalling state, there is nothing left to do except get out:

> *Arise and go,*
> *for this is no place to rest;*
> *because of uncleanness that destroys*
> *with a grievous destruction* (10).

Their homes and their smallholdings ought to have been places of safety, where they could rest and be content. But the rapacity of a few had brought defilement to the whole land and complete chaos for the many. Their transgressions and sins, their wickedness and evil, had contaminated everything – to the point where there could be absolutely no remedy. Instead of a home there was a hell. So they could no longer stay.

Micah is, in effect, acknowledging that the nation has reached the place of no return. If there is to be any more preaching, it certainly would be a waste of breath to speak the truth:

> *If a man should go about and utter wind and lies,*
> *saying 'I will preach to you of wine and strong drink,'*
> *he would be the preacher for this people!* (11).

Preachers are meant to proclaim the word of God, but Micah's audience had so rejected such a message that it was useless saying any more about God. No; speak sweet nothings and empty clichés to this people. Tell them what they want to hear, not what they need to hear. Talk to them about the things they really enjoy, like wine and strong drink. If you do that, you *would be the preacher for this people.* But don't talk to them about God and what God wants.

3. And yet . . . and yet . . . (2:12–13)

There could hardly be a bleaker scenario or a more depressing conclusion than Micah's prophecy of utterly destructive pollution in the land, followed by the instruction to get up and go far away from all the uncleanness. The prophet's words seem final and finished.

And yet the LORD speaks into the darkness with the first explicit mention of a *remnant*:[17]

> *I will surely gather all of you, O Jacob,*
> *I will gather the remnant of Israel;*
> *I will set them together*
> *like sheep in a fold,*
> *like a flock in its pasture,*
> *a noisy multitude of men* (12).

Although commentators vary in their understanding of this passage, some seeing it as a prophecy of disaster and others as a prophecy of hope and salvation, it seems right to follow Waltke's conclusion that it 'stresses the remnant's salvation but implies the destruction of Judah'.[18] This interpretation, with hope breaking into the despair and destruction, is consistent with the outline of the whole book.[19]

These two verses mark the end of the first cycle in the book (1:2 – 2:13) and offer a glimmer of light at the end of a dark tunnel. Such light in even the deepest darkness is the characteristic provision of God. Paul testifies to it in a memorable passage: 'God is faithful, and he will not let you be tempted beyond your strength, but with the temptation will also provide the way of escape, that you may be able to endure it' (1 Cor. 10:13).

There is a strong certainty within the promise of God (12), expressed in the word *surely* and the repetition of *gather*, as the LORD speaks of his intentions. Given the utter hopelessness of what has been prophesied, only God himself could speak hope and life into the despair. This assurance could be trusted because God is speaking.

The phrase *the remnant of Israel* is both chilling and creative. The words leave no doubt that *this is no place to rest*, because destruction will inevitably ensue. The very notion of a remnant suggests survival by the skin of one's teeth for a small minority; the bulk of the nation will not survive. There is an anomaly in the first phrase, *all of you*, which initially suggests a complete rescue and restoration; but then the phrase *the remnant of Israel* kills off any false optimism, making it plain that *all* means the entire remnant. Not one of the remnant will be lost.[20]

The imagery of sheep and flocks is, of course, common in both Old and New Testaments when God is referring to his people.[21] He is himself their Shepherd and he supremely is the one who 'gathers'

---

[17] The other references in Micah are 4:7; 5:7–8; 7:18.   [18] Waltke, p. 652.

[19] See the end of the Introduction above.

[20] For a similar qualified use of 'all' see 1 Cor. 15:22–23.

[21] See esp. Ezk. 34:1–31; Jn. 10:1–30.

his sheep, especially when they become scattered and are therefore in danger from wild animals. Here he undertakes to gather together those left after the population is scattered into exile.[22] They will have become *a noisy multitude of men* as a result of their scattering, like a lot of frightened sheep that get lost in a strange place and need to be rescued and gathered. So God's people will need strong, firm leadership if they are to be released from the grip of their masters. This the LORD alone can and will provide. He will open *the breach* and lead them out of captivity: *they will break through and pass the gate, going out by it* (13).

The last two lines stress the direct, personal intervention of *the LORD* as *their king*, as the only possible way of escape and deliverance. Over the centuries since they first asked for a king, Israel had watched the decline and fall of king after king, with the odd exception of a few individuals who tried to stop the rot and bring the people back to God and to the terms of the covenant. What was about to happen by way of appalling destruction would render all human resources futile. God and God alone could bring hope for *the remnant of Israel.*[23]

[22] The reference could, in the nearer future, be to the rescue of a remnant in Jerusalem when the bulk are taken off by the Assyrians, but in the ultimate (always the primary interest of the prophets) to the glorious future the LORD had in mind for his people.

[23] More implications of the 'remnant' will be examined in the next section (3:1 – 5:15).

The second cycle

Micah 3:1 – 5:15
Ungodly leadership and God's promised leader

Micah now directly addresses the leadership of the nation and of the city, specifically targeting different groupings (3:1–12). Desolation is predicted for the city (3:12), but then Micah looks forward to a time of restoration, the impact of which will be worldwide (4:1–8). But the immediate future means exile and a time of bitter travail (4:9–5:1), after which there will be new life, new power and new commitment – all brought about by God himself under God's appointed and anointed leader (5:2–15).

Micah 3:1–12
3. Micah's message to the leadership of the nation

1. A message for the political and secular leaders (3:1–4)

The chapter division obscures the dramatic and devastating contrast between the leadership which the LORD will bring and the leadership which those currently in power are providing: 'the LORD at their head' (2:13) . . . *Hear, you heads of Jacob* (3:1). The current leadership in Jerusalem was a classic example of scattering, rather than gathering, the sheep (2:1–2, 8–9; 3:1–3, 9–11). Their actions and their attitudes had broken up family and community life, bringing the whole nation to the edge of the abyss; hence Micah's insistent call:

> *Hear, you heads of Jacob*
> *and rulers of the house of Israel!* (3:1).

The emphasis on *justice* shows that Micah is addressing those responsible for upholding and enforcing the law – the judges and the magistrates of city, tribe and nation. These men historically had the authority to settle disputes and to make decisions on important matters.[1] They had a particular responsibility to protect the weak and the vulnerable in the community.[2] The early preaching of Micah's contemporary, Isaiah, also minces no words in his message to the 'rulers' in Jerusalem. He addresses them as 'you rulers of Sodom' and tells them:

> . . . cease to do evil,
>   learn to do good;
> seek justice,
>   correct oppression;
> defend the fatherless,
>   plead for the widow (Is. 1:10, 16–17).

Micah is direct in his message to these leaders: *Is it not for you to know justice?* For the judges and magistrates of Israel, justice (*mišpāṭ*) referred to 'the decisions collected in the sacred law and to other verdicts of the court, as well as to the ability to decide cases fairly'.[3] A study of the law's provision[4] for every contingency, activity and emergency gives a clear picture of its attention to detail and its concern for a just and compassionate society. Provision is made, in cases where it is 'too difficult' to reach a decision in the regular courts, for the matter to be decided by 'the Levitical priests'.[5] There were also occasions when the king himself became the supreme judge – as in the case of the two women laying claim to be the mother of a newborn child, where Solomon passed judgment with such astuteness that 'all Israel . . . stood in awe of the king, because they perceived that the wisdom of God was in him, to render justice' (1 Ki. 3:28).

Kings, priests, magistrates, judges – God had seen to it that it was within their combined competence to know justice and apply it in any and every situation. He had revealed his own just character and

---

[1] See Ex. 18:13–26; Dt. 1:15–18; 17:8–13.   [2] See Ex. 21:1–23:19.
[3] Waltke, p. 657.   [4] Ex. 21:1–23:19.   [5] Dt. 17:8–11.

his requirements for justice in his word. He intended that the whole people should live in obedience to his revealed will, and commanded them to do so.

To know justice means more than simply enforcing the law. It entails 'moral taste as well as intellectual prowess' and it implies 'a sympathy for the outcasts of fortune, not merely an intellectual knowing of precise rules'.[6] This wider, deeper understanding of human beings comes from keeping in constant touch with ordinary people and with God himself, the one who framed and formulated the law. Today it is usually apparent when judges and magistrates, while upholding the requirements of the law, reveal complete ignorance of the demands of justice in the fullest sense. Embarrassingly crass and insensitive comments by *rulers* out of touch with the person in the street (and with God in his heaven) have become increasingly common.

'Justice is truth in action,' said Disraeli in the House of Commons in 1851. In Micah's day those entrusted with administering justice no longer had any hold on truth. Their leadership was founded on deception and lying. They had reached the point where, instead of hating injustice and loving truth and equity, they *hate the good and love the evil* (2).

The very simplicity of these four key words, *hate* and *love*, *good* and *evil*, underlines the chaos and the scandal of Micah's situation. When you hate something or someone, you feel a strong aversion and want to distance yourself as far as possible. When you love something or someone, you equally feel spontaneously drawn in that direction and want to stay as close as possible. The *good* and the *evil* describe very fundamental realities: what is intrinsically valuable, pure and attractive on the one hand; what is tawdry, unclean and repugnant on the other. Those responsible for administering judgment in Jerusalem had it all upside down; they loathed anything and anyone that suggested purity and integrity, while they loved perversity and duplicity.

This 'bonding of morally perverse people to evil'[7] had reduced the city's leaders to cannibals:

> *. . . you . . . who tear the skin from off my people,*
> *and their flesh from off their bones;*
> *who eat the flesh of my people,*
> *and flay their skin from off them,*
> *and break their bones in pieces,*
> *and chop them up like meat in a kettle,*
> *like flesh in a cauldron* (2–3).

[6] Waltke, p. 657. [7] *Ibid.*, p. 658.

The bench had become butchers, seeing ordinary people as 'saleable commodities'[8] and treating them as a butcher treats a slaughtered animal – chopping up land, houses and people like so much skin, flesh and bones.

At this point we need to place this denunciation of the legal system in the city alongside Micah's previous denunciation of the business practices of the property magnates in chapter 1. 'The cancer of injustice had spread from the marketplace to the courtroom.'[9] Instead of justice being available to every citizen, whatever their social or economic position, the wealthy and the influential could buy justice. The poor, meanwhile, not merely had the legal stakes stacked against them, but found themselves the victims of rank injustice – the very opposite of God's intention in establishing the law.

Micah is here adding an exposé of iniquitous structures to his castigation of specific sins. He recognized that certain powerful people were getting away, literally and implicitly, with murder. He would have had no hesitation in naming and shaming them. But he also recognized that the whole system played into the hands of such criminals. So he attacks structural sin, institutionalized injustice – the results of decades, if not centuries, of spiritual and moral decadence on the part of those in authority. His strictures have their modern parallels in exposures of police corruption, bent lawyers, intimidation of witnesses and the Mafia-like impact of the underworlds which control drugs, gambling, weapons and prostitution. We also have our own version of one law for the rich, another for the poor, as well as a legal system in danger of pricing itself beyond the reach of any except the wealthy, legal aid or no legal aid.

The time will come when such a brutal and venal regime will be judged and will collapse. Those who have been responsible for it and profited hugely from it will come crashing down. Whether or not Micah sees such a nemesis as the result of Assyrian invasion or Babylonian destruction of the city, *Then they will cry to the LORD* (4). Although there is something rather weird, if not eerie, about people who *hate the good and love the evil* turning to God in their demise and disgrace, it has often happened and will continue to happen. These perverse leaders were, after all, pious worshippers even if they brutalized the people (11).

Normally, those who cry to the LORD in their trouble can be assured that he will both hear and answer. That is the vibrant refrain of Psalm 107: 'Then they cried to the LORD in their trouble, and he delivered them from their distress' (verses 6, 13, 19, 28). Included in those acts of deliverance are the rebellious, the sinful and the

---

[8] Marsh, p. 101.   [9] Craigie, 2, p. 27.

entrepreneur, but not the corrupt leaders in Micah's Jerusalem: *the* LORD *will not answer them; he will hide his face from them at that time.*

Silence and separation can be frightening at the best of times. But the silence and separation of God, at a time when we most need him and long for him, comprise a very heavy judgment. The silence and separation of God will mirror back to these judges and magistrates their own response to the distressed cries, in their own lawcourts, of the poor pleading for justice. These men had turned a deaf ear to their pleas of agony and despair. They had hidden their faces from them and deliberately refused to look them in the eye. Now they would find God treating them in the same way, the God who in fact had come to them in the eyes and cries of the poor, but whom they had chosen to despise and to reject.[10] This would be precise fulfilment of Scripture: 'He who closes his ear to the cry of the poor will himself cry out and not be heard' (Pr. 21:13).[11]

We are bound to ask why this should be the devastating end of the road for these leaders in Jerusalem. Week by week at their prayers they would have heard the priest pronounce the Aaronic blessing over them:

> The LORD bless you and keep you;
> the LORD make his face to shine upon you, and be gracious
>   to you:
> the LORD lift up his countenance upon you, and give you
>   peace . . . (Nu. 6:22–26).

Then, in their utter devastation, *he will hide his face from them.* Why? Why no mercy?

The answer is: *because they have made their deeds evil* (4). In one sense, this statement is plain and unadorned, particularly in comparison with the previous ghastly, gory word pictures (2–3). It seems a bit of an anti-climax hardly severe enough to warrant such an appalling outcome as the unrestrained anger of divine rejection. The phrase speaks, however, of a deliberate, progressive, insistent, defiant series of decisions over many years, which have resulted in a corrupt and callous lifestyle. What Micah describes is not simply a slippery slope and a slide into evil. These leaders have *made* their deeds evil, by choice and with consistency. Nor is he talking about frequent acts of injustice, so much as injustice as a way of life.

There is also the very obvious implication of collusion. These leading figures in the city have conspired together to pervert justice

---

[10] For illustrations of this, see Pr. 14:31; 17:5; 19:17; Mt. 25:31–46.
[11] *Cf.* the story of Jesus about Dives and Lazarus in Lk. 16:19–31.

and substitute the evil for the good. They knew the commandments of God. They knew what – or rather who – lay behind the law which they were bound to observe and apply. They knew the difference between justice and injustice. But they had decided to walk in the opposite direction: *they have made their deeds evil*. There was no way back.[12]

2. A message for the religious and spiritual leaders (3:5–8)

When justice is missing from both the marketplace and the courtroom, a nation has every right to expect its spiritual leaders to speak up and speak out. For the nation of Israel, supremely, such an expectation was appropriate. There had been a long and noble history of courageous confrontation.[13] A measure of the pervasive corruption in Micah's day is not just the absence of such a voice from the religious establishment, but their blatant collusion with the political, legal and business sectors.

The bottom line was money in their pockets (11) and food in their mouths (5). 'Money talked louder than God.'[14] The secular leadership of the city had a grip on the religious leadership of the nation: 'Tell us what we want to hear, and we will pay you well. Speak comforting and approving words, and we will feed you well.' When religious leadership is in the hands of those with political and financial clout, truth goes out the window and justice goes by the board.

What the *prophets* around the city had to say, both publicly and privately, depended on the way they were treated by their listeners. 'What comes out of the mouth of these prophets depends on what has been put into it.'[15] If the fees and the perks were in place, then their cry was '*Peace*' – all smoothness and approval, but no mention of judgment. If no payment had passed hands or if there was nothing tangible in it for them, then they would *declare war* against such non-contributors and offer no spiritual solace whatsoever (6). These false prophets were into war and peace, but their messages to both audiences were self-concocted. The people who ought to have been told about war had peace preached to them. The people who ought to have heard about peace found that the religious authorities, like the rest of those in authority, had declared war on them. No wonder the LORD says they *lead my people astray* – both the wealthy evildoer and the impoverished victim.

[12] For this principle of finding no mercy, see Heb. 6:4–8; 10:26–31.
[13] *E.g.* Samuel, Nathan, Elijah.
[14] J. L. Mays, *Micah*, Old Testament Library (Westminster, 1976), p. 83.
[15] Wolff, p. 102.

There can be few preachers or prophets who do not know the temptation to trim their message according to the influence and importance (real or imagined) of the listeners. In some situations, a congregation's power to 'hire and fire' can stifle true proclamation of God's word. In others, prospects of advancement or appointment often cause a preacher to say what people want to hear, rather than what God wants them to hear. Micah's experience and his exposé of the false prophets have particular relevance when the audience contains those in positions of responsibility and leadership.

Peace (*šālôm*, shalom) can never be a lightweight or casual theme on the lips of a preacher or a prophet. Its biblical significance is far too profound for that. The nature of peace,[16] the conditions of peace,[17] the way to peace,[18] the author of peace,[19] the makers of peace,[20] the cost of peace,[21] the alternatives to peace[22] – these are life-and-death issues. To trivialize them is a travesty of the calling to declare the word of the LORD, which was and still is the high privilege of those entrusted with spiritual leadership. '"There is no peace," says the LORD, "for the wicked"' (Is. 48:22),[23] and it is leading people astray even to suggest that there might be. Several years later the prophet Jeremiah was commissioned to say, about similarly delinquent spiritual leaders, 'They have healed the wound of my people lightly, saying, "Peace, peace," when there is no peace' (Je. 6:14).

Given the extreme, indeed the eternal, implications of both peace and war, it is not surprising to read that the LORD's response to the mouthings of false prophets is to reduce them to emptiness and to silence – a ministry empty of inspiration and a message silenced by the silence of God. The place of prayer, the acts of worship, and the sources of motivation and of inspiration will all dry up. There will be no life, no immediacy, no freshness, no conviction. If they choose to speak out again, they will know that their words are hollow and that they come from an inner hollowness – and those listening will not take long to see the truth and draw their own conclusions. For those dependent on the presence and the power of God's Spirit for authenticity and integrity, that will spell shame and disgrace:

> . . . *the seers shall be disgraced,*
> *and the diviners put to shame;*
> *they shall all cover their lips,*
> *for there is no answer from God* (7).

---

[16] See Eph. 2:11–18.   [17] See Is. 48:16–22.
[18] See Is. 26:3; Acts 10:36; Rom. 5:1.   [19] See Is. 9:6; 2 Thes. 3:16.
[20] See Mt. 5:9; Jas. 3:18.   [21] See Col. 1:20.
[22] See Ezk. 7:23–27; Lk. 19:37–44.   [23] *Cf.* Is. 57:21.

The false prophets had not only compromised their calling by their venality, but they had also resorted to the pagan practice of divination to establish their credentials as experts in manipulating spiritual forces. The Old Testament is against the practice of divination. It was seen as occultic and superstitious.[24] A true prophet had no need to resort to these methods for seeing the unseen world. He stood 'in the council of the LORD',[25] and the LORD communicated his word directly to him. Dreams and visions were acceptable and common means of discerning the will of God. Divination was not. It is unclear precisely what divination entailed, but the Bible mentions various practices including throwing arrows into the air, examining an animal's liver, consulting the dead, astrology, seeing pictures in water, and casting lots.[26]

Whatever methods these prophets were using to establish their credibility and status,

> . . . it shall be night to you, without vision,
>   and darkness to you, without divination.
> The sun shall go down upon the prophets,
>   and the day shall be black over them;
> the seers shall be disgraced,
>   and the diviners put to shame (6–7).

They had sold their souls to wealthy patrons and they were prepared to look anywhere for spiritual light. One of the strange characteristics of those with money and power is the fascination they have for the spiritual – not often directed to the Lord himself (taking God seriously means personal change), but ready to experiment with any source of supernatural guidance, healing or inner strength. It is likely that the wealthy and influential in Jerusalem patronized prophets who were prepared to play around with the paranormal, making use of local pagan practices.

The contrast between these prophets and Micah is complete. Each phrase of Micah's credo (8) throws the venality and the folly of these charlatans into sharp relief:

> But as for me, I am filled with power,
>   with the Spirit of the LORD,
>   and with justice and might,
> to declare to Jacob his transgression
>   and to Israel his sin.

---

[24] See Dt. 18:10; Jos. 13:22; 1 Sa. 15:23. *Cf.* Nu. 23:23; 1 Sa. 28:8; 2 Ki. 17:17.
[25] See Je. 23:16–22.   [26] See art. 'Divination' in *NBD*.

Everything they failed to do and to be as prophets, Micah did and was. In making this assertion Micah was going out on a limb and making himself a target. That is of the essence of the true prophetic calling.

Micah underlines three essential ingredients in his ministry. First, he is filled with God's Spirit. That is the secret of his power as a prophet. Secondly, the result of being filled with the Spirit of the LORD is a proper fusion of justice and power. In the words of the seventeenth-century French philosopher. Blaise Pascal, 'Justice without power is powerless. Power without justice is tyrannical. Justice and power must therefore be connected, so that what is just is also powerful and what is powerful is also just.' In a society riddled with injustice, Micah was fundamentally committed to justice, to a ministry of declaring and applying God's revealed truth. He was a powerful voice for justice: that was the impact of the Spirit.[27]

Thirdly, as a result of allowing his life to be directed by God's Spirit towards justice, Micah found himself addressing the corruption and wickedness in the nation, especially in the corridors of power. Without the Spirit's enabling he would have gone along with the false prophets. But Micah knew that there was no peace for the wicked, and he was not prepared to go soft on the tough parts of God's word. *Transgression* and *sin* have been on Micah's lips from the beginning (1:5, 13). They will remain there until they have been confessed and renounced. He will not get fat fees and special rewards for being obedient to God, but he will continue to live in the light of God's favour and to hear God's voice. Such a blessing is a gift beyond any material reward and is worth maintaining at any cost.

'The presence of the Spirit of the Lord is the *sine qua non* for effective ministry.'[28] Micah's example and declaration here provide some timeless pointers to a truly Spirit-filled ministry. They provide a healthy corrective to other definitions in vogue today. To be filled with the Spirit is to be ranged against all injustice in our society. To be filled with the Spirit is to stand up for, and on the side of, the oppressed and helpless victims of unjust laws and unjust people. To be filled with the Spirit is to speak out God's word fearlessly, even when there is likelihood of personal attack. To be filled with the Spirit means calling sin sin, not being mealy-mouthed about unpalatable parts of the message God has entrusted to us.

---

[27] Passages in Isaiah about the Servant of the LORD and the Spirit of the LORD link justice with the work of the Spirit: *e.g.* Is. 11:2–9; 32:15; 42:1; 61:1.

[28] Waltke, p. 667.

3. A message for the entire leadership of the nation (3:9–12)

Micah draws his denunciation of the nation's leadership to a close in a string of pithy statements summarizing the national crisis. Leaders responsible for administering the law *abhor justice and pervert all equity* (9) and *give judgment for a bribe* (11). Leaders operating in property and business *build Zion with blood and Jerusalem with wrong* (10). Religious leaders are in it up to their necks: *its priests teach for hire, its prophets divine for money* (11).

The entire leadership of the nation was corrupt, and the common denominator was a love of money. They 'all played the game "The Price is Right"'.[29] The god Mammon had got a stranglehold on Jerusalem, with the inevitable result that venality and violence ruled the city. It is not surprising that Paul, who had his fair share of encounters with the wealthy and the powerful, warns Timothy that 'the love of money is the root of all evils' (1 Tim. 6:10).

Micah's description of Jerusalem is vivid and frightening, but it is important to remind ourselves that the picture he is painting bears little or no resemblance to the generally perceived reality of the city's life. Its buildings were impressive; its prosperity was massive; its past was a source of pride – and its temple dominated the whole vista. That is why Micah's next remark is so crucial:

> *yet they lean upon the* LORD *and say,*
> *'Is not the* LORD *in the midst of us?*
> *No evil shall come upon us'* (11).

The leaders of the nation honestly believed that they were both religious and impregnable. They simply could not see any discrepancy between their acts of worship and their acts of wickedness. Yet these are people who ought to 'know justice' (1), but who now *abhor justice* (9). 'The heart is deceitful above all things, and desperately corrupt; who can understand it?' (Je. 17:9). The core of the deceit is self-deception; there are none so blind as those who will not see.

This blindness in the face of overwhelming evidence came from a selective approach to God's word, particularly to his commitment to the temple in Jerusalem. *'Is not the* LORD *in the midst of us?'* they cried, referring to the dominating presence of God's house on God's 'holy hill', Mount Zion. That Jerusalem's existence and identity revolved around the temple is epitomized by the way the city was frequently called *Zion*.[30] The leadership imagined that God's commitment to his house, his hill and his city was irrevocable.

[29] Kaiser, p. 52.
[30] In Micah alone it occurs at 3:10, 12; 4:2. The people collectively are called 'the daughter of Zion' (4:8, 10, 13).

Such reliance was understandable but faulty. From the outset, when Solomon built the house of the LORD, the conditions were clear: 'Concerning this house which you are building, if you will walk in my statutes and obey my ordinances and keep all my commandments and walk in them, then I will establish my word with you, which I spoke to David your father. And I will dwell among the children of Israel, and will not forsake my people Israel' (1 Ki. 6:12–13).

When Solomon finished building the temple, 'the LORD appeared' to him in distinctive fashion and spoke very plainly about the blessings of obedience and the consequences of disobedience, concluding with these words: '... if you turn aside from following me, you or your children, and do not keep my commandments and my statutes which I have set before you ... then I will cut off Israel from the land which I have given them; and the house which I have consecrated for my name I will cast out of my sight ... And this house will become a heap of ruins; every one passing by it will be astonished, and will hiss; and they will say, "Why has the LORD done thus to this land and to this house?" ' (1 Ki. 9:1, 6–8).

Micah has been rehearsing God's commandments and statutes in front of the city's leadership for some time. He had underlined the perils of continuing to defy the LORD and trample on his word. He has forced them to face up to the issues of justice and mercy. Still they chose to block out the warnings and tune in religiously to the promises – and 'religiously' is the word, because their piety was a combination of the mechanical and the magical, repeating religious practices and phrases in some kind of mantra to ward off all *evil* (11). 'They had inured themselves against repentance.'[31]

This kind of piety remains a danger whenever we drive a wedge between our working lives and our worshipping lives. The workplace then becomes a hermetically sealed compartment, from which we routinely exclude any recognition of the presence of God by reserving worship for the holy place. Spiritual and moral perspectives are not considered relevant or practical in such secular space Much local church life buys into this dichotomy, simply by failing to address the realities of the workplace and thus giving tacit endorsement to a Sundays-only faith.

At the heart of this 'double life' is our view of God and attitude to him. Instead of choosing to humble ourselves and bow the knee to him as Lord and Master, we want to have him endorse and bless what we are doing and want to do. Religious actions and words become tools to keep God favourably disposed towards us, to keep him 'on our side', and to make use of him in times of need. We

[31] Waltke, p. 672.

imagine that such regular acknowledgment of God will be a safeguard for this life and an insurance policy for the next. In a word, it is an attempt to control God and make him play along with us, instead of gladly submitting to his control. God's response is tersely summed up by Isaiah: 'I cannot endure iniquity and solemn assembly' (Is. 1:13).

In the end God gets tired of our playing games with him. If we are not prepared to listen to him and do what he requires, he has to call it a day. He can in no way be said to lose patience with us (*cf.* 2:7, 'Is the Spirit of the LORD impatient?'). He is the LORD God Almighty and will not be presumptuously leaned on. We lean on him for mercy and forgiveness, for strength and guidance – or we lean on him at our peril. Micah's contemporary Isaiah spoke to the people of Jerusalem about appropriate and inappropriate leaning, when he described the time when those who survived the Assyrian and Babylonian onslaughts would 'lean upon the LORD, the Holy One of Israel, in truth' (Is. 10:20).[32] The psalmist describes such leaning perfectly:

> ... thou, O LORD, art my hope,
> my trust, O LORD, from my youth.
> Upon thee have I leaned from my birth;
> thou art he who took me from my mother's womb.
> My praise is continually of thee (Ps. 71:5–6).

Jerusalem's leadership had exhausted God's patience by continuous and arrogant wickedness:

> *Therefore because of you*
> *Zion shall be ploughed as a field;*
> *Jerusalem shall become a heap of ruins,*
> *and the mountain of the house a wooded height* (12).

The unthinkable would take place *because of you*. The city would be reduced to rubble, including the temple. The 'holy hill' would become a haunt for wild animals and thus become unclean, unholy.

No mere individual among the people of Israel would have dared even think such wild thoughts, let alone declare them in public and address them directly to the nation's leaders. Such language was tantamount to high treason, as Jeremiah in particular was later to discover. But Micah's logic had been impeccable. He had argued from the basis of God's own word to the only conclusion possible in the face of such pervasive wickedness in high places. His conclusion

[32] *Cf.* Is. 48:1–2; Je. 7:1–11.

crashes like a thunderclap on the city and its leadership: *Jerusalem shall become a heap of ruins*, and it is all *because of you.*

In the time of Jeremiah, these words of Micah were given more than the authority of a courageous and truthful prophet. Speaking to the religious leadership who were baying for Jeremiah's blood because he brought a message virtually identical to Micah's, 'certain elders of the land' quoted these words of Micah to the assembled people with the preface, 'Thus says the LORD of hosts . . .' (Je. 26:18).[33] These leaders, nearly a century later, were quite clear where Micah's message originated. Their intervention at that stage saved Jeremiah's life at the hands of king Jehoiakim. The account also records that Micah's preaching brought king Hezekiah to his knees, even if the leadership addressed in chapters 2 and 3 remained unmoved: 'Did he not fear the LORD and entreat the favour of the LORD, and did not the LORD repent of the evil which he had pronounced against them?' (Je. 26:19).

If the entire leadership of Judah and Jerusalem could, by their wickedness, cause the collapse and ruin of that country and that city nearly three thousand years ago, there seems no sound theological reason why the same disaster could not happen again today. Cities and nations may look secure and actually be prosperous. Leaders may be religious in their acts of worship. But God's keyword is *justice*, not prosperity or piety. Without justice a city will be dismantled as thoroughly as the LORD was to dismantle Jerusalem.

[33] See the whole chapter. Micah 3:12 is the only Old Testament verse quoted verbatim by another Old Testament writer.

Micah 4:1 – 5:15
4. Micah's message of a future beyond the ruin of Jerusalem

1. A glorious scenario (4:1–8)

The appalling gloom of the final verse of chapter 3 is matched by the glorious prospect painted in the opening verses of chapter 4. Here we are given a picture of what God intends as the future of Jerusalem. 'One of the reasons for the beauty of this passage is that it is totally out of harmony with the reality of our world, yet fully in harmony with what we would like the world to be.'[1]

The whole passage (4:1 – 5:15) contains some significant phrases which help us to gain some time-perspective for the outworking of what is prophesied for the city and people of God. In 4:1 is the phrase 'the latter days'. In 4:9, 10, 11 and 5:1 we have the word 'now'. 'In that day' comes in 4:6 and 5:10. In 4:7 we read the phrase 'from this time forth and for evermore'. The significance of each phrase will emerge, but 'there is a temporal thickness to these prophecies',[2] which prevents us from stating categorically when and how they find their fulfilment.

The glorious scenario of this section (4:1–8) is to occur *in the latter days* (1) or 'in the last days' (NIV).[3] Significantly, Moses is recorded as having warned the people of Israel about fierce tribulation, including being scattered and driven into exile, in the event of their acting corruptly in the land God was to give them. But 'when all these things come upon you in the latter days, you will return to the LORD your God and obey his voice' (Dt. 4:30).[4] Generally in the Old Testament the phrase seems to denote an unspecified future time, a prolonged period rather than an actual date, when situations that have remained in place for years, if not for centuries, will be reversed or replaced.

In the New Testament the phrase seems to take on a specific

---

[1] Craigie, 2, p. 32.   [2] Waltke, p. 679.   [3] Mi. 4:1–3 occurs also in Is. 2:2–4.
[4] *Cf.* Ho. 3:5.

reference to everything that results from the first coming of Jesus Christ. It then possesses the eschatological flavour discernible here in Micah, suggested in certain parts of Jeremiah[5] and more obvious in Daniel.[6] This is especially clear in the way Peter uses the phrase in quoting the prophet Joel in his sermon at Pentecost.[7]

Micah, then, was anticipating this transformation some time in the future. Only future events would establish the accuracy of his words, and these events could take place over a long period of time: 'days' could be years, generations or even centuries. But, however long it takes, *It shall come to pass.* If the whole of this section (4:1 – 5:15) describes *the latter days*, then Micah's prophecy 'embraces the remnant's restoration from Babylon (4:9, 10), the birth of the Messiah (5:2) and his universal rule and everlasting peace (4:1–4; 5:3)'.[8] To what, then, could Micah and his contemporaries look forward?

First, *the mountain of the house of the LORD shall be established as the highest of the mountains* (1). This is the same mountain which, at the end of chapter 3, has been reduced to a forest, fit for nothing but marauding wild – and unclean – animals. It now becomes the highest of the mountains – clearly not literally higher than Mount Everest, but supreme over everything and everywhere: *It shall be raised above the hills.* Just as the highest peak irresistibly draws people, not simply to see it, but to scale it, so *the peoples shall flow to* Mount Zion. Stress is laid on the mountain as the place of *the house of the LORD*, and the nations will flow to it because the LORD's house is there, not simply because of its location or its loftiness.

This movement of the nations to the mountain of Zion will be quite clearly in order to worship the LORD in his house. This is shown by the unusual word *flow*, which is a strange word to use for land-locked Jerusalem – in contrast to Babylon on the river Euphrates, to which people flowed in boats in order to worship its patron deity, Marduk. In the latter days Jerusalem will become the place to worship, thus establishing the LORD God of Israel as the God of the nations: 'The enthronement of Yahweh here celebrated carries with it a dethronement of all other gods.'[9]

This flow of the nations to the new Jerusalem is nothing less than a spontaneous pilgrimage:

> . . . *many nations shall come, and say:*
> *'Come, let us go up to the mountain of the LORD,*
> *to the house of the God of Jacob'* (2).

[5] Je. 48:47; 49:39.   [6] Dn. 2:28; 10:14.
[7] Acts 2:17 (see the discussion of Joel 2:28 above).   [8] Waltke, p. 677.
[9] W. Brueggemann, quoted by Waltke, p. 679.

There is no coercion, no reluctance, no hesitation. This is to be a worldwide movement, homing in on Jerusalem and on the LORD's house on Mount Zion. It will indicate rejection of other gods and other forms and places of worship.

There will, moreover, be a humble and teachable spirit within these worshippers from around the world. They will not be chasing the latest trends or the newest experiences of spiritual power. They will have the clear goal of learning what God has to teach them – *that he may teach us his ways and we may walk in his paths.* The pilgrims will be intent on sitting at the LORD's feet and receiving his instruction, not for intellectual titillation or idle curiosity, but in order to do what he says and walk in his paths.[10] They have been drawn to Jerusalem by *the law, and the word of the LORD*, emanating from God's holy hill (2).

The two words *ways* and *paths* (2) speak of God's own pattern of living and the lifestyle he intends his people to follow. This will be worship in spirit and in truth,[11] nothing superficial or temporary. Unless worship involves teachability and issues in practical obedience, it is not worship at all; this was exactly the condemnation levelled by Micah at the current leadership of the city and the nation.

The contrast with the old Jerusalem of Micah's day is total. There those in authority patronized the temple but trampled on the word of God. Its priests and its prophets handled the word of God deceitfully, venally and corruptly – with the result that God's word never travelled anywhere in that society, except through the faithful few like Micah, Isaiah and their disciples.

When God's law and God's word are on the move among the nations, then God himself is seen to act in powerful and life-changing ways: *He shall judge between many peoples, and shall decide for strong nations afar off* (3). As his word infiltrates the minds and meetings of those who have made the journey to the new Jerusalem and back, God himself takes the lead in their cities and their communities. Leaders look to God for wisdom and instruction. Nations base their laws on God's law. Instead of corrupt magistrates and judges, a nation's legislature becomes God-centred. They base their decisions on what God's word teaches, not on anything inferior. It is God who thus does the judging and the deciding: a reality of which we can see glimpses in today's world when rulers listen to his word and place themselves under the authority of God's Son, and a reality which will one day be fully demonstrated when God is all in all.[12]

---

[10] In Isaiah the nations come to the new Jerusalem for other reasons: Is. 56:7; 60:5–18; 66:18–20.
[11] See Jn. 4:23–24.   [12] See 1 Cor. 15:24–29; Heb. 2:8–9.

This arbitration will particularly affect international dealings *between many peoples*, as well as the internal affairs of *strong nations afar off*. This, in its turn, will lead to ultimate disarmament – not unilateral or even multilateral, but omnilateral:

> ... *they shall beat their swords into ploughshares,*
> *and their spears into pruning hooks;*[13]
> *nation shall not lift up sword against nation,*
> *neither shall they learn war any more* (3).

There will be not merely cessation and the absence of war, but the provision of a deep and pervasive peace. This peace will be available to and enjoyed by everyone, especially the humble peasant and the ordinary citizen: *they shall sit every man under his vine and under his fig tree, and none shall make them afraid* (4).[14] Not only will the earth produce its crops and its fruits in abundance, but people will be content with enough – which is the implication of this reference to a vine and a fig tree for every individual, as well as the settled state indicated by the word *sit*. There will no longer be a mentality of 'bigger and better'. People will be content with what they have, instead of being in the grip of consumerism – one of Micah's major criticisms (2:2; 3:1–3, 11; 7:3).

And none shall make them afraid (4). This phrase beautifully summarizes the situation, not just in a renewed Jerusalem, but – as a result of people coming to see, to taste and to learn from the new Jerusalem – in renewed cities and communities all over the earth. Fear, which drives and controls much of human existence, will have been banished. In particular, the fear which inevitably comes from being under God's judgment will be over.[15] People will fear the LORD and thus have nothing else to fear,[16] from their enemies, their leaders or the wild beasts.

How can we be confident that such a wonderful world is anything more than the idealized dream of an optimistic preacher? Micah is clear about this: *for the mouth of the LORD of hosts has spoken* (4). This comes as a kind of divine 'Amen' (= 'so be it'). If these were merely human words, albeit from a very holy man, they would not be worth the paper they were printed on. But they are a statement of intent from God himself, here referred to by his military title, *The LORD of hosts*, which is equivalent to something like 'Supreme Commander of Angelic Forces in Heaven and Earth'.

[13] 'Swords and spears together represent the entire military arsenal' (Waltke, p. 681).

[14] 'Grapes and figs are the most precious fruits of the land' (Wolff, p. 122).

[15] See Lv. 26:6; Ezk. 34:28. [16] See Ps. 34:4, 9.

Micah personally expresses the decision and the determination of the faithful among God's people to see the vision through to reality:

> *... all the peoples walk*
> *each in the name of its god,*
> *but we will walk in the name of the* LORD *our God*
> *for ever and ever* (5).

Micah is confident enough to act as spokesman for the *remnant* (7) who will survive God's judgment.

The word *walk* picks up the commitment, on the part of these pilgrims to the new Jerusalem, to walk in God's paths (2). Walking speaks of steadiness, purposefulness, continuity. That means gaining strength to keep on walking.[17] Other people claim to find such direction and drive from their religions: *all the peoples walk each in the name of its god.* Micah stakes out his position, and the position of all for whom he is speaking, by asserting: *but we will walk in the name of the* LORD *our God for ever and ever.* That means acknowledging the LORD as *our God*, not paying any attention, let alone devotion, to other gods. The vision of a new (or a renewed) Jerusalem, as the focus for international worship and the force for multinational discipleship, will come about not by mixing and matching the worship of different gods, but by single-minded dedication to the one, true God. That is permanently non-negotiable: it continues *for ever and ever.*

God's own commitment to making the vision a reality comes in the next two verses:

> *In that day, says the* LORD,
> *I will assemble the lame*
> *and gather those who have been driven away,*
> *and those whom I have afflicted;*
> *and the lame I will make the remnant;*
> *and those who were cast off, a strong nation;*
> *and the* LORD *will reign over them in Mount Zion*
> *from this time forth and for evermore* (6–7).

The phrase *In that day* refers back to *in the latter days* (1), thus indicating the activity of God in and behind the glorious scenario just painted (1–4). It is probably also intended to connect with the verse immediately preceding, in which Micah's commitment on

---

[17] Walking is a common theme for discipleship in the New Testament; see *e.g.* Jn. 8:12; 12:35; Rom. 6:4; 8:4; 2 Cor. 5:7; Gal. 5:16, 25; 6:16; Eph. 2:10; 5:2, 8, 15; 1 Jn. 1:6–7; 2:6.

behalf of the faithful remnant of God's people has been spelt out; God's work goes hand in hand with the people's walk.

The phrases used here to describe the condition of those who will constitute the remnant are striking: *the lame . . . those who have been driven away . . . those whom I have afflicted . . . those who were cast off.* The scene is of devastation, trauma and weakness. There can be no doubting or downplaying the ghastly events which must inevitably precede recovery and restoration. But the same LORD, who will be responsible for the afflicting of his people, will be responsible for the gathering of his people together again.

The double reference to *the lame* as those who will become *the remnant* and be made a *strong nation* might well be a cryptic reference to God's striking Jacob on his thigh at Penuel, leaving him with a permanent limp.[18] The result of that wrestling-match was a different Jacob, someone who was teachable, humble and able to be used by God. So now with 'the house of Jacob': as God (*the God of Jacob*, 2) moved to bring his people low, he would turn them into a strong nation. They would limp for the rest of their lives, but they would genuinely lean on the LORD and walk in his name – unlike the current leadership of Jerusalem (3:11). As Jacob was, from Penuel onwards, given a new name, Israel, so Micah's Israel would eventually become a new nation, 'the Israel of God' (Gal. 6:16).

Essential to the new Israel and to its strength as a nation will be their submission to the rule of God: *the LORD will reign over them in Mount Zion* (7). That was manifestly not true of Micah's Jerusalem, whose leaders were completely opposed to anyone ruling over them. Just as this faithful remnant's commitment to walk in the name of the LORD was to be *for ever and ever,* so the LORD's rule over his people will last *from this time forth and for evermore.* There is an eternal kernel to the renewed Jerusalem, which will survive time and space. This is in contrast with all other nations in Micah's world, which 'did not survive the upheavals of history because God did not preserve a remnant for them'.[19]

In case the people of Jerusalem failed to appreciate that there would be a straight line from themselves through the catastrophe on the horizon to this glorious new creation, Micah stresses that everything here promised will come to them:

> *And you, O tower of the flock,*
> *hill of the daughter of Zion,*
> *to you it shall come,*
> *the former dominion shall come,*
> *the kingdom of the daughter of Jerusalem* (8).

[18] Gn. 32:22–32.   [19] Waltke, p. 687.

The faithful remnant is just that – a remnant of God's covenant people. This promise of a bright future is not disconnected from God's purposes for Israel from Abraham onwards. Even less does it indicate God reneging on his promises to David. The verse has subtle references to the reign and *former dominion* of David, seen as the greatest king from whose seed the Messiah would one day appear – a theme directly taken up in 5:2ff. God had repeatedly promised David that his kingdom would endure for ever.[20] He was not about to break his word.

The phrase *tower of the flock* again emphasizes what God can do with broken and scattered people. These are the ones he has scattered and then gathered together again. Now they are strong enough to take responsibility for the flock, to take up the position and the responsibilities of sentinels on the 'watchtower' (NIV). Isaiah's vision of someone filled with God's Spirit, coming 'to bind up the brokenhearted, to proclaim liberty to the captives, and the opening of the prison to those who are bound', is of a piece with Micah's words here. When the LORD moves to heal and to deliver, victims and mourners are turned into 'oaks of righteousness', people able to 'build up the ancient ruins' and to 'repair ... the devastations of many generations' (Is. 61:1–4).

This, then, is the scenario to which Micah pointed his contemporaries. Clearly, they saw little or nothing of its fulfilment. In the coming of the Messiah, Jesus of Nazareth, we today can see each detail of the scenario reaching substantial fruition, as people from all the nations turn to him as Saviour and Lord, turning away from other gods and experiencing the power of God's Spirit to make the lame walk and set the captive free. The full consummation is still to come.

2. This present darkness (4:9 – 5:1)

Four times in six verses Micah says, *Now ... now ... Now ... Now ...* as he drags himself and his listeners back into the harsh realities of their present situation. He faces up to this present darkness in the light of the glorious future just described, both because he cannot avoid doing so and because the future must always be rooted and grounded in the present if it is to have any reality – just as the present must be rooted and grounded in the future if it is to have any meaning. Once Micah has come back to the present and absorbed more of its pain, he is ready to describe more of what will happen in the future (5:2–15).

The first two *nows* are: *Now why do you cry aloud?* (9) ... *now*

[20] Expressed in several psalms, *e.g.* 46; 48; 76; 84; 87; 122.

you shall go forth from the city (10). The people of Jerusalem are addressed as *daughter of Zion* (10), a description used twice earlier (8) and repeated later (13). The content of this section (especially 9–10) shows why Micah has chosen this name: *pangs have seized you like a woman in travail* (9). The people are crying out like a woman having her contractions before giving birth, such is the agony of what they have been compelled to go through over the years as a result of the city's corrupted leadership.

Micah first acknowledges the extreme pain of their situation (9), but then tells them that they are to keep on writhing and groaning, for something even worse is about to happen:

> *for now you shall go forth from the city*
> *and dwell in the open country; you shall go to Babylon* (10).

Those pangs will last a long time, until they are then delivered and find new life back in their homeland:

> *There you shall be rescued,*
> *there the* LORD *will redeem you*
> *from the hand of your enemies* (10).

To cry aloud, to writhe and to groan are all absolutely appropriate when a woman is in travail. *The daughter of Jerusalem* has every reason to be in travail; but she must not forget her *king* and her *counsellor* (9) – references to the LORD himself. He has neither left her nor *perished*. He is at her side in her travail, ready to give wise counsel. He is there to counsel her during the pangs of her present distress, but he will continue alongside her throughout the extended travail of exile in Babylon. Ultimately, however, the message is one of substantial hope: these sufferings will not be endless or meaningless. Something better, something new, awaits.

Jeremiah often likens the people's agony during captivity to labour pains,[21] and Jesus himself uses the same experience to encourage his disciples on the verge of his departure from this earth to return to his Father, before sending them the gift of the Counsellor, the Holy Spirit.[22] The same principle holds good for any time of suffering for the people of God. However endless or meaningless it seems, our King, Jesus, is alongside us and our Counsellor, God's Holy Spirit, wants to bring strength and encouragement to hang in there.

The next paragraph (11–13), again prefaced by an emphatic *Now*, brings another perspective to bear on the people's suffering, namely

---

[21] Je. 4:31; 6:24; 13:21; 22:23; 49:24. [22] Jn. 16:16–22.

the *thoughts* and the *plan* of the LORD (12). In context, these are a complete mystery to the *many nations* assembled to create mayhem among the people of Jerusalem, demoralized by the degenerate activities of their leaders. The people of the city seem easy pickings for the marauding profiteers hovering on its borders. They are already gloating over the city: *'Let her be profaned, and let our eyes gaze on Zion'* (11). Godless people always take a perverse delight in the downfall of those who have been held up as God-fearing and distinctive. These invading forces eagerly anticipate the prospect of ravaging the temple on Mount Zion, ransacking the Holy of holies and exposing the sacred rituals and vessels to desecration.

But, in their greedy glee, they fail to understand God's plan: *He has gathered them as sheaves to the threshing floor* (12). This is the immutable purpose of God, which no historical turn of events can thwart but must simply fulfil. God's ultimate plans for his people do not involve destruction at the hands of Assyrians, Babylonians or any other empire. They are, in the words of Jeremiah, 'to give [them] a future and a hope'. They are plans 'for welfare and not for evil' (Je. 29:11). Their enemies will come to thresh, and will be threshed themselves. God's winnowing-fork is already in his hand.[23] The daughter of Jerusalem is God's winnowing-fork, and she is commanded to 'arise and thresh' like a vigorous heifer: *For I will make your horn iron and your hoofs bronze* (13).

This strenuous activity will completely turn the tables on the *many nations* intent on shattering and stripping Jerusalem:

> . . . *you shall beat in pieces many peoples,*
> *and shall devote their gain to the LORD,*
> *their wealth to the Lord of the whole earth* (13).

The plausibility of such a prediction is underlined by these last few words. The LORD is not just king over Jerusalem and counsellor to his people. He is *the Lord of the whole earth*, Lord of every one of these encircling nations. Their soldiers may derive great *gain* from their expansionist campaigns, but it all belongs to the LORD, and his faithful people will see that it is returned to him to be dealt with in the way he shall choose.

On previous occasions in Israel's history, devoting the possessions of pagan cities and nations to the LORD meant their complete destruction, to avoid any contamination arising from their use in idolatrous worship.[24] The context of these commands, a passage dealing with a renewed Jerusalem and worldwide worship of the LORD, indicates that the meaning is similar to a later vision of the

[23] See Je. 15:7; Mt. 3:12.   [24] See Jos. 6:17; Is. 43:28.

wealth of the nations being brought into the city and the kingdom of God.[25] This is certainly the ultimate plan of the LORD, something which the Assyrians could not understand.

But for now the picture is very different:

> *Now you are walled about with a wall;*
> *siege is laid against us;*
> *with a rod they strike upon the cheek*
> *the ruler of Israel* (5:1).[26]

Surrounded and humiliated, they seem to have no hope of deliverance. Their ruler is completely unable to defend himself and is reduced to public disgrace, further demoralizing the people. Micah places himself among the citizens of the besieged city (*us*), and it is likely that he was present when the king was struck on the cheek (if it was a literal event). The events described here fit best with what happened under King Hezekiah when Sennacherib besieged Jerusalem in 701 BC – a situation which also ties in well with the previous events in this section (4:9–13).

The four *nows* in this passage give a timelessly accurate description of the consequences of sin and disobedience. There are personal consequences for the individual (4:9) – pangs like a woman in travail. There is all the isolation and deprivation to which persistent sin inevitably leads – being cut off from fellowship with the LORD and his people (4:10). Circumstances and events often begin to pile up and everything seems to be set against us: our world can collapse under such hammer-blows (4:11). The end result is being walled up in a narrow place, brought down and led into a lifestyle in which we become despised and despise ourselves (5:1).

Micah's description of such darkness, which in his day was about to envelop Jerusalem, brings despair as deep as the hope and reassurance brought by his description of a renewed Jerusalem. In order to live with such a tension, the people of God need an altogether different calibre of leader. Micah now proceeds to announce that leader's coming.

3. The coming deliverer (5:2–15)

Allusions to Israel's glorious past under King David (4:8) now become explicit in the appearance of *one who is to be ruler in Israel* (5:2). That is plain in Micah's reference to *Bethlehem Ephrathah*, the

[25] See Is. 61:6; Rev. 21:26.
[26] The translations of this verse vary considerably (see *e.g.* RSV and NIV). These comments are based on the RSV rendering. (English versions' 5:1 is 4:14 in the Hebrew text.)

home of Jesse and the birthplace of his sons, including David, the youngest. Bethlehem was a little town, so insignificant that it was not even mentioned in a list of place-names in Judah when Joshua divided the land.[27] When we realize that 115 towns and cities were named, 'with their villages', which remained without a name, it becomes plain just how insignificant Bethlehem was.

Micah's reference to Bethlehem as the birthplace of Israel's new ruler is, therefore, a powerful pointer to the way God raises up the weak and the despised. Just as God instructed Samuel to go to lowly Bethlehem to look for the man born to be king, and then passed over all of Jesse's sons until he eventually had David brought before the prophet, so the coming Messiah will emerge from the little town of Bethlehem – a place so small that it was scarcely worth a mention *among the clans of Judah.*

This prediction about Bethlehem is also a smack in the eye for the haughty leadership in Jerusalem. Like powerful people in most capital cities, they would have imagined that leadership began and ended in the metropolis. When Micah highlighted Bethlehem as the place from which this ruler would emerge, they might have had a dim recollection of Jesse's birthplace, but they may well have had to get out their maps of Judah to locate it.[28]

And yet Micah's description of this ruler's origin as being *from of old, from ancient days* (2), brings a double nuance. It stresses the historic link with King David many centuries before, but it also strongly suggests even older lineage. The word for *old* is used of God himself in two other passages in the Old Testament, notably in Habakkuk: 'Art thou not from everlasting, O LORD my God . . .?' (Hab. 1:12).[29] It is possible, therefore, that 'Micah expected a supernatural figure'.[30] The coming ruler is certainly in radical contrast with any other leader, but still in real continuity with the lineage of David.

The phrase *for me* (2) also has an intriguing parallel in Samuel's discovery of David at Bethlehem. When the LORD sent Samuel to 'Jesse the Bethlehemite', his actual words were: 'I have provided *for myself* a king among his sons' (1 Sa. 16:1). If we can hear the LORD's own voice speaking through Micah, this phrase finds an echo in the LORD's plan for a renewed Israel: *from you shall come forth for me one who is to be ruler in Israel.* The coming Messiah is a provision not so much for Israel as for the LORD himself. He will fulfil all his purposes, not simply the people's deepest longings.

[27] Jos. 15:20–63.
[28] King Herod had to consult his experts when 'wise men from the East' asked him about the birthplace of another 'king of the Jews'; see Mt. 2:1–6, where this verse from Micah is quoted to Herod.
[29] *Cf.* Dt. 33:27.   [30] McComiskey, p. 427.

In the meantime, the prophet and the people can only wait. The coming of the Messiah is assured, but what will happen until that time?

> *Therefore he shall give them up until the time*
> *when she who is in travail has brought forth* (3).

Again the picture of pregnancy, travail and childbirth comes to the fore, as in the previous chapter (4:9–10). Micah could be referring to 'the daughter of Zion' continuing with the travail of her sufferings under the judgment of God. He could also, under special prophetic inspiration, be foretelling the physical birth of this Messiah in Bethlehem at some unknown date in the future – as we now know with hindsight.

But the unnerving message for the people of Jerusalem is in that phrase *he will give them up*. There will be a period of unknown length when God will let them alone, leaving them to their own devices. In her extended and excruciating travail, the daughter of Zion will be on her own. The LORD will not be there to hold her hand and see her through the pain. It is a scenario painted in vivid colours by Jeremiah, when 'the whole land shall be a desolation'. The prophet says,

> I heard a cry of a woman in travail,
>   anguish as of one bringing forth her first child,
> the cry of the daughter of Zion gasping for breath,
>   stretching out her hands,
> 'Woe is me! I am fainting before murderers' (Je. 4:27, 31).

The book of Lamentations, in particular, gives vent to the experience of being given up by God. There Jeremiah, the weeping prophet who, nearly a century later, had to pick up the pieces of a people shattered by the fulfilment of this word from Micah, grieves over the desolation of a city which God has disowned. Lamentations 2 refers to 'the daughter of Zion' six times.[31] The last reference in the book draws a line under these sufferings: 'The punishment of your iniquity, O daughter of Zion, is accomplished' (La. 4:22). There *will* be an end: *he shall give them up until the time when she who is in travail has brought forth* (3).

We must not underestimate the cost either to God or to people of his giving them up. He had done it before in the face of their wickedness in the reign of Jeroboam: 'he will give Israel up because of the sins of Jeroboam, which he sinned and which he made Israel to sin'

[31] La. 2:1, 4, 8, 10, 13, 18.

(1 Ki. 14:16). But it was a deep agony to the LORD to do so, as Hosea's poignant words reveal:

> How can I give you up, O Ephraim!
>> How can I hand you over, O Israel! ...
> My heart recoils within me,
>> my compassion grows warm and tender (Ho. 11:8).

But when there is eventually no option, because of people's refusal to bow the knee to him, then Paul's triple refrain comes hauntingly into our consciousness: 'God gave them up ... to impurity ... God gave them up to dishonourable passions ... God gave them up to a base mind and to improper conduct' (Rom. 1:24, 25, 28). This threefold abandonment by God of the people he has made for himself leaves them at the mercy of their own desires and of their enemies, none of which have any mercy. 'It is a fearful thing to fall into the hands of the living God' (Heb. 10:31), but it may well be an even more fearful thing to be given up by the hands of the living God.

But the tide will turn when Bethlehem's royal child is born. Those scattered to the four winds in the wake of God's decision to give them up will return from exile: *then the rest of his brethren shall return to the people of Israel* (3). 'Now' it is bleak and traumatic. 'Now' the people of God are facing disintegration. But when God's true ruler emerges from the little town of Bethlehem, God's family will be together again, united around their new head. The word *return* has the sense of being converted or turning back. This will be a new unity based on a fundamental heart-conversion as the people return to the LORD under the leadership of his Messiah.[32]

The community of the Messiah's rule with the kingdom of David is particularly stressed in a reversion to the 'shepherd and sheep' metaphor of leadership:

> *He shall stand and feed his flock in the strength of the LORD,*
> *in the majesty of the name of the LORD his God* (4).

David, who shepherded his father's flock on the hills around Bethlehem, was taken from the sheepfolds to shepherd God's people.[33] A shepherd is a strong, fit, unflinching and courageous leader. This *ruler in Israel* will stand firm in the face of every peril and pressure. He will be resolute in making sure that the sheep are fed, not fleeced. Again, the contrast with the leadership in Micah's

[32] Jesus is called 'the first-born among many brethren' (Rom. 8:29) and 'he is not ashamed to call them brethren' (Heb. 2:11).
[33] Ps. 78:70–72.

time is clear-cut. His secret lies in his personal relationship with *the LORD his God*, from which he derives his inner strength and in which he expresses single-minded devotion to the honour and glory (*majesty*) of the LORD. In so doing, he gives personal and practical expression to the people's resolve to 'walk in the name of the LORD' (4:5).

Under such high-quality leadership, the people *shall dwell secure*. Security is not to be found in wealth or technology or status, but in quiet trust in the great Shepherd of the sheep. His greatness extends, not simply over the territory of Israel, but *to the ends of the earth* (4). The security he brings does not depend on being in a particular place or in particular circumstances. It is to be experienced in any place throughout the entire world.

It will, moreover, be intact and inviolable even *when the Assyrian comes into our land and treads upon our soil* (5). In the face of such disaster, which was imminent as Micah spoke, the coming of the promised Messiah and his sovereignty to the ends of the earth become a rock-solid assurance: *And this shall be peace* (5), possibly meaning 'this (man) means peace', referring to the new ruler who is to come. Israel's current leadership talked flippantly and cynically about *peace* (3:5), about 'shalom'. The new leader would himself embody true 'shalom'.[34]

When there is leadership of that quality, providing security of such inner depth, a people's expectations are transformed. Instead of quivering in fear at the invader's threats and taunts, Micah expresses complete confidence for a future and a hope: *we will raise against him seven shepherds and eight princes of men* (5). With a great shepherd at our head, we will be able to find quality leadership again. There will be no shortage of people equipped, not simply to stand firm and victorious against the Assyrians when they come into our land, but to establish our authority in their land. *Seven* is the perfect number; *eight* is one more still. *Rule* (6) literally means 'shepherd' – in other words, these shepherds will truly shepherd, unlike the nation's current leadership.

When the Messiah is in charge, the people of God find a new unity, a new strength and a new purpose (all three realities expressed in the use of the number seven). They move from defeatist mode to a dual focus, both cleansing and expanding their territory. *Nimrod* (6) stands for the mightiest forces around. The grandson of Noah, Nimrod 'was the first on the earth to be a mighty man . . . The beginning of his kingdom was Babel . . . in the land of Shinar. From that land he went into Assyria, and built Nineveh . . .' (Gn. 10:8–11).

---

[34] Paul says of Jesus, in a single passage, that 'he is our peace . . . so making peace . . . he . . . preached peace . . .' (Eph. 2:14, 15, 17).

Babel (or Babylon) and Nineveh are both indicated by Micah's mention of Nimrod. When God's ruler is on the throne of the new Israel, even the greatest cities of the earth cannot withstand him.[35] Whether on the attack or on the defensive, there is victory.

The remnant will then come into their own. *The rest of his brethren* (3), who have returned to the places from which they have been scattered, will unite under their new ruler and a renewed Israel will at last begin to be the people God created them to be.[36] Micah sees the remnant, not as a holy huddle gathered together for mutual protection and mere survival, but a force *in the midst of many peoples . . . among the nations* (7, 8). They will, moreover, be a force both for refreshment and for rending: *like dew from the LORD* (7), and *like a lion among the beasts of the forest, like a young lion among the flocks of sheep* (8). These two contrasting images point up the double impact of a people united and committed to the LORD's Messiah; to some they are 'a fragrance from life to life', to others 'a fragrance from death to death' (2 Cor. 2:16). The same quality of life, the same lifestyle, affects different people in dramatically different ways: some feel blessed and renewed, others feel battered and shredded.

The remnant have this impact among the nations solely because of their relationship with the LORD. They take on his character and impart something of his qualities wherever they go. This is probably the force of the phrases about the origin and the impact of the dew and the rain, *which tarry not for men nor wait for the sons of men* (7). The LORD's own words to Israel through Hosea make this clear:

> I will heal their faithlessness,
>   I will love them freely . . .
> I will be as the dew to Israel;
>   he shall blossom as the lily,
>   he shall strike root as the poplar;
> his shoots shall spread out;
>   his beauty shall be like the olive,
>   and his fragrance like Lebanon.
> They shall return and dwell beneath my shadow,
>   they shall flourish as a garden (Ho. 14:4–7).

Drawing on the LORD's resources, his people become providers of life and growth: 'I will make them and the places round about my

---

[35] Speaking of his church, Jesus said, 'Even the gates of Hades shall not prevail against it' (Mt. 16:18 mg.).

[36] See Is. 49:6, 'a light to the nations', and Gn. 12:3 mg., 'in you all the families of the earth shall be blessed'.

hill a blessing; and I will send down the showers in their season; they shall be showers of blessing' (Ezk. 34:26).

Equally, the remnant will take on God's sterner qualities as they deepen their relationship with him – his justice, his purity, his hatred of sin in all its forms, his resistance towards human pride and self-sufficiency. Whereas both Egyptian and Assyrian kings likened themselves to a lion, it is Hosea again who expresses this aspect of the LORD's character:

> I will be like a lion to Ephraim,
>   and like a young lion to the house of Judah.
> I, even I, will rend and go away,
>   I will carry off, and none shall rescue (Ho. 5:14).

Micah recognizes that, when such an impact is made among the nations, the reason is the sovereign action of God himself:

> *Your hand shall be lifted up over your adversaries,*
>   *and all your enemies shall be cut off* (9).

It has never been easy to be the LORD's instrument 'to pluck up and to break down, to destroy and to overthrow', rather than 'to build and to plant'.[37] But when God puts his words in our mouths and his Spirit in our bodies, both ministries will affect those around us.

What will happen *then* (7) is the exact reverse of what is happening 'now'. That is the difference between corrupt leadership and consecrated leadership, between a city in rebellion against the LORD's sovereignty and a faithful remnant secure in the LORD's sovereignty. Micah now proceeds (10–15) to summarize what will happen *in that day* (10) when, having given up his people to the fruits of their disobedience, he regathers them under the shepherd from Bethlehem.

What will happen *in that day* complements what Micah has already said will happen (4:6–7). There he emphasized the LORD's decision to assemble and gather the 'lame' as the remnant. Here he emphasizes the LORD's decision to *cut off* (10, 11, 12, 13) and to *root out* (14) every alien influence, practice and object from the renewed Jerusalem and the new Israel. This double action is parallel to his qualities likened to dew and a lion: he restores the battered and bruised, and he removes what is alien to his kingdom.

The repetition of *your* (ten times) and *you* (five times) shows that the LORD's target is apostate Jerusalem. He will purge the city of all evil. There are four primary evils: urban self-sufficiency, military

---

[37] This was the LORD's commission to Jeremiah (Je. 1:9–10).

might, occult practices and idol worship. All are centred in Israel's *cities* and *strongholds*. With all these there can be no compromise. It is not a question of scaling them down or getting them in proportion. They are to be *cut off*. The phrase comes four times, as an expression of the LORD's determination to get rid of them once for all; it is taken up from the last phrase of the previous paragraph: *all your enemies shall be cut off* (9).

In other words, these four evils within the nation are enemies of equal virulence and viciousness as any Assyrian invader or Babylonian empire-builder. The thrice-used phrase *from among you* (10, 13, 14), underlines the way the four evils have taken hold of Israel's national life. They have burrowed their way into the heart of the nation and become endemic. As such, they need to be rooted out (14), as well as cut off. That these evils were a notorious presence in the land is shown by the fact that Isaiah, also, stresses the last three.[38] The potential for arrogance and self-sufficiency in all cities is eloquently expressed in the account in Genesis of the tower of Babel.[39] Then, and ever since, human beings have expressed their determination to control their own lives and destinies by building their dream of the perfect community, expecting to discover security and unity along the way, but independently of God.[40]

Military might, the second evil Micah denounces, is defined as *horses* and *chariots* as well as *cities* and *strongholds* (10–11). Horses and chariots have been mentioned in reference to Lachish, one of the major centres of the Shephelah, which had developed a wide reputation for its chariot brigade, with horses bought from the Egyptians to develop a formidable war machine of virtually impregnable capability. In the military might based at Lachish, Micah had seen 'the beginning of sin to the daughter of Zion' (1:13). Their military strength produced in them pride in their own achievements and a sense of invincibility. This arrogance God intended to cut off.

When a nation prospers, the capacity and the desire to build up its military resources inevitably follow. Micah presumably lists this first because nothing so erodes trust in God as quickly or as remorselessly as the ability to look after oneself. If we can make ourselves secure in the material sense, even if only by the provision of so-called 'security devices', we come to believe that God is superfluous. That happens to a city and a nation as much as to individuals.

[38] Is. 2:6–8. There is evidence that, in his response to Micah's words, King Hezekiah set about dealing specifically with the last three evils (see Je. 26:16–19 and 2 Ki. 18:1–8).

[39] Gn. 11:1–9.

[40] For a powerful, biblical analysis of this theme, see Jacques Ellul, *The Meaning of the City* (Eerdmans, 1970; reprinted in the Biblical and Theological Classics Library by Paternoster, 1997).

From the time of Moses, God had made it abundantly clear that any king of Israel must put his trust in the LORD for military security, not in horses: 'he [the king] must not multiply horses for himself, or cause the people to return to Egypt in order to multiply horses, since the LORD has said to you, "You shall never return that way again"' (Dt. 17:16). Time and time again down the years, Israel had attempted to establish national security by strengthening their military resources, not least by alliances with other nations. The message of the prophets had consistently been one of condemnation.[41]

So long as people called by the LORD continue to put their trust in military might, or in any other human resources, Micah's vision of a time when war shall be no more (4:1–4) remains a pious hope. One of the strategies of Micah's day, when a nation or a city was attacked, was for the entire population to withdraw within fortified cities and towns, or *strongholds*. This had been developed into such a highly skilled tactic that it was virtually impossible to breach the stronghold – impossible, that is, until the Assyrians appeared. They had pioneered and perfected the science of siege warfare. No longer was even the strongest stronghold secure. In this way God used Assyria as 'the rod of my anger' (Is. 10:5) to flush out the people of Israel, not simply from their strongholds, but from their haughtiness: *I will . . . throw down all your strongholds* (11).

Occult practices, Micah's third evil, have already come to our notice in the divination practised by the false prophets (3:6–7). These practices had been part and parcel of the land of Canaan, when the people of Israel first entered the land. They had been plainly and powerfully ordered not to touch them with a barge-pole.[42] No compromise was even to be considered. God's way of communicating to his people was by the law and the prophets, not by mediums, diviners or sorcerers.

But as time went on and the spiritual leadership of the nation became lax and slipshod, they allowed some, and gradually all, of these pagan practices to infiltrate the worship of the people. It was expected and acknowledged that other nations worshipping other gods would virtually depend on occult practices; that was the nature of paganism. But not for God's people. 'When they say to you, "Consult the mediums and the wizards who chirp and mutter," should not a people consult their God? Should they consult the dead on behalf of the living? To the teaching and to the testimony! Surely for this word which they speak there is no dawn' (Is. 8:19–20).

The LORD will, therefore, summarily cut off everything of that kind from the renewed Jerusalem and the new Israel under the

---

[41] See *e.g.* Is. 30:1–2; 31:1–3.   [42] Lv. 19:31; 20:6; Dt. 18:9–14.

Messiah's leadership. *I will cut off sorceries from your hand, and you will have no more soothsayers* (12). Sorcery was, in fact, a capital offence under the old covenant in Israel,[43] and it remains explicitly forbidden in the kingdom of God under the new covenant.[44] In Micah and Isaiah's day, sorcery and divination were identified with the Philistines and with eastern cultures.[45] The same anathema was applied to practitioners of the magic arts, therefore, as was applied to those who relied on horses from Egypt.

It is the same issue with all three of these evils. On whom do the people of God rely? Whether the question is urban self-sufficiency, military security or personal security, is the LORD adequate or not? And it is the same issue when we come to Micah's last evil, idol worship (13–14). *Images, pillars* and *Asherim* are the items mentioned (13–14). They were all *the work of your hands*. The LORD says that he will cut them off and root them out: *You shall bow down no more to the work of your hands* (13).

The *images* were idols, made out of wood, stone, gold, silver or any suitable and available material. Where idols are part of modern worship, a huge industry always grows up and thrives around the shrines. Paul discovered that in Ephesus,[46] and any traveller today can see the same thing. The LORD's condemnation of all such idolatry is plain to any reader of the Old Testament, from the second commandment ('You shall not make for yourself a graven image'; Ex. 20:4) on through prophet after prophet and their remorseless, often ribald, denunciation of idol worship.[47]

Pillars and *Asherah* stand for the male and female deities in the most widely practised religion of the region, Baal and Asherah. The worship of these two deities was blatantly erotic and sexually explicit. Cult prostitution, by both men and women, was an essential ingredient. The *pillars* were normally stones, while the Asherim were trees. 'Stones and trees murmur and whisper.'[48] The message was one of fertility: follow these practices, and fruitfulness is guaranteed in your fields and in your wombs.

Fertility brought prosperity, not just for a few individuals, but for the national economy. A basically agricultural nation, like the Israel/Judah of Micah's day, depended on the fruitfulness of the land. Today the issues in most western countries are very different. The worship of Baal in modern cities and nations is evidenced by the virtual worship given to production, performance and profits. Market forces and the Gross National Product seem to be the powers which control and enslave us. Everything is seen as subservient to such realities, even to the point of losing true health and happiness.

---

[43] Ex. 22:19; Mal. 3:5.   [44] Gal. 5:20; Rev. 21:8; 22:15.   [45] Is. 2:6.
[46] Acts 19:11–41.   [47] E.g. 1 Ki. 18:17–40; Is. 44:9–20.   [48] Waltke, p. 721.

This idolatrous worship was and is fundamentally perverted. It inevitably led to perverse lifestyles. It was the result of worshipping the creature rather than the Creator. It held its worshippers to no ethical norms or boundaries. It was a licence for licentiousness. And it could take over whole communities or entire cities – hence the LORD's pronouncement, *I will . . . destroy your cities* (14). There can clearly be no 'both . . . and' when it comes to the worship of idols and the worship of God. It is plainly 'either . . . or'. The time is coming, says the LORD, when all fudge and flippancy will be rooted out and cut off.

The closing verse of this fifth chapter and this second cycle (15) brings God's judgment to bear, not just on Israel under her new leader, but on *the nations that did not obey*. This is the statement of 'the LORD of the whole earth' (4:13) in the light of the coming of a ruler who *shall be great to the ends of the earth* (5:4). Many nations and many peoples will have found their way to the mountain of the LORD (4:2). They will have learned God's ways and will have begun to walk in God's paths. As a result, God's law will have gone forth from Jerusalem, the renewed Jerusalem, to instruct people all over the world. But not all will obey, and they will be dealt with in accordance with God's righteous judgment.

The words used of this process are bald and dramatic: *In anger and wrath I will execute vengeance* (15). This process is essentially protective: God will keep everything unclean out of his city, the renewed Jerusalem. The visions of John in Revelation explain it well: 'But nothing unclean shall enter it, nor any one who practises abomination or falsehood' . . . 'Outside are the dogs and sorcerers and fornicators and murderers and idolaters, and every one who loves and practises falsehood' (Rev. 21:27; 22:15). God does not have a raging temper which flares up. He has a settled hatred of sin, which ultimately excludes from his presence and his kingdom all that is opposed to him. What he avenges is his sovereignty, wherever and whenever it is flouted.

The third cycle

Micah 6:1 – 7:20
A time of disintegration and desolation

Micah begins with a passionate plea to the people from the heart of God (6:1–5). He then responds to God's pleading with a clear statement of the proper way for human beings to behave (6:6–8), before again attacking the corruption of the city (6:9–16). By this time it is beyond hope (7:1–6), and all he or they can do is wait in hope for God to lift them out of and beyond the judgment that must fall. He is confident for himself (7:8–10) and for the faithful remnant who will survive (7:11–17). His confidence is based solely, but strongly, on the faithful, forgiving character of God (7:18–20).

Micah 6:1 – 7:7
5. A message of gloom and doom

1. The Lord's case against his people (6:1–5)

The third cycle begins with another summons to his people to pay attention: *Hear what the* LORD *says.*[1] 'Summons' is the word, because this opening section is couched in the form and atmosphere of a lawcourt. In this court the people of Israel are in the dock, and

---

[1] It is possible that this call is to everyone who is reading the book (so Waltke, p. 727). The word 'hear' is plural, while the word 'arise' is singular, clearly addressed to Israel.

the mountains are called in as witnesses (the second *Hear* is addressed to *you mountains . . . and you enduring foundations of the earth*). The mountains and the hills must hear the voice of God's people as they face up to the charges that he is levelling against them.

There is an ongoing fascination about any legal drama. They are the stuff of television and cinema. As we look at this case between God and his people, 'the heart must be dull that does not leap to the Presences before which the trial is enacted'.[2] God's insistence that the trial should be heard, not just in public, but in the presence of the mountains and the hills, underlines his intention that his dealings with his covenant people should be in the public domain and that people should live in the light of his certain judgment. His *saving acts* (5) down the years have been manifest for all to see, so that the whole world will sit up and take notice of his ways and his word.

Whenever God's people hide themselves away and shun exposure to and involvement with the wider world, they betray God's purpose for them. God wants his people to be distinctively holy in the very midst of the general corruption that surrounds us – to be in the world, but not of it.[3] We, however, have an instinctive inclination to keep our internal lives to ourselves, to hush up any hint of scandal and not to parade our shortcomings – often with the result that unbelievers have little or no genuine encounter with authentic Christian discipleship and little or no concept of what it might mean to hold ourselves accountable to God for our lives. Not infrequently, this is due to a general misconception on the part of believers that the world expects God's people to be spotless and above reproach, when in fact they long to see authenticity and realism in acknowledging our vulnerability and our weaknesses. The essence of God's activity, from the creation of the world through the covenant with Israel to the coming of Christ and the proclamation of the gospel, has always been its openness and its accessibility. As Paul said when on trial before King Agrippa, 'this was not done in a corner' (Acts 26:26).

So the LORD has decreed that his people should go on trial before the watching world, epitomized in dramatic terms by its oldest inhabitants – the mountains and the hills, who have been silent witnesses to his dealings with people and to their dealings with him right from the beginning. Now it is time for them to speak out: *for the LORD has a controversy with his people, and he will contend with Israel* (2). So Israel is told: *plead your case before the mountains* (1). The LORD is the plaintiff; Israel is the accused. The LORD is entering a charge; Israel must bring her defence.

[2] G. A. Smith, p. 449.   [3] See Jn. 17:1–26.

The mountains were there to witness the LORD's original action in entering into a covenant with his people. Three times the LORD had declared through Moses: 'I call heaven and earth to witness.'[4] On each occasion it had been a witness 'against' his people in the event of their breaking his covenant. Now, with all the evidence, by Micah's day, stacked up against them, the witnesses are called to take their stand. The whole of creation is under the authority of its Creator. It does his bidding[5] and he intends it to bear witness to his goodness, justice and truth, as Jesus himself asserted on Palm Sunday, when his followers in Jerusalem hailed him as Messiah and King but were condemned by the Pharisees: 'I tell you, if these were silent, the very stones would cry out' (Lk. 19:40).[6]

In the context of the pagan worship of Baal so prevalent in Judah and Jerusalem in Micah's time, this theology of nature is a sturdy antithesis to such fertility cults and any modern versions of the same. Israel's orthodoxy was healthily and extravagantly committed to celebration of the good earth and all its infinite variety; but it never countenanced anything less than exuberant praise of its Creator, not the deifying of its living organisms. The earth and everything in it are God's witnesses and they do what they are told.

What is the kernel of God's *controversy* with his people? Significantly, it is not a catalogue of crimes, sins, failures or shortcomings. Given the long list of offences itemized earlier by Micah, this is striking. The entire mood of his case against Israel has changed. This is shown by the LORD's opening form of address: '*O my people*' (3), which is repeated for emphasis (5). If the whole passage evokes the atmosphere of a lawcourt, the language here is personal and passionate, far more like a father's pleas to his child or a husband pleading with his wife. The LORD is not intent on reading out a long list of grievances: 'You have done that; you always do this, you always do that.' This is the plea of a loving God, whose heart has been broken by his people's rejection of him. 'Love . . . keeps no record of wrongs' (1 Cor. 13:5, NIV),[7] and at this point God is concerned for the relationship, not for the record. In fact, his opening question turns the situation on its head. Instead of reprimanding them for the countless things they have done to him,

---

[4] Dt. 4:26; 30:19; 31:28. *Cf.* Ps. 50:1–6; the whole psalm evokes a similar court drama. In Ezk. 36:1–8, God speaks to the mountains about what he is going to do in judgment on the nations.

[5] This is the thrust of those psalms which speak of the glories and the functions of the created world, *e.g.* Ps. 148:8, 'stormy wind fulfilling his command'. *Cf.* Pss. 107:25–29; 147:15–17.

[6] *Cf.* Mt. 8:24–27.

[7] The Greek word here is used in accountancy; from it we derive the appropriate word 'logbook'.

he asks them, *'what have I done to you?'* (3). He wants to hear the evidence.

The next question is also the question of a fervent lover: *'In what have I wearied you?'* (3). 'You have grown tired of me. You are bored with me. It is all such an effort to be with me, to give me any time or affection. What have I done – or failed to do – to bring about such a sense of tedium and lack of interest?' We can almost see Israel toss her head, turn away and say absolutely nothing. So God almost blurts out, *'Answer me!'* (3). In a court of law, witnesses have the right to silence, to avoid self-incrimination. But this right can be abused, and in Israel's case the situation required them to speak – or was their reluctance a silent admission of guilt? 'Yes, I am bored with God.'

In fact, of course, 'it was God who had a right to be weary',[8] weary with his people for their sins and transgressions. A similar accusation is levelled at Israel through Isaiah:

> You did not call upon me, O Jacob;
> > but you have been weary of me, O Israel!
> You have not brought me your sheep for burnt offerings;
> > or honoured me with sacrifices.
> I have not burdened you with offerings,
> > or wearied you with frankincense . . .
> But you have burdened me with your sins,
> > you have wearied me with your iniquities' (Is. 43:22–24).

God's people were bored stiff with the mechanics and the routine of worship. They found it a chore and a weariness, to the point where they now defaulted on observing their obligations. They had more interesting and stimulating things to do. God denies the suggestion that, by his requirements for their worshipping life, he has overburdened them. They have lost the plot and the passion. It is no wonder that they see it as a charade. If truth were told, they have really wearied the LORD. The words of another prophet, Malachi, explain why and how: 'You have wearied the LORD with your words. Yet you say, "How have we wearied him?" By saying, "Every one who does evil is good in the sight of the LORD, and he delights in them." Or by asking, "Where is the God of justice?"' (Mal. 2:17).[9]

But the LORD wants his people to concentrate on his *saving acts* (5), because he is aware that the only adequate motivation for a restored and renewed relationship between them is gratitude for all that he has been and done for them over the years. So he highlights

[8] R. L. Smith, pp. 50–51.   [9] *Cf.* Is. 7:13.

three or four key events in their history, times when they walked hand in hand and were very close to one another. The name of a place or a person is sufficient to bring back a whole host of memories: *Egypt*; *Moses, Aaron and Miriam*; *Balak* and *Balaam*; *Shittim* and *Gilgal* (4–5). When a relationship has lasted a long time, certain places have particular associations and key individuals continue to carry special significance.

> *'I brought you up from the land of Egypt,*
> *and redeemed you from the house of bondage'* (4).

That had always been the high point of Israel's relationship with the LORD. It was celebrated systematically and dramatically in the feast of the Passover.[10] Like any routine, it could go dry and appear dead – but only if they failed to identify imaginatively with the events thus re-enacted, *the saving acts of the LORD* (5). How could they find it wearisome and boring, let alone forget that God had rescued them from bondage?

The trouble is that certain people like bondage. They get a perverse pleasure out of being under someone else's power. They prefer to be slaves rather than to be free. They pay for the privilege of being whipped and beaten. What is called sado-masochism in the physical sense is surrender to self-centred drives and desires in a spiritual sense. Whatever the resultant pain and misery, 'my people love to have it so' (Je. 5:31). In the words of the LORD through Jeremiah:

> . . . wicked men are found among my people;
>   they lurk like fowlers lying in wait.
> They set a trap;
>   they catch men (Je. 5:26).

More bondage, more perverse pleasure in being caught in the house of bondage, rather than choosing to be rescued and redeemed.

God had always found it easier to get his people out of Egypt than to get Egypt out of his people. The words *I . . . redeemed you* (4) were wonderful, but it now looked as though they had become a memory, not a motivation. *I brought you up* (4) had all the right associations – the past behind, the journey completed, the land possessed – but now they were down and virtually out. Could a relationship of faith, hope and love really be re-established?

The major problem for God's people in Micah's time was leadership. It was completely corrupt. The people had no role models, no

[10] See Ex. 12:1–51.

inspirational examples. The business high-flyers were sharks (6:11–12). The political and legal leaders were entirely out for themselves (3:1–4). The religious hierarchy was a joke (3:5, 11). Remember Moses? And Aaron? And Miriam? Where did they come from? Did they just happen? No, says the LORD, *I sent them before you* (4). He did not just send them; he sent them *before you* – to go in front of you, to lead you, to be your leaders. It was no simple matter to get Moses, at least, to take on such leadership. He had thought of every excuse in the book, and a few more.[11] Nor was he a paragon of virtue.[12]

Leadership does not appear out of thin air. It comes from people whom God has created, chosen, called and commissioned with his authority. I did it back then, says the LORD through Micah, and I can do it again now. You may be wearied beyond belief with your present so-called, or self-styled, leaders, but I am still in the business of sending men and women (and Miriam was one of those leaders) to go before my people.

> '*O my people, remember what Balak king of Moab devised, and what Balaam the son of Beor answered him*' (5).

Remembering in the Bible is not merely a matter of calling to mind, but of 'actualizing the past into the present'.[13] That kind of remembering brings events so vividly into people's experience that they take part in them afresh for themselves:[14] 'Remembrance equals participation.'[15] Such participation in 'virtual reality' ought not to be beyond the grasp of our modern video (Latin for 'I see') and audio ('I hear') generation. The LORD wanted his people in Micah's day, in their particular circumstances, to remember Balak and Balaam.[16]

The events referred to take place at Shittim at the beginning of 'Israel's triumphant march into the promised land'.[17] When they reached Gilgal, with the torrential waters of a swollen river Jordan safely negotiated, they were home and dry, though with the land still to be possessed.[18] But in first remembering Shittim, they were to bring Balak and Balaam into focus.

When, in the time of Joshua, the LORD was reminding the people of Israel about significant events in their history so far, he spoke

[11] Ex. 3:1 – 4:17.   [12] Ex. 3:11–15.   [13] Waltke, p. 730.

[14] The most significant example in the New Testament is in our Lord's words at the Last Supper: 'Do this in remembrance of me' (Lk. 22:19; 1 Cor. 11:24–26). Remembering is, therefore, at the heart of the worshipping life of God's people in both Old and New Testaments. For the key role of remembering at Passover, see Dt. 16:1–3.

[15] B. S. Childs, quoted by Waltke, p. 731.   [16] Nu. 22:1 – 24:25.

[17] Waltke, p. 731.   [18] Jos. 4:19–24.

about the Balak and Balaam affair: 'Then Balak the son of Zippor, king of Moab, arose and fought against Israel; and he sent and invited Balaam the son of Beor to curse you, but I would not listen to Balaam; therefore he blessed you; so I delivered you out of his hand' (Jos. 24:9–10). It is probable that this summary is in Micah's mind and that these are the lessons God wants his people once again to recall and make their own: a powerful army threatening their very existence, a particular individual failing in his duties to be God's person for the crisis, and a sovereign intervention by God to thwart human perverseness and to deliver his people.[19] It all involved, as we might recall, God speaking through a donkey. Now, we can almost hear God saying through Micah, will you believe I can deliver *you*? You have the Assyrians instead of the Moabites and you have a corrupt leadership instead of a delinquent prophet: but I remain the constant in the equation.

God's saving acts were not isolated incidents at key moments, like the exodus and the entry into the promised land. They happened regularly *from Shittim to Gilgal* (5) – virtually the period covered in the book of Joshua. That series of divine actions records the commitment of the LORD to establishing his people in the land. He had demonstrated his commitment to them over the years, and the evidence lay in the ground underneath their feet. He was a God of actions, not merely words. Just as he had put all their enemies under their feet in those days, so he would put all their current enemies under their feet.

The last chapter of the book of Joshua records what happened beyond Gilgal: '. . . you went over the Jordan and came to Jericho, and the men of Jericho fought against you, and also the Amorites, the Perizzites, the Canaanites, the Hittites, the Girgashites, the Hivites, and the Jebusites; and I gave them into your hand. And I sent the hornet before you, which drove them out before you . . . it was not by your sword or your bow. I gave you a land on which you had not laboured, and cities which you had not built, and you dwell therein: you eat the fruit of vineyards and oliveyards which you did not plant' (Jos. 24:11–13).

If they exercise their memory properly, therefore, the people must *know the saving acts of the LORD* (5). They know from firsthand, personal experience; it is not simply an intellectual awareness of them. God's acts of salvation become the living possession of his people in each generation, as they *remember* in order to *know*. Such remembering and knowing will bring constant renewal to our personal relationship with him in love, faith and hope. God may

---

[19] It is worth comparing the lessons of the Balak/Balaam story drawn by New Testament writers: see 2 Pet. 2:14–16; Jude 11; Rev. 2:14.

confront us in an atmosphere coloured by the law; but he deals with us from his heart of love. He enters pleas against us, but he constantly pleads with us.

2. The LORD's requirements for everyone (6:6–8)

In face of such an emotive plea from the LORD, Micah, as representative of the people of God, is moved to return to him. But *'With what shall I come before the LORD, and bow myself before God on high?'* (6). Moved and humbled by God's pleading, the prophet wants to see the relationship restored. Micah may be speaking more for the people as a whole, and the nation's leadership in particular. The immense scale of the sacrificial offerings he goes on to mention may either be rhetorical exaggeration or indicate the response of the wealthiest citizen of Jerusalem, even of the king himself. There is, in any case, a new recognition of personal *sin* and *transgression* (7). God's passionate and personal plea has produced the desired effect: this representative of the people now *wants* to come before him and make atonement for his sin.

But, as is usually the case when people with a religious background resolve to take God seriously again, the individual concerned begins by wanting to step up his acts of piety:

> *'Shall I come before him with burnt offerings,*
> *with calves a year old?*
> *Will the LORD be pleased with thousands of rams,*
> *with ten thousand of rivers of oil?'* (6–7).

He fondly imagines that quantities of transgressions can be swept away by quantities of sacrifices. This notion of atonement by means of costly gifts, of virtually buying God off, dies very hard in the human heart.

In the venal, money-mad world of Micah's Jerusalem, paying the right price was the only known currency. If all human relations in the city were conditioned by mercenary considerations, how could they view their relationship with God in any different way? Everybody else had their price: why not the LORD? Just add a few noughts (*thousands . . . ten thousands*) and the problem is solved. Instead of seeing all relationships between human beings, and between a human being and God, as a covenant to be cherished and explored, the people of Jerusalem thought in terms of a contract – cold, formal, legal, with penalty clauses, rules and regulations; a document that could be torn up and rewritten if necessary.

Writing about 'the good society', John Tusa (Managing Director of the Barbican Centre in London) has commented, 'The language

175

of the market has now taken over most other human transactions. Any organization worth its salt is supposed to exist by an internal market. This means that each and any transaction must be costed and should only occur if a price is put upon it.'[20] This is how Micah's speaker sees his relationship to God.

As soon as these words were out of his mouth, the person knows that with God it does not and cannot work like that: '*Shall I give my first-born for my transgression, the fruit of my body for the sin of my soul?*' (7). To offer up your eldest child to pay for your sin is the ultimate sacrifice, however appalling such a practice might be (and it was an integral part of the Baal worship which had been allowed to infiltrate the life of the nation). In the history of God's people, also, there was some precedent for that option. Had not God told Abraham to sacrifice his only son, Isaac?[21] It had not actually reached that far, of course, but the thought was there. But even that proposed act of sacrifice by Abraham was not to atone for sin, but to demonstrate the obedience implicit in faith.

Micah was involved in a situation where transgression and sin had riddled a whole nation from top to bottom. No one individual could begin to make adequate atonement, and, in any case, *the fruit of my body* can have no impact on *the sin of my soul*. Moreover, 'Yahweh does not make these kinds of demands upon his people,'[22] because God never requires what we are in no position to give, or what there is no point in giving. The New Testament teaches us what God has done in Jesus Christ to answer Micah's rhetorical question about atonement for *the sin of my soul*.

So we come to Micah's best-known and fundamental teaching:

> *He has showed you, O man, what is good;*
> *and what does the* LORD *require of you,*
> *but to do justice, and to love kindness,*
> *and to walk humbly with your God?* (8).

In other words, God wants our very selves, our lives and our love. That is the costliest sacrifice we can bring, a living sacrifice of our souls and bodies.[23] This is the only reasonable response we can make to his redeeming love. It is on the basis of 'the mercies of God' that Paul makes his appeal to God's people at Rome, mercies which he has been expounding in the first eleven chapters of his letter.

Micah's summary also encapsulates all that he has said up to this point about justice, mercy and humble fellowship with God – or the

[20] *The Independent*, August 1997.   [21] See Gn. 22:1–19.   [22] Wolff, p. 179.
[23] See Rom. 12:1–2.

lack of all three in his generation of leaders. He has shown his audience what is evil. Now he stresses that God has shown *what is good*, even though the leaders of his own generation had chosen to 'hate the good' (3:2). The word translated *man* is *'āḏām*. This explicitly refers back to the Genesis account of Adam and Eve turning their back on God as provider and definer of *what is good*.[24] Israel may have had much greater revelation about God's idea of the good life, notably in the Ten Commandments; and those who have been given knowledge of God's Son, Jesus, have even fuller revelation. But the fundamentals are available to everyone from the evidence of creation and the witness of conscience.[25]

The impact of revelation shakes us into facing up to the question, *What does the LORD require?* (8). When God speaks through his commandments, his creation and our conscience, it is not to titillate us or to intrigue us, but to call forth our repentance and faith. For repentance and faith are the necessary prerequisites for living with justice, mercy and humility before God as our priorities. Micah's contemporaries were living evidence of what happens to people who decide to dispense with God, to walk in pride without God. Instead of responding to the imperative of doing justice in humble obedience to God's commandments, they had reached the point where they had come to 'abhor justice' (3:9). Rather than show *kindness* (or 'compassion' or 'steadfast love'), particularly to those less fortunate and less successful, they pursued a ruthless policy of exploitation, greed, fraud and murder.

Micah's threefold requirement cannot, therefore, be conveniently dissected, packaged and labelled. The three qualities hold together. It is only by applying ourselves to the third (*to walk humbly with your God*), that we can begin to practise the first two (*to do justice, and to love kindness*). That is, also, what it means to love the Lord your God with all your heart, soul, mind and strength, and to love your neighbour as yourself.[26] Justice and kindness are, in fact, essential qualities in the nature of God himself.[27] They do not come down from heaven wrapped in parcels. They are expressed in and through people who walk humbly with their God.

To walk humbly with your God cannot, in the context of Micah's prophecy and of the Scriptures as a whole, be taken to mean 'God as you know him', but 'God as he has revealed himself to you', as creator, redeemer, father and judge. This is the only God, fully incarnate as Emmanuel (God with us) in Jesus of Nazareth, who invites each person into a living relationship and a loving friendship

---

[24] Gn. 2:15; 3:1–7; note particularly the use of 'good' and 'very good' in the first three chapters of Genesis.
[25] Rom. 1:19–20; 2:14–16.   [26] See the account in Mk. 12:28–34.
[27] See Ps. 119:156; Is. 30:18; Ho. 2:19.

with himself, to walk with him and to ensure that there is no day when we walk without him – or away from him.

One person who found the reality of such a walk with God commented: 'For the first time in my life I feel accompanied.' That is the core reality which God has shown to enshrine *what is good*. This is the good life, and it produces the fruit of goodness in the covenantal blessings of justice and kindness (or goodness and mercy)[28] – *mišpaṭ* and *ḥesed* – the Hebrew terms for the qualities which make for peace, or shalom. By ignoring these, Jerusalem had sentenced herself to war, not peace – as she did in the time of Jesus, to his deep sadness.[29]

To be committed to and express both justice and kindness, goodness and mercy, it is necessary to *walk humbly*, not haughtily (2:3). Both justice and kindness stem from humble people. If we do not walk humbly in relation to God, it is unlikely – if not impossible – that we shall walk humbly with other people. If we love kindness, mercy and compassion, we shall act justly.

Micah's response to God's cry from the heart is, therefore, the perfect response to the people of God in his generation. He may necessarily be silent about atonement: but his words are of universal application, relevant to any city, in any nation, in any century. Young people today, in their desire for the good life, stress in their own way the same priorities as Micah: justice, compassion and spirituality. The good life is accessible to those who listen and respond to what God has shown to be good.

3. The Lord's judgment on the city (6:9–16)

Micah cannot leave his threefold definition of what God has shown to be good and requires of everyone, without addressing the people of Jerusalem directly about the numerous ways in which they have rejected God's will. The phrase with which he begins this diatribe is unique: *The voice of the Lord cries to the city* (9). It seems to have even more urgency and intensity than the usual prophetic words, 'Thus says the Lord', or 'The word of the Lord came to me'. There is passion and pathos in his voice. In addressing *the city*, God is like a town crier, calling publicly for the attention of every citizen, because what he has to say is so important.

Micah adds his own measured, almost *sotto voce* and perhaps awed, comment about the Lord's urgent summons to Jerusalem: *and it is sound wisdom to fear thy name* (9). It is as though he is responding to the Lord on his own account, even if his fellow

---

[28] See Ps. 23:5, where the Lord, 'my Shepherd', will see to it that 'goodness and mercy shall follow me all the days of my life'.
[29] Lk. 19:41–44.

citizens choose not to pay attention. Micah knows that 'the fear of the LORD is the beginning of wisdom' (Ps. 111:10). He has learned to listen when God speaks and to let the Spirit of God fill him for his prophetic ministry (3:8).

The book of Deuteronomy clearly states the basic covenantal position of the LORD's people. Hearing God's voice and obeying what he says form a constant refrain in the book: 'Out of heaven he let you hear his voice, that he might discipline you' (Dt. 4:36). They had forgotten the immense privilege of having God speak to them at all – something their ancestors under Moses had recognized: 'For who is there of all flesh, that has heard the voice of the living God speaking out of the midst of fire, as we have, and has still lived?' (Dt. 5:26). When the voice of God spoke, there was only one option: obey, or disobey.[30] Obedience would bring blessings in abundance; disobedience would unleash curses without number.[31] Because Micah's Jerusalem was fundamentally disobedient to the voice of the LORD, they were inevitably heading for the curses – as Micah points out (13–15).

So it is *sound wisdom* to fear the revealed will of God. Wisdom in Scripture is intensely practical, focusing on the best way to achieve the desired results.[32] The *tribe and assembly of the city* (9), in any culture or generation, are supremely interested in practical results. In the city's welfare resides their personal welfare. If the city experiences a slump, their fortunes go into decline. So the question of prudent management of the city's affairs is fundamental to its leaders. The NIV rendering is entirely different: 'Heed the rod and the one who appointed it.' This would probably be a veiled reference to the Assyrians (called by God in Is. 10:5 'the rod of my anger') as the agent of God's coming judgment – a perspective crucial for sound wisdom in the leadership of any city or nation.

Micah's comment about sound wisdom could well be a faintly ironic reference to the concern of the city fathers for good business practice. The problem was that for them good business practice meant solely practices which increased their profits. Business ethics were an embarrassment. But they, together with today's business leaders, needed to learn that obeying God's commandments is not just good business practice but good for business.

So Micah now proceeds to spell it out:

> *'Can I forget the treasures of wickedness in the house of the wicked,*
> *and the scant measure that is accursed?*

---

[30] See Dt. 8:20; 13:18; 15:5; 26:14; 27:10.   [31] Dt. 28:1–68.
[32] See art. 'Wisdom' in *NBD*.

*Shall I acquit the man with wicked scales
and with a bag of deceitful weights?'* (10–11).

Micah gets very specific. He could name names. There are big
mansions and prosperous business houses which owe their size and
wealth to corrupt commercialism. It has, moreover, been going on
for years, to the point where any sensitivity to God's standards and
sanctions has long been eroded: God has forgotten – if he ever took
any notice in the first place.

But God cannot forget and does not forget. The corrupt
traders and merchants of Jerusalem are guilty of *wickedness*
(the word comes three times in two verses) and God will not *acquit*
(11) the guilty, because he is the God of justice. Jerusalem's
merchants were guilty of the standard business practice of rigging
weights and measures – a small weight to cheat the buyer, so that he
paid more for less; a larger weight to cheat the seller, so that he
received less for more (*wicked scales and . . . a bag of deceitful
weights*, 11).

In the time of Micah, a time of immense economic prosperity,
Jerusalem was a city where there were vast fortunes to be made. It
was the marketplace of the nations, a place of pilgrimage, a tourist
trap, a city of history and culture. It was the capital city of a
relatively small, but extremely fertile, hinterland. It was the place of
the great temple of Solomon, to which the whole nation resorted at
times of great festival and high celebration. At such times the
marketplace would have become one huge and hectic bazaar. It must
have been expensive at the best of times to visit Jerusalem – simply
to spend time there, let alone to fulfil one's religious obligations.
Entrepreneurs in such a metropolis would have been two a penny;
their prices somewhat higher.

A counter to such potential for dishonesty and corruption
had been provided in the Mosaic law, not just by specific legislation,
but backed by the full dignity of the LORD's personal authority,
and by a sharp reminder of his redeeming activity on behalf of his
people when they were the victims of oppression in Egypt: 'You
shall do no wrong in judgment, in measures of length or weight or
quantity. You shall have just balances, just weights, a just ephah, and
a just hin: I am the LORD your God, who brought you out of the land
of Egypt' (Lv. 19:35–36).[33] Business is a matter of justice – and kindness, because the just trader does not exploit the vulnerable and
ignorant. Only those who 'walk haughtily' (2:3), rather than humbly
with their God, choose to ignore such self-regulating checks and
balances.

---

[33] *Cf.* Dt. 25:13–16.

Commerce is always with us, as it must be, and its activities are regulated by law. But at the bottom, the integrity of commerce must rest with its practitioners, not with the law. When justice and kindness are among the virtues of business practice, and when these balance the desire for profit and expansion, men like Micah will finally be out of work. And that is one kind of unemployment which the business community may reasonably choose as a goal.[34]

The true state of the city's marketplace is summarized:

> *'Your rich men are full of violence,*
>   *your inhabitants speak lies,*
>   *and their tongue is deceitful in their mouth'* (12).

The whole system has been corrupted. The rich started it and must take the major responsibility, but their example has permeated the whole city. The key insight here is that the violence of a few leads to dishonesty by the many. A city where brutality and ruthlessness are the order of the day[35] inevitably becomes a place where people lie and deceive for survival. Nobody can be trusted. No longer is people's word their bond.

Whenever the god Mammon is allowed to rule, hard-headed business people become ruthless and prepared to resort to anything to boost profits and personal gain. In today's major cities the evidence for this syndrome is obvious. Methods of trading and dealing have become increasingly brutal. Companies and businesses go to the wall with alarming frequency, especially 'little people'. The loyalty of employers to their workforce has dramatically diminished. People are made redundant in droves, at a moment's notice and at extremely vulnerable times in their lives (with major responsibilities still to be fulfilled with respect to mortgages and family support). This has, in its turn, created a climate of opportunism in the workforce, in which loyalty to one's employer is at a premium.

The net result is an atmosphere of serious distrust. It is assumed by the professionals that clients are lying and that customers will not keep their word. Deals cannot be made unless there are lawyers covering every possible loophole. When it comes to interviews for, and contracts of, employment, it has become virtually accepted that you cannot trust what people tell you – about themselves or about somebody else. The violence of the marketplace creates a climate of fear, and fear produces a culture of economy with the truth.

---

[34] Craigie, 2, p. 50.
[35] 'A favourite instrument of "violence" is false accusation and injust judgment' (Haag, quoted by Waltke, p. 740). See Pss. 25:19; 27:12; 55:10; 58:3.

Against such a backcloth, in Jerusalem then or any modern city, the following comment makes complete sense: 'To us injustice is injurious to the welfare of the people; to the prophets it is a deathblow to existence; to us an episode, to them a catastrophe, a threat to the world.'[36]

'A threat to the world' is the gist of Micah's next sentence as he listens to the voice of the LORD:

> *'Therefore I have begun to smite you,*
>   *making you desolate because of your sins'* (13).

There is a chilling impact in that initial phrase, *I have begun*. The punishment will be long drawn-out and progressive. It is also something that God has already begun. He has finished warning and waiting. There is no going back, no possibility of cancellation. And the end result will be the desolation of the city. It will be 'ploughed as a field . . . . . . a heap of ruins . . . a wooded height' (3:12).[37]

This must happen *because of your sins* (13). The next two verses (14–15) make it plain that God's acts of judgment are entirely consistent with his word to his people in the time of Moses. The language of these two verses is taken from the curses in Deuteronomy 28, which give a comprehensive account of what happens to a city and a nation which, having heard the voice of the LORD, deliberately and persistently choose to disobey.

The five disasters mentioned here are those directly or indirectly connected with the commercial life of the marketplace, but God's overall judgment extends further than that. 'Cursed shall you be in the city, and cursed shall you be in the field. Cursed shall be your basket and your kneading-trough. Cursed shall be the fruit of your body, and the fruit of your ground, the increase of your cattle, and the young of your flock. Cursed shall you be when you come in, and cursed shall you be when you go out' (Dt. 28:16–19).[38]

There is actually no watertight division between 'the city' and 'the field', or between work and family, or work and leisure. All life is of a piece and interconnected. What affects our home life affects life in the workplace. That is plain from the whole panorama of blessings and curses in Deuteronomy. The evidence is all around us today as well. Those who try to keep their family life and their working life separate, rather than in balance and in proportion, are attempting not just the unrealistic but the impossible.

---

[36] A. J. Heschel, quoted by Waltke (TOTC), p. 198.

[37] *Cf.* Is. 24:10–12; 27:10; 32:13–14.

[38] It is worth reading the whole of Deuteronomy 28 before absorbing what Micah says here.

What will be the signs of God's judgment on the city? First, their appetites will be unsatisfied ('*You shall eat, but not be satisfied*', 14). This is more than simple physical hunger, because there will not necessarily be any shortage of food – not for some time, anyway. But their food will not satisfy them. *There shall be hunger in your inward parts* (14); they will lose their appetite for it, even though they may have the fruits of the whole world on their table. It will begin to pall in their mouths. As another prophet put it: 'you eat, but you never have enough; you drink, but you never have your fill' (Hg. 1:6).

It is important to note the corporate nature of the city's suffering under the judgment of God. These miseries are not seen as a personal visitation on particular individuals. There will be a general malaise, an air of discontent and of wanting more. This desire to get more food, not merely for sustenance but to find satisfaction, will be all-demanding and will never be fulfilled. Systemic sin, as prevailed in the city of Jerusalem then, brings societal suffering as part of God's judgment. It is hard not to ask leading questions along similar lines about the modern curses of anorexia and bulimia.

> '*You shall put away, but not save,*
> *and what you save I shall give to the sword*' (14).

Their savings will be eroded and eventually be swallowed up by the military machine of invading armies (*the sword*). It is human nature, and not a little wisdom, to 'put a little bit away for a rainy day'. Such insurance has at times been wrongly castigated as the opposite of trust in God, which it can become but need not be. But it is biblically sound to use years of plenty as investment for the future, which inevitably contains times of frugality, if not famine.[39] The principle is to use times of prosperity, not to live in luxury and extravagance,[40] but to provide for the needs of the less fortunate[41] and to lay aside sufficient to look after one's family when their needs are urgent.[42] That could be when a regular income has ended, when there is illness or lack of work, or when elderly relatives need special care.

We can see the judgment of God in operation when such use of material resources is linked to illegitimate business activity (such as insider dealing), exorbitant rewards for minimal risk or effort, or unethical investment in profiteering enterprises which exploit the

---

[39] See God's way of using a dream about years of plenty and famine to secure Joseph's position with Pharaoh, and the ultimate future of his family (Gn. 41:1 – 47:28). Joseph's business acumen, inspired by the Lord, led him to conclude that God had intended all his earlier sufferings to be for good. And so he promised his eleven brothers, 'I will provide for you and your little ones' (Gn. 50:20–21).
[40] Ja. 5:5.   [41] Is 58:6–7; 2 Cor. 8:12–15.   [42] 1 Tim. 5:8.

poor or wreck the environment – God's poor and God's creation. When God's judgment begins to bite, individuals suffer, often intensely. But systems and structures also begin to creak, crack and eventually collapse. Contemporary concern about the security of the ordinary (as distinct from the wealthy) person's pension is, on this principle, well founded.

> 'You shall sow, but not reap;
>   you shall tread olives, but not anoint yourselves with oil;
>   you shall tread grapes, but not drink wine' (15).

Although this refers directly to the produce of 'the field', these three basic commodities – grain,[43] oil and wine – and their innumerable derivatives would have been the heart of the Jerusalem marketplace. With the help of the fraudulent trading condemned earlier (10–11), people were making huge profits in this sector – as they do in today's international markets, with the added potential provided by modern technology and high-risk stakes in the futures and options market.

The market in commodities and their derivatives rises and falls with supply and demand. What Micah predicts here is not necessarily the failure of grain, oil and wine, but the absence of any benefits for the traders of the city: You shall ... not reap ... you shall ... not anoint yourselves with oil ... you shall ... not drink wine. They will put in all the effort and spend much time and many resources in production, but there will be nothing to show for it. Their hard work will prove useless. Worse than that, the benefits will be reaped by others; the profits will go to boost the revenues of competitors. This was exactly what had been predicted long ago: 'A nation which you have not known shall eat up the fruit of your ground and of all your labours; and you shall be only oppressed and crushed continually; so that you shall be driven mad by the sight which your eyes see' (Dt. 28:33–34). There are few things more intolerable for city traders than that.

The scenario would have been particularly appalling for the wealthy people of the city, because most of life's essential goods, and a few of its luxuries, come from grain, oil and wine. They are also the staple sources of many of the necessities in the religious life in the temple. Grain, for example, produced bread and cakes. The olive tree was regarded as 'the king of the trees by both gods and humans',[44] because it was used for cooking, cosmetics, fuel, medicine and anointing. The fruit of the vine was highly prized, and

---

[43] In Is. 28:25 five crops are named as commonly sown in the land in those times: dill, cummin, wheat, barley and spelt. The most important product was, of course, daily bread.
[44] Waltke, p. 742.

was not just a special boon on special occasions, but part of everyday life. Remembering that daily life in those days was relatively unsophisticated, we can see that a curse on grain, oil and wine (which were regarded as God's gifts in the first place)[45] would depress the markets and destroy the economy – irretrievably, if the LORD chose to perpetuate the curse.[46]

Micah keeps the LORD's fundamental charge against the city to the last:

> *. . . you have kept the statutes of Omri,*
> *and all the works of the house of Ahab;*
> *and you have walked in their counsels* (16).

The leading personalities of the city have adopted a lifestyle characterized by ruthless brutality in pursuit of profit. They have created a climate of fear which has encouraged ordinary people to operate without integrity and contrary to truth. But the bottom line, as far as God is concerned, is not business ethics, but spiritual priorities. Their corporate behaviour demonstrates that they have chosen to worship other gods, as deliberately and culpably as Omri and Ahab, the former kings of Israel in Samaria, who had provoked the LORD to such anger and brought about the uncompromisingly prophetic stance of Elijah and Elisha about 150 years earlier.[47]

The city fathers in Jerusalem would have been shaken rigid to be compared to the generation of Omri and Ahab. Not only were they part of that other place, Samaria, and those other people in the north; they were the epitome of unauthorized and ungodly leadership. 'Omri did what was evil in the sight of the LORD, and did more evil than all who were before him' (1 Ki. 16:25). When Omri died, Ahab, his son, 'did evil in the sight of the LORD more than all that were before him. And as if it had been a light thing for him to walk in the sins of Jeroboam, the son of Nebat, he took for wife Jezebel, the daughter of Ethbaal, king of the Sidonians, and went and served Baal, and worshipped him. He erected an altar for Baal in the house of Baal which he built in Samaria. And Ahab made an Asherah. Ahab did more to provoke the LORD, the God of Israel, to anger than all the kings of Israel who were before him' (1 Ki. 16:30–33).

Jerusalem, says the LORD through Micah, has chosen the *statutes*, the *works* and the *counsels* of Omri and Ahab. Omri was the founder and builder of Samaria, but his spiritual mentor was Jeroboam, who had defiantly set up two golden calves, one at Bethel, the other at

---

[45] See Ho. 2:8.

[46] In Rev. 18, there is an apocalyptic vision of what will happen when 'mighty Babylon' is destroyed, to the utter consternation of 'the merchants of the earth'.

[47] See 1 Ki. 16:21ff.

Dan, and told the people: 'You have gone up to Jerusalem long enough. Behold your gods, O Israel, who brought you up out of the land of Egypt' (1 Ki. 12:28). There was nothing subtle about Jeroboam's *statutes*, which Omri and Ahab reinforced: 'Don't worship the LORD; worship the golden calf.'[48] It was impossible to get more theologically and evocatively idolatrous than that. *The statutes of Omri* enshrined rank rejection of the LORD and blatant worship of Mammon.

The works of the house of Ahab were, quite simply, appalling. The moving spirit behind his actions was Jezebel, an out-and-out Baal-worshipper. She egged her husband on to more and more Baalist practices, explicitly linking fertility in the womb and in the fields with sexual promiscuity of all kinds, under the pretext of worshipping the Baals and the Asherim. This was 'natural religion' in its most debased and demonic form, and it was perpetuated in the northern kingdom for several generations.[49] The business, legal and political leaders of Jerusalem had now taken up these abominations – with not a little tacit connivance, if not actual involvement, from the religious leadership.

Instead of walking in God's laws, they actually *walked in the counsels* (16; NIV 'traditions') of Omri and Ahab. They took their priorities and their principles, not from the book of the law of the LORD, but from the prophets and priests of Baal. The content and the quality of *their* counsels can be gauged from their performance in a national crisis during the contest with Elijah on Mount Carmel. There had been a crippling drought in the land for three years, and their only course was to 'rave on' uselessly.[50] They were talking to themselves and any counsel they might offer came from themselves – a state of affairs into which Israel had often been seduced: '. . . this command I gave them, "Obey my voice, and I will be your God, and you shall be my people; and walk in all the way that I command you . . ." But they did not obey or incline their ear, but walked in their own counsels and in the stubbornness of their evil hearts, and went backward and not forward' (Je. 7:23–25).

So the nub of the LORD's accusation against the city was one of idolatry, a covetousness that was self-serving in its devices, brutal in its execution, demoralizing in its impact, self-reliant in its counsel. The leadership of a city does not need to set up statues of Baal and Asherah or to worship at their shrines. No mention is made of statues, but of *statutes*; none of worship but of *works*; none of cults but of *counsels*. For these things, which characterize modern city life as much as Micah's city life, the LORD guarantees judgment: '*that I*

---

[48] See Ex. 32:1–29.
[49] At least until the time of Athaliah, Omri's great-great-grandson; 2 Ch. 22:2–7
[50] 1 Ki. 18:17–46, esp. verse 29.

may make you a desolation' (cf. 13), *'and your inhabitants a hissing'* (16). They were meant to be a light to the nations; but now they would bear *the scorn of the peoples* (16).

To be hissed at is indescribably shameful, the ultimate rejection. Jerusalem's citizens would find themselves in that appalling situation. It was predicted by the prophets for Edom,[51] Babylon[52] and Tyre[53] – symbols of civic pride and commercial prosperity – but for Jerusalem it was almost unthinkable. Only when it actually happened did Jeremiah put the horror into words:

> All who pass along the way
>   clap their hands at you;
> they hiss and wag their heads
>   at the daughter of Jerusalem:
> 'Is this the city which was called
>   the perfection of beauty,
>   the joy of all the earth?'
> All your enemies
>   rail against you;
> they hiss, they gnash their teeth,
>   they cry: 'We have destroyed her!
> Ah, this is the day we longed for;
>   now we have it; we see it' (La. 2:15–16).

God's judgment on the city, *his* city, has been declared. This is the city of peace. This is the city for which every member of every tribe was under solemn obligation regularly to pray: 'Pray for the peace of Jerusalem! . . . Peace be within your walls, and security within your towers!' (Ps. 122:6–7). Peace and security had been sought in other directions and from other gods, especially in material prosperity for its own sake. But peace is to be found only in the Prince of peace, whatever the name of the city.

4. The prophet's summary of the situation (7:1–7)

Having been the mouthpiece for 'the voice of the LORD' (6:9) to the city, Micah now takes another walk through its streets (either literally or in his imagination). He seems to be absorbing both the appalling scale of the wickedness and the implications of the doom he has just declared. He is overwhelmed: *Woe is me!* (1). He had pronounced woe on those in the city who devised 'wickednes . . . upon their beds' (2:1). But now he feels the woe deep within his inner being. In the authentic tradition of Israel's prophets, the

[51] Je. 49:17.   [52] Je. 50:13.   [53] Ezk. 27:36.

impact of God's holy judgment on sin – his own, or particularly that of his contemporaries – sears Micah through and through.[54]

He likens himself to a poor person going into the vineyards to gather a little sustenance, an odd fig and a bunch of grapes, from what would normally have been left after *the vintage has been gleaned* (1). Such provision for the poor was made explicit in the law.[55] Farmers were not allowed to go back a second time to gather what they might have missed. As Micah paces the streets and looks for something good to sustain his spirit, almost hoping to persuade himself that the LORD might have missed something worth applauding, he has to conclude that *The godly man has perished from the earth, and there is none upright among men* (2). Wickedness has become endemic and the whole fabric of city life has become unravelled.

Micah's painful conclusion, that *there is none upright among men*, is a significant blend of personal despair and theological accuracy. In the streets and homes of the city there were those who had remained faithful to the LORD, people who resisted the 'statutes of Omri' and the 'counsels of the house of Ahab' (6:16). Not everyone was irretrievably wicked. But, in two important senses, Micah's conclusion was right: first, everyone had been infiltrated and influenced by the pervasive corruption at the heart of city life; and secondly, as far as God was concerned, everyone was guilty by the standards of his holiness and fell short of his glory.[56]

The heart of the problem is still one of leadership: *the prince ... the judge ... the great man ... The best of them* (3–4) – the great and the good of the land. Those who ought to have set an example for good, and to have pursued it *diligently* (3), have set their hands *upon what is evil* (3) and thrown all their energies into that. Due diligence was applied to their brutal business deals: *Each hunts his brother with a net* (2). They have used their contacts to *weave ... together* (3) a patchwork of conspiracy against ordinary people, unashamedly ready to *ask for a bribe* (3), before using their clout to provide what people needed. It was the kind of culture, sadly still prevalent in many parts of the world today, where nothing happened without greasing the palm of some petty official or *great man* (3) – which has to be a sarcastic comment.

Any shame about being responsible for such a climate of bribery and corruption had disappeared. *The great man* was brazenly ready to declare aloud *the evil desire of his soul* (3). The overall result was that, between them, the leaders of the city's whole life had it sewn up to their own advantage: *thus they weave it together* (3). Micah had

---

[54] Is. 6:5; Je. 15:10.   [55] Lv. 19:9–10.
[56] Rom. 3:9–26 (esp. verse 23). *Cf.* Ps. 14:1–3; Is. 59:1–15.

gone looking for something to sustain and refresh him (a fig or a few grapes). What he found was that *The best of them is like a brier, the most upright of them a thorn hedge* (4): try to get past them and you get lacerated; cross them and you know all about it. Micah knew what it meant to fall foul of the law. Like many disadvantaged minorities today, he experienced the entire legal and law-enforcement system as hostile, prejudiced and the very opposite of God's intention, which was to reward the good and punish the evil.[57]

Given such a situation in the city, what can be said and done? Micah makes three points: God's judgment is at hand (4); everyone must watch their backs (5–6); he is going to look to the LORD (7).

First, judgment is at hand: the same message as before, but expressed succinctly:

> *The day of their* [or 'your'] *watchmen, of their* [or 'your']
> *punishment has come;*
> *now their confusion is at hand* (4).

All three are new words for Micah, which suggests that walking around the city, in the wake of the LORD's pronouncements (6:9–16), has brought home to him the full reality of the situation in a new way.

Every city appointed sentinels to keep watch on the city walls, so that they could warn the city authorities about imminent threats from invaders. Historically, the LORD's prophets were appointed by him to be the spiritual watchmen of the nation.[58] They looked in two directions – outwards to warn of approaching attack, inwards to warn of internal vulnerability through self-absorption, self-confidence or sheer negligence. Along with other prophets, Micah had been blowing the trumpet to warn Jerusalem for many years. Now *the day of your watchmen* has come: what the watchmen had been saying would happen is about to happen. Because their responsibilities were a matter of life and death, watchmen were liable to the death penalty if they failed to blow the trumpet and disaster then fell.[59]

Punishment has a connotation well expressed in the old word 'visitation', because it speaks of God coming to visit his people in order to make a full audit of their behaviour, and then to call them to account and impose appropriate sanctions and penalties. The day of God's visitation on the city has come.[60] It is no longer a diary date,

---

[57] See Rom. 13:1–7; 1 Pet. 2:13–14.
[58] See Is. 52:7–10; 56:10; Ezk. 3:17–21; 33:1–9; Hab. 2:1 (and exposition of this passage, below).
[59] Ezk. 33:6.
[60] Lk. 19:44; 1 Pet. 2:12. The Greek word is *episkopē*, the word for episcopal responsibility or oversight.

but an actual event. God's visits are not necessarily for the purpose of punishment. Indeed, his preference is to visit for the purpose of salvation.[61] But for Micah's city and generation, it was curtains.

This visitation from God will be a day of *confusion* (4) for the leaders of the city. The people so accustomed to having it all together and being in control will be in complete confusion, as the sovereign Lord calls them to account and opens the books. They will be speechless and reduced to complete panic. Used to giving orders and manipulating people for their own sinister purposes, they will find themselves face to face with one with complete authority, who can never be manipulated and who refuses to be used.

Micah's second point, in the light of the crisis of leadership, is that everybody in the city must watch their backs in such a violent and corrupt environment:

> *Put no trust in a neighbour,*
>   *have no confidence in a friend;*
> *guard the doors of your mouth*
>   *from her who lies in your bosom;*
> *for the son treats the father with contempt,*
>   *the daughter rises up against her mother,*
>   *the daughter-in-law against her mother-in-law;*
>   *a man's enemies are the men of his own house* (5–6).

There is an increasing scale in the intensity of the precautions advocated by Micah: neighbours, friends, family. You expect neighbours occasionally to stab you in the back. You are prepared for the odd friendship to turn sour and produce real problems. If your own kith and kin turn the knife, it is difficult to know where to turn. Whom can you trust?

It is a sick society where such basic trust and confidence have been completely eroded. It may be a boon for the legal profession, and today's climate is increasingly litigious as a result; but it is not hard to identify with Micah's hard-headed pragmatism. Because we feel we cannot trust friends and neighbours, we keep ourselves to ourselves and take endless security measures against violence and fraud. Anyone involved in family affairs, for example in settling estates of deceased relatives, may sadly become aware of the way that *a man's enemies are the men of his own house.*[62]

Micah's three examples of family friction and faction have an uncanny relevance to the contemporary disintegration of family life

---

[61] See Lk. 1:68; Acts 15:14.

[62] Jesus uses this phrase to describe the upheaval in extended families caused by an individual who responds to his call to wholehearted discipleship (Mt. 10:21, 35–36 and parallels).

and, as a result, of society in general. Society today is full of examples of sons holding fathers in contempt and daughters in fierce conflict with their mothers. Problems with in-laws are proverbial, and often exaggerated for cheap comic effect; but nobody would deny the reality of daughters-in-law rising up in fury at the way mothers-in-law have conditioned their husbands, whether to encourage chauvinism by cosseting and smothering in earlier years, or by constant interference and nagging criticism long after they are married. Breakdown in marriage is regularly traced to this kind of conflict. There is no trust or confidence in such situations, and, when occurrences are multiplied throughout a city and nation, the general situation deteriorates to a frightening degree.

Because our modern societies so accurately mirror Micah's description of contemporary Jerusalem, it is particularly striking to note the diagnosis which he provides – throughout the book, but especially in this passage. Political comment on social disintegration today often revolves around the need to focus, not so much on crimes and criminals, but on the causes of crime. Micah would direct us all back to the way we have steadily ignored, and often directly flouted, the requirements of God for our personal, social and working lives, as well as for our nation. This defiant rejection of God's revealed truth is the fundamental reason for the social disintegration we see around us.

After pinpointing the imminence of God's judgment and urging inhabitants of the city to be on the alert against personal attack, Micah makes his own stance plain:

> *But as for me, I will look to the LORD;*
> *I will wait for the God of my salvation;*
> *my God will hear me* (7).

These statements look both backwards and forwards. They express Micah's response to the bleakness around him, and his resolve for the future awaiting him (7:8–20).

One of the striking features of the book is the prophet's pre-occupation, not with himself and his calling, but with God and his people. There are only three other occasions when Micah self-consciously refers to himself: when he laments and wails for the incurable sickness of his people (1:8); when he expresses the heartbeat of his ministry over against the ministry of the false prophets (3:8); and when he cries *Woe is me!* as he realizes the finality of God's judgment on the city (7:1). Here he again stresses his own bottom line, which is the antithesis of the position taken up by the leadership of the city.

They trusted in their own resources and devices; he trusted in

God. There were three key elements in this trust. First, *I will look to the LORD*. This was his regular practice (the verb can be translated 'I keep looking'), not something he brought into play in emergencies. It was the tenor of his entire life.[63] Secondly, *I will wait for the God of my salvation* (7). As for the leaders, the only time they were prepared to wait was to catch and control other people in their brutal schemes. Otherwise, their watchword was *hate*, not *wait* – 'hate the good' (3:2). Micah knew his need (and the people's need, including the leaders) of a Saviour. He was prepared to wait for God, who had demonstrated his 'saving acts' (6:5) over centuries, to act again on his behalf.[64] The prophet candidly looks forward to his personal vindication (*my salvation*), but he knows that it will extend way beyond himself. Thirdly, Micah knew that *my God will hear me*, whereas 'he will not answer' (3:4) the guilty leaders of the city when they cry out to him.

With such quiet confidence in place, Micah knows that he can face whatever the future may bring. Like many people today, the pressurized leaders of the city probably cried out 'My God!' in surprise, but never with any meaning attached to the words. For Micah, *my God* meant everything. It summarized his life and his work. It was the most eloquent expression he could apply to the realities of the city in which he was operating.

---

[63] The word translated 'look to' is from the same root as 'watchmen' (7:4). Micah's whole life was spent watching and looking in this sense.

[64] Waiting is 'the most powerful form of action by the helpless' (Waltke, TOTC, p. 202). *Cf.* Pss. 38:15; 42:5, 11; 43:5; 130:5.

Micah 7:8–20
6. A message of light and love

1. The LORD is light in the darkness (7:8–10)

Once Micah again focuses his attention on the LORD, 'my God', everything begins to get into another perspective. Most of all, he begins to see aspects of God's character and activity which he has been in danger of forgetting amid all the personal trauma caused by the wickedness around him. He becomes buoyant and upbeat:

> *Rejoice not over me, O my enemy;*
> *when I fall, I shall rise;*
> *when I sit in darkness,*
> *the LORD will be a light to me* (8).

The word *enemy* is feminine in the Hebrew, indicating that Micah might be identifying with the city of Jerusalem ('the daughter of Zion') and seeing Nineveh, the Assyrian capital, as the *enemy*. This is further underlined by the triple reference to the enemy as *her … her … she …* (10). The enemy is not actually named. Whoever or whatever the enemy, whether it is Micah's personal enemy or the nation's, the message is: *Rejoice not over me, O my enemy*.

The most piercing wound the enemy of God's people or of God's representative can cause is the gloating mockery enshrined in the defiant challenge: '*Where is the LORD your God?*' (10).[1] There is nothing an enemy enjoys more than rubbing our noses in the dust and ashes of unanswered prayer and the apparent absence, lack of interest, or even death of God. This proved to be the mocking tone of Sennacherib's commander-in-chief, the Rabshakeh, when he had Jerusalem apparently at his mercy. He tried to persuade the people of Judah not to listen to any pious talk along the lines of 'The LORD

---

[1] See Pss. 42:3, 10; 70:10; 115:2; Joel 2:17 (and exposition, above). *Cf.* Jesus on the cross (Mt. 27:43).

will deliver us'. Similar appeals to the gods of other cities, such as Samaria, had not saved them from the Assyrians; why should Jerusalem's God be any different? 'Where are the gods of Hamath and Arpad? Where are the gods of Sepharvaim?' (Is. 36:19).[2] And now, *Where is the* LORD *your God?*

Wherever the opposition comes from, its ultimate source is 'your adversary the devil'.[3] To him we say, with Micah: *when I fall, I shall rise; when I sit in darkness, the* LORD *will be a light to me* (8). Micah is not presumptuous enough to say that he will not fall. He knows that he can and will. But the LORD will pick him up. Neither is he naïve or triumphalist, to the point of thinking that life with the LORD will be all sweetness and light. There will be darkness, and the darkness will not be a passing cloud. He will find himself sitting in darkness and in the shadow of death.[4] But there the LORD himself will be a light to him. He will not need human sources of light, however pleasant and positive they might be. The LORD will be enough.

The darkness Micah particularly has in mind is what he calls *the indignation of the* LORD (9). When God finally acts 'in anger and wrath' (5:15), it gets very dark indeed. This darkness will last an inordinate length of time. But *He will bring me forth to the light; I shall behold his deliverance* (9). Micah asserts that he and his people will endure whatever it takes to exhaust the LORD's anger and reach the point where he chooses to execute *judgment* for him (9), instead of against him, and where 'the accuser'[5] is silenced and God *pleads* his *cause*.

The darkness, even this darkness, can be borne provided that people face up to their sin: *I have sinned against him* (9). As long as we either excuse ourselves for our sins or blame God for their consequences, we will have no light in our darkness. Micah is under no illusion about sin's consequences, because he understands that sin is against God. He also knows that God, not sin, has the last word, as the last three verses of the book gloriously affirm. He, therefore, fully expects the gloating of the enemy to be turned back on their heads:

> *Then my enemy will see,*
> *and shame will cover her . . .*
> *My eyes will gloat over her* (10).

She may tread down the people of Jerusalem in the not-so-distant future. But then, when God's deliverance has been achieved, *she will be trodden down like the mire of the streets.*

---

[2] See the whole section Is. 36:1 – 37:28.   [3] 1 Pet. 5:8.   [4] Lk. 1:79.
[5] Rev. 12:10.

Micah's crucial function at this point is to articulate his own quiet confidence in the LORD on behalf of his people and in spite of his people's sad condition. As the prophet discovers the LORD to be light in the darkness, hope is kindled for the people.

2. The LORD is shepherd to his people (7:11-14)

As in the previous passages of hope at the conclusion of the book's first two cycles (2:12-13; 5:4), Micah's imagery returns to the people as a flock to be shepherded. So here he directly prays to the LORD: *Shepherd thy people with thy staff, the flock of thy inheritance* (14). As we have seen in looking at 5:4, this language is directly reminiscent of David's reign in Jerusalem, Israel's great shepherd king. Once again, therefore, Micah's vision of the future becomes messianic. This is seen also in the repeated phrase *In that day* (11; cf. 4:6, 5:10), which will be *A day for the building of your walls* – not just rebuilding what will have been destroyed, but *In that day the boundary shall be extended.*

In that day, the LORD will be shepherd over a people greatly increased in number:

In that day they will come to you,
    from Assyria to Egypt,
    and from Egypt to the River,
from sea to sea and from mountain to mountain (12).

This expansion could have a double reference: to Israel's returning exiles, and to the gathering-in of the Gentiles under the rule of the new shepherd king. For them all, 'Zion's walls will be expanded to embrace all the elect from the ends of the earth'.[6]

As the LORD gathers all his redeemed people into the fold, his judgment will fall on those who have rejected his rule. This judgment will be worldwide, and *the earth will be desolate because of its inhabitants, for the fruit of their doings* (13). This desolation, which is parallel to the imminent desolation of Judah and Jerusalem (6:13, 16) at the hand of invaders, will be in stark contrast with the prosperity and fertility of the new Jerusalem, whose citizens will 'dwell apart' (NIV) *in a forest in the midst of a garden land* (14). While the rest of the earth is laid waste, the land of the renewed Israel will be teeming with good things – like *Bashan and Gilead as in the days of old.*

Every phrase in verse 14 'reinforces the idea of security and well-being'.[7] Bashan and Gilead were 'proverbial beauty spots in the Holy Land',[8] with lush grazing pasture and farming land. Bashan

[6] Waltke, p. 756.   [7] *Ibid.*, p. 759.   [8] Kaiser, p. 89.

was noticeable for splendid trees and fat cows.[9] Gilead was the first part of the land to be possessed by the people of Israel and was known to be good pasture land. The reference to a *garden* could be to Carmel (the actual word in the Hebrew). This will be the place where God's people will dwell 'apart'. *Dwell*, in a context such as this passage, has the connotation of permanence, while 'apart' (RSV *alone*) speaks of separation from any alien influences or hostile forces.[10]

If we link the references to Carmel, Bashan and Gilead (14) with the vision of Jerusalem extending its boundaries (11), we have a thrilling scenario. The whole of this territory will be contained within the rebuilt walls of the new Jerusalem – geographically impossible but theologically powerful. This also corresponds to the perfection, beauty and fruitfulness of the holy city which John saw 'coming down from God out of heaven' at the end of the book of Revelation.[11] Micah's phrase *as in the days of old* indicates the continuity of God's people and God's city under the old covenant with this vision for God's people and God's city under the shepherd-king Messiah.

Such an expanded and secure flock will certainly evince strong and wise shepherding. It would have no chance of survival without the leadership of the good and great 'shepherd of the sheep' (Heb. 13:20). Indeed, no such splendid event would even look like occurring unless the LORD himself shepherded the sheep from the four corners of the earth into the sheepfold of the new Jerusalem. As Jesus himself said: 'I have other sheep, that are not of this fold; I must bring them also, and they will heed my voice. So there shall be one flock, one shepherd' (Jn. 10:16). The sheep, we notice, belong to the LORD: *the flock of thy inheritance* (14). They are his by right of creation and by right of redemption.

The LORD's shepherding of his people is done with his *staff* (14), a symbol of rulership and leadership. When Jacob blessed each of his sons before he died, he prophesied over Judah:

The sceptre shall not depart from Judah,
    nor the ruler's staff from between his feet,
until he comes to whom it belongs;
    and to him shall be the obedience of the people (Gn. 49:10)[12]

---

[9] See Dt. 32:14, and Amos's reference to Israel's wealthy and self-indulgent women as 'cows of Bashan' (Am. 4:1).
[10] See Je. 50:19–20 for a similar series of promises, which is explicitly linked to 'the remnant'.
[11] See Rev. 21:10 – 22:5.
[12] Jacob's actions on his deathbed are held up as examples of faith in Heb. 11:21.

– a remarkable prophecy, partially fulfilled in David, but only properly fulfilled in Jesus. With his staff and his rod, both alike emblems of executive authority, the LORD comforted his people,[13] and Micah prays that he will continue to do so.

3. The LORD is God over the nations (7:15–17)

Like verse 7, verse 15 looks both backwards and forwards. *As in the days* picks up 'as in the days of old' (14), and *I will show them marvellous things* looks forward to what the LORD will be doing among the nations and with his people (16–20). Micah has already spoken of people coming from many nations to become part of the people of God in the new Jerusalem (11–12). He has spoken also of God's judgment on the earth as a result of the behaviour of the rest of its inhabitants. This whole process underlines God's sovereignty over the nations and is further evidence of his supreme power, as demonstrated in *the land of Egypt*.

In saying to Micah's generation, *you came out of the land of Egypt* (15), the LORD indicated that even their persistent sinning and his coming judgment did not disinherit them from being his people and, as such, from being in line for *marvellous things* (or 'wonders') to come. The exodus, throughout the history of God's people, was more than a wonderful deliverance at a crucial stage of their history. It was re-enacted in their liturgical worship.[14] It was passed on from one generation to the next.[15] It was recited in the course of the Ten Commandments.[16] It was frequently on the lips of the prophets.[17] It was a constant source of encouragement to faith and hope in times of despair and darkness, as well as a challenge to repentance in times of disobedience.

But even more than all these things, 'because God is unchanging and his attributes timeless, his people could expect his acts to be repeated again and again in history... The Exodus would occur again, but in a new and greater way'.[18] In particular, it would be repeated in the way the nations of the world, like the Egyptians and surrounding nations at the exodus, would come to acknowledge the LORD as God of the whole earth: *The nations shall see and be ashamed of all their might* (16). God will act dramatically to redeem his people from bondage – a different bondage from the one in Egypt, but a dense and dire bondage – and the watching world will be amazed into silence.[19] Such an act of redemption will render all normal expressions of

---

[13] *Cf.* Ps. 23:4. [14] Dt. 16:3; Ps. 105:23. [15] 1 Ki. 8:9. [16] Dt. 5:6, 15.
[17] Je. 7:25; Ho. 2:15. [18] McComiskey, p. 444.
[19] *Cf.* the predicted impact of the suffering servant of the LORD (Is. 52:13–15).

human power impotent. The folly of trusting in human power will be exposed.

Shorn of their strength and forced to face up to their inability to be effective in the things which really matter, the nations will shut their mouths and close their ears. They will have nothing to say and they will not want to know – either when God speaks or when anyone else makes a comment. Instead,

> *they shall lick the dust like a serpent,*
> *like the crawling things of the earth;*
> *they shall come trembling out of their strongholds* (17).

This humiliation of the nations and vindication of God and his people, prophesied in Isaiah[20] and expressed at the exodus,[21] will be fully demonstrated when God finally establishes his Christ as King of kings and Lord of lords, as acclaimed in the 'song of Moses and the song of the Lamb' in the book of Revelation:

> Great and wonderful are thy deeds,
> O Lord God the Almighty!
> Just and true are thy ways,
> O King of the ages!
> Who shall not fear and glorify thy name, O Lord?
> For thou alone art holy.
> All nations shall come and worship thee,
> for thy judgments have been revealed (Rev. 15:3–4).

Micah also emphasizes this healthy fear of God which will characterize the attitude and the worship of the nations, when they ultimately come out of their strongholds to acknowledge the LORD as God of the whole earth:

> *they shall turn in dread to the LORD our God,*
> *and they shall fear because of thee* (17).

The fear begins when people are forced out of their *strongholds*, the places of security where for centuries human beings have barricaded themselves against God. On the lips of prophet after prophet, the word of the LORD promised to lay low such strongholds,[22] both in the nations and among his own people.[23] They represented human pride at its most defiant, human security at its most determined.

---

[20] Is. 45:14–25.   [21] Ex. 15:1–18 (the song of Moses).
[22] *E.g.* Is. 23:11; Je. 48:41; Ezk. 33:27; and eleven times in Amos.
[23] Mi. 5:11.

Before the LORD both physical and spiritual strongholds must fall.[24]
When any such strongholds fall, as fall they must, people become
afraid. When it is the result of God's activity, vindicating his own,
they shall turn in dread to the LORD our God, afraid not because of
the LORD's people, but because of the LORD (*because of thee*).

> Who would not fear thee, O King of the nations?
> For this is thy due (Je. 10:7).

4. The LORD is the one and only saviour (7:18-20)

If the LORD is light in the darkness (8–10), shepherd to his people
(11–14) and God over the nations (15–17), it is not surprising to find
Micah exclaiming, *Who is a God like thee?* (18). What is surprising
is that these are not the characteristics of the LORD in which he
proceeds to exult. What marks the LORD out from all other gods is
his *steadfast love* (*ḥesed*, 18, 20), a love located in the will which
stresses mainly unchanging commitment; and also his *compassion*
(19), a love that is mainly emotional.

The qualities the LORD requires of humanity in walking humbly
with him, as we have seen (6:8), are justice and *ḥesed* (mercy, kindness, steadfast love). Having thoroughly dealt with the realities of
God's justice, Micah draws to this glorious climax by acclaiming
God's steadfast love, mercy, kindness and compassion. This supreme
quality is, of course, heightened by his justice. If God did not remain
entirely just, his compassion and mercy would be neither remarkable nor reliable. In the light of what the future will hold for Micah's
people, God's steadfast love is nothing short of astonishing. There
will be severe judgment; but there will also be full restoration.

As Micah expands on the uniqueness of the LORD's unchanging
nature, he returns to the theme with which he began and which he
has regularly addressed throughout the book – the transgressions
(wilful rebellion) and sins (specific misdemeanours) of the people
(1:5, 13; 3:8; 6:7). They are many and blatant. But such is the
steadfast love of the LORD that *He does not retain his anger for ever*
(18). *He delights in steadfast love*: to behave in a kind, merciful and
compassionate way is a sheer delight for the LORD our God. That is
why he wants everyone to 'love mercy' (6:8) – to act justly, yes, but
to love kindness, compassion and steadfast love. He wants us to
delight in it as much as he does. It is a very distinctive mark of God's
nature, *the* distinctive characteristic.

How does God express his delight in showing steadfast love to his
people? By *pardoning iniquity and passing over transgression* (18).

---

[24] *Cf.* 2 Cor. 10:3–6.

These two phrases encapsulate Micah's understanding of God's 'name' as it was revealed to Moses by the LORD in the wake of the people's appalling idolatry of the golden calf: 'The LORD, a God merciful and gracious, slow to anger, and abounding in steadfast love and faithfulness, keeping steadfast love for thousands, forgiving iniquity and transgression and sin, but who will by no means clear the guilty, visiting the iniquities of the fathers upon the children and the children's children to the third and the fourth generation' (Ex. 34:6–7).

Time and again this description of the LORD's character and covenant relationship with his people was emphasized down the centuries,[25] sometimes in an extended form, often in calling him 'gracious and merciful'.[26] In his sheer grace he pardons sinners. He pardons *iniquity* – referring to our warped human nature, which God himself lifts up and bears[27] (the literal meaning of the word translated 'pardon'). In George Herbert's words, 'Though my sins against me cried, thou didst hear me; and alone, when they replied, thou didst clear me.'[28] God acquits and absolves the guilty.

This is the one who challenged corrupt traders in the city, entrenched defiantly in their iniquitous practices: 'Shall I acquit the man with wicked scales and with a bag of deceitful weights?' (6:11). What he could not and would not do for the criminals in the city he delighted to do *for the remnant of his inheritance* (18), for those who, in the midst of his visitation (7:4), respond to his leadership.[29] Their sins he will pass over, not punish, as he passed over the houses of his *inheritance* on that fateful night in Egypt when the LORD dealt death to the firstborn among the Egyptians but spared the people of Israel.[30]

Because it is in the nature and heart of God to pardon, Micah is sure that *He will again have compassion on us* (19). God delights to do this, and so he will not be content with doing it simply two or three times for his people, nor will he eke out the time of withholding forgiveness unnecessarily. He will be looking eagerly for an opportunity to show his steadfast love. This conviction leads Micah again to meditate creatively on the events of the exodus, where the LORD overwhelmed the enemies of his people in the waters of the Red Sea and, as it were, trampled them under his feet.[31]

In similar fashion, declares Micah, *Thou wilt cast all our sins into the depths of the sea* (19). First, *he will tread our iniquities under foot* (19), trampling any remaining breath out of them. Then God will see

---

[25] *E.g.* by Moses, David, Hezekiah, Ezra, Joel and Jonah.

[26] Particularly in the Psalms, *e.g.* 111:4; 112:4; 116:5.

[27] See Is. 53:6; 'The LORD has laid on him the iniquity of us all.' *Cf.* also the references to a scapegoat in Lv. 16:1–34.

[28] In the hymn 'King of glory, King of peace'.   [29] *Cf.* 2:12; 5:7–8.

[30] Ex. 12:21–32.   [31] This is the language of Ex. 15:1–10.

to it that they are buried in *the depths of the sea*, out of reach, out of sight, and (as far as God is concerned, anyway) out of mind: 'I will remember their sin no more' (Je. 31:34). The *depths of the sea* could well be a reference to the drowning of the Egyptians (when they were pursuing the Israelites) in the depths of the Red Sea. When we today find ourselves mentally harping on sins which the LORD has forgiven and forgotten, he points out the notice at the water's edge: 'No fishing.'

> Once every year, on Rosh Hashanah, the Jewish New Year, the orthodox Jew goes to a stream or river and symbolically empties his sins from his pockets into the water as he recites Micah 7:18–20. This is the 'Tashlich' service, named after the word 'You shall cast'. It symbolises the fact that God can and will take our sins, wash them down the streams of running water and bury them deep in the depths of the ocean. God not only forgives our sins, he forgets them.[32]

Micah, then, has come as close as can be to the provisions of the new covenant in the body and blood of God's Son, Jesus Christ. Because he cannot look forward in that dimension, he ends by looking back to Jacob and Abraham. It is the tenth time he has mentioned Jacob, but the first time he has mentioned Abraham:

> *Thou wilt show faithfulness to Jacob,*
> *and steadfast love to Abraham* (20).

The LORD had been delighting in showing steadfast love for a very long time, from the beginning of Abraham's call to become the father of a special nation under God. Towards the end of Abraham's life, when God's promises to bless the whole world through his family looked like foundering, Abraham sent his servant to find a suitable wife for his son Isaac and thus perpetuate his line. When the man discovered Rebekah, he knew that God's promises would not fail. There and then, 'The man bowed his head and worshipped the LORD, and said, "Blessed be the LORD, the God of my master Abraham, who has not forsaken his steadfast love and faithfulness toward my master"' (Gn. 24:26).

Abraham's servant clearly understood the bottom line in the LORD's dealing with Abraham, even if we have no record of Abraham himself expressing any such recognition. What the servant declared then has been recognized by believing men and women ever since: the LORD is gracious and merciful.

[32] Kaiser, p. 92.

> He does not deal with us according to our sins
>> nor requite us according to our iniquities.
> For as the heavens are high above the earth,
>> so great is his steadfast love toward those who fear him;
> as far as the east is from the west,
>> so far does he remove our transgressions from us
>>> (Ps. 103:10–12).

That is the thrust of what God has *sworn to our fathers from the days of old* (20). What was good enough for Abraham, Isaac and Jacob was good enough for Micah. And, because of God's steadfast love in dealing with our sins once and for all in the atoning death of his Son Jesus Christ, it is even better for us. The LORD truly is the one and only Saviour.

Introduction to Habakkuk

Habakkuk lived at a time when society was shaken by violence. As Judah and Jerusalem had sunk deeper into disobedience towards God and his requirements, so the fabric of national life had begun to come apart at the seams. The prophet lived and spoke in the inexorable build-up to the invasion of Judah and ultimate destruction of Jerusalem by the Babylonians – in the years following the reign of Josiah when Jehoiakim succeeded as king in 609 BC.

Josiah had been a just king,[1] ruling and administering justice in the spirit of Israel's covenant law: 'He judged the cause of the poor and needy; then it was well' [Je. 22:16]. Jehoiakim inherited none of his father's qualities. He exploited his subjects for his own aggrandisement and had no concern for justice and mercy.[2] Those who held subordinate positions of power in the land – governors and judges – took their cue from him. The result was widespread oppression, injustice and violence. There was no hope of redress except in God: and God did not seem to be taking any action to vindicate his own law or indeed his own character.[3]

When Jeremiah challenged Jehoiakim about his corrupt ways, he spoke with characteristic vigour:

> You have eyes and heart
>   only for your dishonest gain,
> for shedding innocent blood,
>   and for practising oppression and violence (Je. 22:17).

Habakkuk, a contemporary of Jeremiah, directs his passion and despair at God himself, rather than at the king. In this sense he is an

---

[1] See 2 Ki. 22:1–2.   [2] 2 Ki. 23:36–37.   [3] Bruce, p. 844.

unusual, if not unique, prophet in the Old Testament. We are given profound insight into the prayer life of the prophet and, in the process, his whole relationship with God becomes public. It is a moving and challenging experience.

Habakkuk burned with zeal for God as much as, if not more than, with pain for the people. He poured out his heart to God in prayer, rather than (or before) pronouncing doom on the guilty. He was moved by the offensiveness to a holy God of people's sins, not by any personal sense of injury or rejection within himself. He was concerned equally for the people's violation of *both* tables of the law – the first three commandments covering responsibility to God, the remaining seven covering responsibility to family and neighbour.

In all these distinctive ways Habakkuk epitomizes what Voltaire, of all people, has been quoted as saying: 'Habakkuk was capable of anything.' With Habakkuk, 'larger questions quickly engulfed the local concerns',[4] which initially sparked the prophet's interaction with God. This is essentially the reason for the continuing relevance of Habakkuk's message. Beginning with his own situation, he found himself articulating timeless questions – about the problems of evil and the character of God, about the apparent pointlessness of prayer and impotence of God, about the oppressiveness of unrestrained violence and the silence of God.

The dilemmas and the traumas are timeless, but so is the overwhelming power of violence. Our own societies today, over two and a half thousand years after Habakkuk and Jeremiah, are being torn apart by violence of all kinds. The violence of war is now reproduced, in a dangerously sanitized fashion, in our own homes through television. At any one time, we are told, there are between twenty-five and thirty wars being fought around the world. We see pictures of a very few. But it is not so much the prevalence of war, in whatever format it touches us, that has turned our societies into theatres of violence. Violence seems to have taken hold of so many aspects of our lives – on our streets and in our schools, making it dangerous to walk alone in both city and country, and placing teachers in physical danger if they exercise a discipline which children will not countenance. Violence in the home has become widespread – by husbands to wives, by parents to children. In particular, we hear increasingly frequent accounts of women being battered by their partners, of children being abused by adults. To all this must be added psychological and verbal violence, which may stop short of beating people up, but is only one step away from it. There is road rage, mob violence, drunken mayhem, gang warfare,

---

[4] Armerding, p. 494.

drug-induced assault. In the words of Salman Rushdie, 'The barbarians were not only at our gates but within our skins.'[5]

There is violence, also, in the womb. What was institutionalized as acceptable legal and medical practice in the 1960s has now manifestly spawned a sinister callousness about the sanctity of human life. *The Times* of 16 August 1996 carried side by side a news item and an advertisement which (one assumes inadvertently) epitomize the state we have reached. In the news item the story emerged that a career woman in her late twenties, married to a company director and already living comfortably, obtained the professional acquiescence of two senior obstetricians in London to have one of twins she was carrying aborted – because her 'psychological well-being' was deemed to be at risk. She felt able to look after only one child. The adjacent advertisement was placed by the World Wide Fund for Nature, asking the public to subscribe as 'godparents' for a baby rhinoceros called Mbolifue, born in Zaire. The advertisement runs, 'Before Mbolifue's arrival, there were just 29 northern white rhinos alive in Garamba National Park: the last surviving population in the wild. You can imagine the excitement when a tiny baby calf was spotted from the air, moving slowly through the grass with her mother. In March this year, a pregnant female was shot and brutally butchered by poachers. The birth of Mbolifue goes some way towards compensating for that tragedy . . .' Readers could join the WWF adoption scheme 'for just £2 a month'. The baby rhino's name means 'Gift from Heaven'.

Violence against unborn babies; violence against women and children; violence by the strong against the weak, by the many against the few, by those in authority against those unable to resist or get redress; violence which goes unchecked and unpunished. We, like Habakkuk, live in a violent world. In the words of Salman Rushdie, 'Violence today is *hot*. It is what people want.'[6]

Like Habakkuk, we need to reach the place where we can quietly say, 'Though . . . yet I will rejoice in the LORD' (3:17–18). But, like Habakkuk, we need to start where he begins in his dialogue with God: How long . . .? Why . . .? (1:2–3). To assert the former without starting with the latter is glib and slick. 'The whole value of this prophecy is its revelation of the process that led to the song of 3:17–18.'[7]

Isaiah had a vision of someone yet to come, the one we call the suffering servant of the Lord, who would attract to himself all the violence inherent in human nature. It would, Isaiah said, be visited on this man in appalling suffering, 'although he had done no

---

[5] *The Moor's Last Sigh* (Vintage, 1996), p. 372. [6] *Ibid.*, p. 306.
[7] Campbell Morgan, p. 116.

violence' (Is. 53:9). Only by such an act of atonement could the reality of human violence be finally and fully resolved. Then, in the ultimate perfection and peace of the new Jerusalem, 'Violence shall no more be heard in your land' (Is. 60:18). Because violence is noisy as well as destructive, its termination will spell peace, perfect peace. But, like Habakkuk, we must make the journey from here to there. As we enter into the prophet's experience, we shall trustfully be strengthened to keep pressing onward and upwards.

Habakkuk 1:1–17
1. Dialogue with God

1. Preface (1:1)

'There is not much to tell about the man Habakkuk. He is simply a "prophet" and he is given a "burden".'[1] Later (3:1) we are given 'a prayer of Habakkuk the prophet'. This crisp designation could indicate that Habakkuk was one of the official prophets at the temple in Jerusalem, a possibility strengthened by the musical ascriptions and instructions at the start and finish of chapter 3 ('according to Shigionoth' and 'To the choirmaster: with stringed instruments', 3:1, 19).

The Hebrew word *maśśā*, translated *oracle* or 'burden', has the literal meaning of something that has been lifted up and is being carried. It is consistently used by several Old Testament prophets to describe the message which God had laid upon their hearts.[2] In the earlier chapters of Isaiah it is a refrain introducing messages of judgment on various countries.[3] 'This word never occurs . . . except when it is evidently grave and full of weight and labour.'[4]

Habakkuk's message was indeed a heavy one to carry and to convey; it 'possesses a burdensome dimension from start to finish'.[5] By using this particular word, the prophet emphasizes that this is not a message that he has dreamed up himself. In a very real sense he neither looked for it nor likes it. He would rather be rid of it, but it weighs heavily on him and he cannot escape the responsibility of declaring it. It is of *God*, and therefore is not to be ignored, trimmed or trivialized.

It is, of course, possible to invest our own ideas with such *gravitas*, and to attribute what we feel we must proclaim to the weight of divine inspiration. Jeremiah was particularly sensitive to this kind of prophetic manipulation, and he calls to account many of

---

[1] Kaiser, p. 143.   [2] Na. 1:1; Zc. 9:1–2; Mal. 1:1.
[3] Is. 13:1; 15:1; 17:1; 19:1; 21:1, 11, 13; 22:1; 23:1; 30:6.
[4] Jerome, quoted by Goldsmith, p. 14.   [5] Robertson, p. 135.

his contemporaries who have taken upon themselves to declare 'the burden of the LORD'.[6] It had become a pious catchphrase in the mouths of ordinary people in general, and of priest and prophet in particular.

For Jeremiah, as for Habakkuk, declaring the message of the LORD to his compatriots was costly and traumatic. They both experienced – not just once or twice but continually over long periods of time – the personal anguish of being spokesmen for God in days of deep darkness in the nation. But, for Habakkuk, God's message was a burden, supremely because it contained at its very heart an uncompromising and chilling declaration of judgment on his own country.

Habakkuk tells us that he *saw*[7] this *oracle* or 'burden'. The content of the book is so vivid, the word pictures so dramatic, that we today can almost 'see' what the prophet is describing. Habakkuk lived his message, not merely spoke it.

The Hebrew verb used here (*ḥāzâ*) is 'a loan word from the Aramaic, where the verb and its derivatives are the usual words used to denote the act of seeing ... It refers both to the natural vision of the eyes and to supernatural visions of various kinds. In the OT the verb and its derivatives appear alongside the verb *rā'â* for all kinds of sight and vision, but are especially associated with the visions of the prophets.'[8] To what degree a particular passage may be referring to literal sight or to understanding and insight depends largely on the context. It is possible that sometimes both are intended, the one leading to the other, much as we today might see something unfolding in front of our eyes, but gradually see its significance the more we look at it and ponder it. At least part of the divine revelation to Habakkuk is called a 'vision', and he is commanded to write it down (2:2–3). Habakkuk 'may have been an eyewitness to at least some of what God wants him to communicate'.[9] Indeed, he himself says that he will 'look forth to see what he will say to me' (2:1).

Old Testament prophets went around with their eyes, as well as their ears, open to God. On occasions a prophet is specifically asked by God, 'What do you see?'[10] The LORD then interprets the special significance of that object or event in terms of his word to and through the prophet. This explains much of the visual nature of prophetic messages. It is underlined in the book of Revelation, which is called 'the words of the prophecy of this book'.[11] It

---

[6] Je. 23:33–40.
[7] *Cf.* Is. 1:1; Am. 1:1; Ob. 1; Mi. 1:1; Na. 1:1. 'Isaiah's prophecy contains a great deal more than visionary material, yet the whole is termed "that which he saw"' (Patterson, WEC, p. 136).
[8] J. A. Naude, in *NIDOTTE* 2, p. 56.   [9] Patterson (WEC), p. 136.
[10] *E.g.* Je. 1:11, 13; 24:3; Am. 7:8; 8:2; Zc. 4:2; 5:2.   [11] Rev. 1:3; 22:7.

contains a record of what the apostle John saw and heard when he looked through heaven's open door.[12] Prophecy (in both Testaments) comes through seeing and hearing. It contains the visual and the verbal. It makes both audible and pictorial contact with its hearers. That is one of the reasons why prophetic ministry of this kind is so relevant in today's audiovisual society.

2. Habakkuk speaks to God (1:2-4)

Habakkuk has been crying out to God for a long, long time. He is now completely overwhelmed by the situation in which he lives. 'He was living in the midst of terrible anarchy – violence abounded, cruelty was rampant, crime was flagrant, lust was everywhere.'[13] As he turns to God once again, he uses two phrases which were used by psalmists in their cries of lament,[14] and which remain today the heart cry of men and women at the end of their tether as they call out to God: O LORD how long...? Why...? (2–3).

Behind how long? is the unspoken cry, 'I have my limits.' Behind why? is the insistence, 'I must have reasons.' God's silence is impenetrable and intolerable. Habakkuk believes that the limits of his tolerance will be extended if he is able to understand why God is acting – or not acting – in a particular way. Habakkuk's fundamental lament and complaint before God is expressed in one word, violence (ḥāmās, 2–3). The word comes six times in the prophecy,[15] fourteen times in the Psalms, and seven in Proverbs. It is, therefore, a key word in this book. It 'denotes flagrant violation of the moral law by which man injures primarily his fellow-man',[16] or 'continued oppression'.[17]

The prophet lived in a violent society. He chose to speak in general terms about the endemic, systemic violence all around him. No doubt he could have given specific examples. For horror and ghastliness, they would have been on a par with accounts we could give to illustrate the violence of our generation and our nation. Within a few weeks in the first four months of 1996, we were shaken by massacres of children at school in Scotland and of tourists in Tasmania. Destruction and violence are before me (3).

It is debatable, however, whether one generation is more violent than another. The biblical record suggests that violence has been pervasive and typical in human society from the earliest times. In the days of Noah, 'the wickedness of man was great ... every imagination of the thoughts of his heart was only evil continually ... the

[12] Rev. 4:1.   [13] Campbell Morgan, p. 117.
[14] E.g. Pss. 10:1, 13; 13:1–2; 22:1; 35:17; 42:9; 43:2; 44:23; 74:1, 10, 11; 79:5, 10; 80:4, 12; 88:14; 89:46; 90:13; 94:3.
[15] 1:2, 3, 9; 2:8, 17 (twice).   [16] Armerding, p. 500.   [17] Baker, p. 51.

earth was corrupt in God's sight . . . all flesh had corrupted their way
. . .' The result? 'The earth was filled with violence' (Gn. 6:5–11).

Violence does, nevertheless, escalate. It had escalated in the Judah
and Jerusalem of Habakkuk's time. This is indicated, first, by the
combination of horror words piled up by the prophet: *wrongs* and
trouble, destruction and violence, *strife and contention* (3). In the
Old Testament, generally speaking, injustice and wrongdoing are
correlated and used predominantly in contexts of perverted justice
and social oppression. *Destruction and violence* are similarly
correlated – associated with 'the unjust oppression of the weaker
members within a community'.[18] Habakkuk's society was an ugly,
cruel, vicious society, where the weak went to the wall unnoticed,
unsupported and unlamented.

All this took place in a context of *strife and contention* (3).
Although, at one level, this couplet refers to a general atmosphere of
confrontation, hostility and aggression, the specific meaning of both
words has a litigious connotation. Habakkuk's world had become
plagued by continuous resorting to the lawcourts to get one's
'rights'. In the words of one American commentator: 'Welcome to
the litigious society.'[19] Quarrels and lawsuits were everywhere;
justice and the law were nowhere.

But the most profoundly disturbing aspect was what had
happened to *the law* (or, in Hebrew, *tôrâ*, without any definite
article; 4). *The law is slacked* – 'paralysed', 'numbed' or 'slackened'.
The suggestion is that this may refer to a general, pervasive lawlessness in society, or, more likely, to a virtually universal rejection of
God's law as the basis for personal and social behaviour – resulting
in its being not simply ignored, but deliberately perverted. Those
who should have upheld and applied the law had become venal and
corrupt. There is even a suggestion in the word 'paralysed' that the
law itself had lost power and become ineffective.

Violence is fanned by such a lawless situation. *Justice never goes
forth* or, if it does, it *goes forth perverted* (4). The essential evil of the
situation is summed up in the phrase, *The wicked surround* (or 'hem
in', 'encircle') *the righteous* (4). Habakkuk's use of these two
categories, often on the lips of psalmists and prophets, indicates the
essential godlessness of contemporary society. Wickedness is always
seen as defiant transgression of God's law. Righteousness comes
from obedience to God's law. If the wicked encircle the righteous,
that means at the very least that godless people outnumber
Godfearers. Inevitably it points also to the oppression of righteous
people by the wicked, the immoral majority.[20]

The law (*tôrâ*) was mediated primarily through the Levitical

[18] Armerding, p. 500.   [19] Kaiser, p. 154.   [20] *Cf.* Is. 10:1–2.

priesthood,[21] in close conjunction with the king and others in authority. What Habakkuk is describing, therefore, is a nation where the religious and civil leaders had become corrupt, resulting in paralysis for the law. God had set it in place to be 'the soul, the heart of political, religious and domestic life'.[22] But this socio-political glue had come unstuck. Society had come apart at the seams, its very fabric unravelling with every misapplication or rejection of the law's demands. 'The best law in the world profits nothing if its statutes are not maintained.'[23]

In Old Testament terms, *justice* (*mišpaṭ*) is the application of *the law* (*tôrâ*) by means of 'all the functions of government'.[24] Wherever Habakkuk looked, those in authority ignored the law and 'no one dared to oppose the torrent, though frauds, rapes, outrages, cruelty and even murders everywhere prevailed: if any righteous men still remained, they dared not come forth into the public arena, for the wicked beset them on all sides'.[25]

So Habakkuk feels trapped by the violence of wicked men. The leadership of his people, God's covenant people, has allowed wickedness to prevail and has brought God's law to a state of paralysis. He is facing the kind of situation we face today, and he begins to ask the questions we want to ask: Why, then, does God not do something? How long will God stand back and do nothing, say nothing? Habakkuk cries for *help* (2). God's personal intervention is their only hope. But *thou wilt not save* (2). God is not listening (*thou wilt not hear*, 2). The prophet is at the point where he doubts whether God is interested in sorting out the situation. But he is also near to concluding that God is incapable of putting things right. Either possibility is too frightening to contemplate. But what if God is neither willing nor able to do anything about it?

Habakkuk suggests that he personally would be very glad to be rid of the whole situation: *Why dost thou make me see wrongs and look upon trouble?* (3). He feels that God is rubbing his nose in all this violence. He wants none of it. He would prefer to be out of it. But God makes him look at it, compels him to take in its force and ugliness, and requires him to feel its impact in his own soul.

'Habakkuk was an unhappy, perplexed and greatly frustrated prophet.'[26] Why do good people suffer? Why do the ungodly flourish? Why are justice and mercy flouted with impunity? What is the point of praying? What is the point of having faith in God? What kind of God is he? Why put up with the hassle of being a prophet? Why not take the wings of a dove and opt out? Why is it all such a

[21] Dt. 33:10.   [22] F. Delitzsch, quoted by Keil, p. 57.   [23] Robertson, p. 140.
[24] Armerding, p. 500.   [25] Calvin, 15, p. 23.   [26] Patterson (WEC), p. 141.

211

burden? 'Habakkuk raises openly the kind of questions any thinking and believing person ought to ask.'[27]

3. God replies to Habakkuk (1:5–11)

Most people . . . who have longed for the privilege of arguing with God, of questioning the way he does things, of seeking God's explanation of his ways, have not been given that opportunity . . . What Habakkuk has recorded here is something extraordinary: a dialogue in which he twice complains to God about the world's injustice, and twice God answers him.[28]

And yet, as the dialogue proceeded, Habakkuk began to wonder whether he had been wise to raise such huge issues with God. By the time he had begun to absorb something of the implications of God's reply to his initial lament, he realized that he had walked into something of immense and intense significance. His 'burden', rather than being lightened and lifted, became frighteningly heavier.

God begins by taking the prophet up on his complaint: 'Why dost thou make me see wrongs, and look upon trouble?' (3). God tells him: *Look among the nations, and see* (5). Habakkuk had been forced to watch violence gradually taking over his own city and nation. But as it had escalated, he had become progressively depressed and desperate about the situation. Like us today, he might well have reached the point when he no longer wanted to know. But God would not let him pull out of his prophetic responsibilities. God kept on compelling Habakkuk to look at the violence and to feel its impact in his sensitive soul. Now, in answer to his honest prayer, God tells him to look again, and to look further afield. The prophet is to look *among the nations*, to *look . . . and see*, to take in what God will bring to his attention.

Habakkuk is thus instructed – he and his people – to turn his eyes away from his own little world and watch God at work on a wider canvas. Like us, the prophet had become preoccupied, if not obsessed, with his own situation. His horizons had narrowed to the limits of his own vision and experience. He could not lift himself above the daily events of his particular circumstances. Because God seemed to be inactive, indeed absent, he was becoming sucked into a downward spiral of doubt and despair.

Look among the nations, urges God, *and see*. God has been listening to Habakkuk's prayer very carefully, taking in the actual words the prophet has used to pour out his heart to God. God then

[27] Craigie, 2, p. 84.
[28] Donald E. Gowan, *The Triumph of Faith in Habakkuk* (John Knox, 1976), p. 20.

responds specifically to Habakkuk's prayer by taking up his own vocabulary: his lament about the paralysis of the law and the perversion of justice (4, 7), and his central theme of violence (2, 3, 9). There is nothing vague or generalized about this answer to prayer. God listened to Habakkuk and addressed the prophet's burning concern in specific detail. He still does so today.

But we need, like Habakkuk, to be open to God's lateral thinking. His perception and perspective are much wider than ours. He sees the end from the beginning and he sees the whole picture. His purposes and activity are based on this knowledge and understanding. Our judgments are radically affected by time, space and mortality. God stands outside all three. Yet, in his compassion and concern, he takes our prayers very seriously.

It may well be that it was out of compassion that God had held back from responding to Habakkuk. God knew that the events which would contain his answer to his prophet's dilemma would bring untold agony and distress.[29] This is hinted at in these words:

> *... wonder and be astounded.*
> *For I am doing a work in your days*
> *that you would not believe if told* (5).

Once he had listened to God's reply and absorbed its implications, however incompletely, Habakkuk's stunned incomprehension is obvious (12–17).

God hesitates to divulge what we would be unable to take on board regarding his ways and means of dealing with endemic violence and systemic injustice. We may be properly convinced that God is 'able to do far more abundantly than all that we ask or think' (Eph. 3:20): but, given the limitations we share with Habakkuk, we tend to restrict that ability to what we can cope with. Because God's ways are not our ways and because God's thoughts are not our thoughts,[30] he paces the publication of his purposes.

The nub of God's answer to Habakkuk is that, contrary to the prophet's personal conviction, he is already very active in pursuing his purposes: *I am doing a work in your days* (5). 'The "work" that God is doing is actually going on at the very time when Habakkuk is complaining and God is answering his complaint.'[31] That *work* may be invisible, but it is in operation. This activity is directly related to the nub of Habakkuk's prayer. Nor is it a vague promise for the future. It is time-specific: *in your days.*

---

[29] *Cf.* God's soliloquy in the face of Abraham's intercession for Sodom: 'Shall I hide from Abraham what I am about to do?' (Gn. 18:17).
[30] *Cf.* Is. 55:8.   [31] Goldsmith, p. 22.

For lo, I am rousing the Chaldeans (6). 'The focus of Habakkuk's prayer had been local ... To these local issues he had been able to discern no local response that could be traced to God. But ... far away in Babylon events were taking place which would change the course of human history; they were not random events, nor merely the independent actions of a human state. Rather, in the larger scheme of things, they were a part of God's participation in human history which eventually would have their impact on the prophet's nation.'[32]

This was no new revelation. About a century earlier, God had announced a similar operation in similar language:

> Because this people draw near with their mouth
>   and honour me with their lips,
>   while their hearts are far from me,
> and their fear of me is a commandment of men learned by rote;
>   therefore, behold, I will again
>   do marvellous things with this people,
>   wonderful and marvellous;
> and the wisdom of their wise men shall perish,
>   and the discernment of their discerning men shall be hid
>   (Is. 29:13–14).

At that time 'the Assyrian came down like the wolf on the fold',[33] as Sennacherib invaded the northern kingdom, ruthlessly putting the nation to the sword and capturing Samaria, its capital. Habakkuk must have felt an icy chill course through his soul when he began to absorb the implication of God's new initiative with the Chaldeans, a superpower on a par with the Assyrians and destined to outstrip them by far in imperial domination.

Because we cannot be sure precisely when this prophecy was written, it is difficult to know just how great a frisson the mere mention of the Chaldeans would have caused. It is reasonable to suppose that ripples were already being felt in Judah and Jerusalem, if only the impact of dark rumours from a distant land. If the first verses of this prophecy refer to the time after the death of King Josiah in 609 BC and before the Babylonian king, Nebuchadnezzar, defeated Pharaoh Neco of Egypt at the battle of Carchemish in 605 BC,[34] then the Chaldean/Babylonian factor was already a major force in the region when Habakkuk was engaged in this dialogue with God. They had conquered the old capital of Assyria in 614, Nineveh in 612 and Harran in 610. They were on the march.

---

[32] Craigie, 2, pp. 86–87.   [33] Byron, *The Destruction of Sennacherib.*
[34] So Bruce, pp. 847–848.

The Chaldeans had come so far so fast, virtually from nowhere:

Kaldo was a country situated along the Euphrates and Tigris rivers between the Persian Gulf and the southernmost cities of Babylonia. It was a region of swamps, canebrakes and lakes with few urban areas. The inhabitants seem to have relied on fishing, hunting, small-scale agriculture and some cattle-breeding for their livelihood. The region was divided into tribal areas. The people lived in loosely organized tribal groups and were fiercely independent of each other and especially of the major cities of the north, such as Babylon and Nineveh.[35]

These 'natural enemies of all urbanized societies'[36] were a *bitter and hasty nation* (6), ruthless and impetuous. Such an arrogant bully is part of God's working purposes: *I am rousing the Chaldeans* (6). This Chaldean development moved at an astonishing speed: 'They became the world rulers over Babylonia, Assyria, Syria, Palestine and Egypt, when twenty years previously they hardly were known to exist.'[37]

They pursued a scorched-earth policy: they *march through the breadth of the earth, to seize habitations not their own* (6). The essence of this international terrorism is summed up in the hauntingly simple words, *they all come for violence* (9). Violence had been the cry of Habakkuk (2–3), unprecedented and unchecked violence by ruthless people in power in his own land. Here was God responding to his cry with a promise of yet more violence in store for his people, at the hands of a rapacious invader on the rampage at the instigation of God himself.

God virtually flings Habakkuk's own words back in his face: *Dread and terrible are they; their justice and dignity proceed from themselves* (7). This is a clear echo of Habakkuk's lament (4) about the erosion of law and justice in Judah. The Chaldeans make up their own rules as they go along. They are a law to themselves. 'They set their own standards of justice and dignity, regardless of the opinions of others.'[38] So God's answer to Habakkuk's lament about lawlessness and injustice is greater lawlessness and more injustice at the hands of an evil empire of terrifying cruelty.

Part of the terror inspired by the Chaldeans was the sheer speed with which they moved when on the march:

Their horses are swifter than leopards
more fierce than the evening wolves;

---

[35] R. L. Smith, p. 101.   [36] Armerding, p. 502.   [37] Robertson, p. 149.
[38] Bruce, p. 849.

> *their horsemen press proudly on.*
> *Yea, their horsemen come from afar;*
> *they fly like an eagle swift to devour* (8).

Leopards, wolves, eagles – animals renowned for their speed and aggression in pursuing their victims. Hasty and impetuous by temperament, the Chaldeans 'could dart from place to place to snatch victory, to plunder and to devastate'. Because of their 'practised, skilled and trained efficiency',[39] these Chaldean soldiers were consummate professionals and together constituted a fearsome war machine: *terror of them goes before them* (9).

Chaldean warfare was, in this sense, a precursor of the astonishing technological precision of modern weaponry. We sat in front of our television screens during the Gulf War in 1991 stunned by the sight of Tomahawk missiles being guided down streets in Baghdad, turning corners and homing in on a particular building. One shudders to think of what might be perpetrated if this firepower were in the unrestrained hands today of a vicious, evil empire like the Chaldeans in Habakkuk's time. This is at the heart of the world's ongoing concern about Saddam Hussein's present capacity for nuclear, gas and germ warfare.

They gather captives like sand (9). Here Habakkuk's language seems to be a deliberate echo of the original promise made by God to Abraham: 'I will indeed bless you, and I will multiply your descendants as the stars of heaven and as the sand which is on the seashore. And your descendants shall possess the gate of their enemies' (Gn. 22:17).[40] Now, many centuries later, here was God speaking of Abraham's descendants being possessed *like sand* by their enemies, who would carry them off as *captives* into a foreign land.

Such a scenario had, of course, come to pass in about 722 BC, when the Assyrians under Sennacherib had invaded the northern kingdom of Israel and had taken off huge numbers of people into exile. About that catastrophe Isaiah declared: 'Though your people Israel be as the sand of the sea, only a remnant of them will return. Destruction is decreed, overflowing with righteousness' (Is. 10:22). Now the people of the southern kingdom, inhabitants of Judah and Jerusalem, were staring a similar disaster in the face.

God's description of the Chaldean invasion draws to a close with a vivid description of their sheer arrogance. Utterly self-confident,

---

[39] Goldsmith, p. 25.

[40] These particular words are used by Jacob in prayer for God's blessing (Gn. 32:12). *Cf.* 1 Ki. 4:20: 'Judah and Israel were as many as the sand by the sea; they ate and drank and were happy' (*i.e.* in the halcyon days of Solomon).

the Chaldeans feared no king, no ruler, no fortress in opposition to their advance:

> *At kings they scoff,*
> *and of rulers they make sport.*
> *They laugh at every fortress,*
> *for they heap up earth and take it* (10).

The Chaldeans swept everything before them. Not just petty kings and local potentates, but rulers of well-established kingdoms (such as Pharaoh Neco of Egypt) were treated like a joke. Fortified cities, impregnable for generations, capitulated like so many sandcastles before the advancing tide of Babylonian cavalry and infantry. They simply built up huge mounds of earth and then walked in over the level walls of the city. It was so simple a manoeuvre as to make resistance look foolish and pointless.

This contempt for all authority is the inevitable corollary of self-sufficient autonomy: *their justice and dignity proceed from themselves* (7). The Chaldeans needed no other authority, except as fodder for their voracious appetite for domination. They respected no other authority. They recognized no other authority. They paused in their empire-building only as long as was needed to conquer and to possess: *then they sweep by like the wind and go on* (11).

But God then makes plain to Habakkuk that the very pride and self-confidence of the Chaldeans contained the seeds of their own downfall: *guilty men, whose own might is their god!* (11). So the sting is in the tail, and God gives Habakkuk and his people early notice of the demise of the Chaldeans: 'Sweep past they may, but the final verdict was already in.'[41]

Categories of sin and guilt would have been entirely alien to the Chaldean mindset. They made up their own rules, and chief among them was the belief that might is right. They despised the very notion of accountability. They regarded themselves as answerable to nobody. They justified their actions – if they ever needed to do so – by attributing both their goals and their successes to their great god Marduk.

But, as Habakkuk says, their *own might is their god* (11). 'Ruthless arrogance is rightly epitomized as a form of self-deification.'[42] Their particular pantheon, with Marduk at its head, was a manmade system of idolatry; and the Chaldeans had developed a religion which legitimized unbridled cruelty and savage expansionism. The rise and fall of Marxism have given us a modern parallel of equivalent

---

[41] Armerding, p. 503.   [42] *Ibid.*

savagery and similar transience: both empires emerged and then evaporated within eighty years.

But the implied eventual termination of Chaldean tyranny could scarcely have registered with Habakkuk. He had pleaded with God to end the violence. All God had promised was more violence and more vicious violence. When this is the nub of God's message, it is hard to pick up the nuances which point to an ultimate day of reckoning for all perpetrators of violence.

Nevertheless, Habakkuk is being told that it is 'not by their own instinct, but by the hidden impulse of God'[43] that the nations rise and fall. If he can receive it, he is being encouraged to believe that 'God can employ the vices of men in executing his judgments – the wicked are led here and there by the hidden power of God'.[44] God has been telling Habakkuk, however opaque and shattering the message, that evil does not go unpunished and that even the most brutal aggressor, backed up by immense military might, is not merely under the authority of God, but is even an instrument of the divine purpose.

4. Habakkuk speaks again to God (1:12–17)

As God himself had indicated (5), Habakkuk could not believe what he was hearing from God. The answer to his complaint had opened up a far more frightening scenario than the one he had brought to God in agony of heart. The violence all around him, which dominated his horizon and dogged his footsteps, was going to be met with even greater violence. 'The "cure" of Babylonian invasion is worse than the "illness" of Judean sin.'[45]

Habakkuk was shaken to the core by God's answer. The phrase *their god* (11) seems to have sparked off in him what might have been a semi-desperate plea to *my God* (12). The self-appointed god of the Chaldeans, people who were worshipping their own power and might, had appalled the sensitivities of this Hebrew prophet. And so he invokes God in a string of resonant phrases and titles, which together calm him down and allow him some breathing (and thinking) space, so that he can absorb the impact and implications of God's reply.

First, he rehearses the unchanging characteristics of God (12a). Secondly, he receives within his soul the truth about God's sovereign use of the Chaldeans as his own instrument (12b). Thirdly, he begins to remonstrate with God about the inherent contradiction (as Habakkuk sees it) between the kind of God he is and the kind of action he is pursuing (13–17).

---

[43] Calvin, 15, p. 27. [44] *Ibid.*, p. 28. [45] Baker, p. 47.

Habakkuk feels himself floundering and he reaches for the *Rock* (12); he speaks to God in prayer. We need to steel ourselves to come first to God in both private and public prayer, rather than discuss the problems with friends or counsellors first. Today, the abundance of human resources can subtly erode this foundational relationship with God, with the result that we come to him often as our last resort, rather than as our first resource and our best friend.

Habakkuk rehearses qualities in God which are basic, simple and strong: *Art thou not from everlasting, O* LORD *my God, my Holy One?* (12). The Chaldeans were a relatively recent phenomenon on the world stage. Their power and presence were growing all the time; but they were only human beings, with all the frailty and foibles of mere mortals. Even if Habakkuk remained unconvinced of their vulnerability and their ephemerality, simply recollecting the everlasting nature of God introduced a different perspective.

The secret is not so much to persuade ourselves that powerful people and monolithic structures are only temporal and temporary as to focus on God's eternal changelessness and essential divinity. Habakkuk's language in this prayer is reminiscent of Moses' final prayer of blessing for the people of Israel, with its affirmation that 'underneath are the everlasting arms' (Dt. 33:27). Equally (and especially if he was a professional prophet in the temple in Jerusalem), it is likely that Habakkuk was instinctively drawing on the psalmody of the nation's worship.[46]

In the face of the arrogance of the Chaldeans, lifting themselves up, Habakkuk could remind himself that the LORD already reigns on high, far above all self-appointed upstarts. However much the violence thunders and roars within the nation and upon it, what God decrees and ordains is rock solid.

God is called 'the LORD' (Yahweh) twelve times in this prophecy, six times in direct address. This emphasizes the covenant relationship between God and his people, and between God and his prophet. This is the name by which he made himself known to Moses when he established his covenant with the people of Israel.[47] The Hebrew word has four letters, YHWH, and is connected with the verb *hayâ*, 'to be'. It is best rendered 'I am who I am', and, as the divine name, is usually rendered 'I AM'. The Hebrew word, though transliterated 'Yahweh', is actually intended to represent the sound of someone breathing or expelling air, rather than giving the substance of an actual name. Devout Jews today still regard it as blasphemous to utter God's name, because he is too holy: so this word is breathed as a sound, not uttered as a name.

Habakkuk, therefore, is humbling himself before God, daring to

---

[46] See Ps. 93:1-5.   [47] Ex. 3:13-15.

breathe out an inward invocation to him, but reminding himself and God of the covenant relationship between God and his people, on the basis of which alone he can continue his dialogue. He is also reminding himself that this God is the living God, the great I AM – no doubt in contrast to the gods and self-aggrandizement of the Chaldeans.

Habakkuk then makes two personal declarations of faith in, and submission to, the everlasting Lord: *my God, my Holy One* (12). In the searing light of what the LORD has just revealed to him about the role of the Chaldeans under God, Habakkuk is affirming that his life and identity are inextricably intertwined with the life and identity of the LORD. He has no existence apart from the LORD. He has no definitive reason for living except in relationship to 'the Holy One of Israel'. Habakkuk knows that he is now standing absolutely naked before God. He realizes that he is utterly dependent for the breath of life on this God to whom he has presumed to bare his soul. 'In him we live and move and have our being' (Acts 17:28).

The poignant, personal phrase, *my God*, seems to contain a mixture of passion and defiance: 'Whatever you do and say, LORD, I am not going to let you go; nor am I going to let you get away with it. I am yours and you are mine: so be it.' The prophet's cry echoes a frequent refrain in the Psalms, in particular the psalmist's cry of dereliction, which Jesus Christ himself uttered from the cross: 'My God, my God, why have you forsaken me?' (Ps. 22:1; Mk. 15:34).

When we are driven to our knees by pressures external and internal, similar to those faced by Habakkuk, we need to examine afresh what God really means to us. In particular, in our experience of being stripped down to fundamentals, we need to ask whether we can look the Lord in the eye and say, 'my God'.

This profound encounter is sharpened further by the prophet's other personal and intimate way of addressing the LORD: *my Holy One*. This description of God stresses his otherness, his essential difference from human beings and from other 'gods'. By his otherness in the midst of Israel, he makes them different, distinct from other nations. This distinctiveness is to express itself in a consecrated lifestyle, cleaving to the LORD and obeying his word, especially in the deep darkness surrounding the prophet – and the even deeper darkness on the horizon.

When Habakkuk, therefore, calls God *my Holy One*, he is taking this distinctive otherness into his own soul, and, under the particular pressures he is facing, declaring himself set apart for the LORD. He is not going to allow himself be assimilated into the violent culture in which he is living, nor is he prepared to surrender his conviction about the otherness of God. His faith is under severe trial and his experience contradicts his beliefs. But he has decided to settle his heart and his soul in the LORD, *my Holy One*. Habakkuk is prepared to stand out among his contemporaries as a man of God.

Having rehearsed these four qualities of God, Habakkuk then declares: *We shall not die* (12). This statement has caused considerable discussion among the commentators. An alternative reading is 'You shall not die', addressed to God. Whether this phrase expresses the prophet's confidence in the people's future security or in God's own indestructibility, it reflects the way his faith is beginning to rise, as he rehearses the attributes of God in prayer. Such growth in faith can come to us also, when we deliberately turn our eyes away from the gods of secular society to the LORD God – 'a real God of objective power, rather than the subjective deification of their own strength worshipped by the Babylonians'.[48]

Having heard God's statement about using the Chaldeans as the instrument of his purposes, Habakkuk is now willing to receive the bitter truth of this fact in his inner soul.

> O LORD, *thou hast ordained them as a judgment;*
> *and thou, O Rock, hast established them for chastisement* (12).

If this is the decision of the covenant-making and covenant-keeping God, the LORD (Yahweh), Habakkuk accepts its wisdom.

God had warned disobedient Israel about invasion and destruction at the hands of foreign powers:

> The LORD will cause you to be defeated before your enemies; you shall go out one way against them, and flee seven ways before them ... Your sons and daughters shall be given to another people, while your eyes look on and fail with longing for them all the day; and it shall not be in the power of your hand to prevent it. A nation which you have not known shall eat up the fruit of your ground and of all your labours; and you shall be only oppressed and crushed continually; so that you shall be driven mad by the sight which your eyes shall see ... The LORD will bring you, and your king whom you set over you, to a nation that neither you nor your fathers have known; and there you shall serve other gods, of wood and stone ... The LORD will bring a nation against you from afar, from the end of the earth, as swift as the eagle flies, a nation whose language you do not understand, a nation of stern countenance, who shall not regard the person of the old or show favour to the young ... (Dt. 28:25, 32–34, 36, 49–50).

[48] Baker, p. 55.

The vivid picture of an enemy swooping on the people *like an eagle* (8) would have aroused the prophet's memory of this passage, one of the most frightening statements about God's judgment in the Old Testament. Given the depths to which Judah and Jerusalem had plunged, there was nothing else for Habakkuk to do except bow his head in awed submission before the just decrees of a holy God and say: *thou hast ordained them as a judgment* (12). Like the Assyrians a century earlier in their devastating descent upon Samaria, so the Babylonians will execute the judgment of God on Jerusalem. What more is there to say? *Thou ... hast established them for chastisement* (12), and 'chastenings must be taken with a sober humility'.[49]

Habakkuk has rehearsed God's eternal attributes; he has received God's sovereign decrees; he now begins to remonstrate with God about the glaring contradiction between his own experience of God's goodness and this latest revelation of God's intentions (13–17). The question *Why?* is back on his lips:

> *Thou who art of purer eyes than to behold evil*
> *and canst not look on wrong,*
> *why dost thou look on faithless men,*
> *and art silent when the wicked swallows up*
> *the man more righteous than he?* (13).

It was one thing for the prophet to be compelled to *see wrongs and look upon trouble* (3); it is quite another for God himself to *behold evil and ... look on wrong* and *on faithless men* (13). Habakkuk could not look upon all-pervasive evil, because his own soul was tortured by it and he could do nothing about it. God continued to look upon such evil (unless he was turning a blind eye), abhorred it and condemned it, but did nothing about it – even though he was well able to do so. What did that say about the intentions and the very character of God? What did it say about what God can and cannot do? Habakkuk's creed told him that *Thou ... canst not look on wrong*, but here was God looking on it and letting it intensify. God must be immoral or impotent – or even both.

Habakkuk has become free to remonstrate with God at this level only after planting his feet firmly on the *Rock* (12), on God's eternal changelessness and on his personal commitment in a covenantal relationship between God and the prophet. Habakkuk is not a drowning man about to go under for the last time. Paradoxically, his very strong inner security, as a person beloved by and belonging to God, releases him to batter the gates of heaven and berate the living God. There has always been this important distinction between

---

[49] Robertson, p. 160. See the New Testament perspective in, *e.g.*, Heb. 12:5–11.

bitter cynicism and believing confrontation: one is a denial that refuses to believe, the other is a belief that refuses to deny; one makes assertions and will not stay for an answer, the other makes assertions and will not move until there is an answer.

Having accepted the rightness, the justice, in God's sovereign choice of the Chaldeans to bring correction and chastisement to Judah, Habakkuk cannot but point out the inherent contradiction to which this testifies: the Chaldeans are *faithless men* (13). However corrupt and violent the people of Jerusalem have become, the people of Babylon are the epitome of *the wicked* (13) – and there is absolutely no justice, no rightness, in God allowing, let alone commissioning, such people to swallow up those *more righteous than* they (13).

Habakkuk's approach here is an intriguing example of the way human beings, especially those sensitive to the holiness of God, instinctively assume a competence to be moral judges, comparing themselves with others in terms of ethical standards (*the wicked . . . the righteous*), both as individuals and as groups or nations. However wicked his own people have become, they are *more righteous* (13) than the Babylonians. Claiming the moral high ground has become one of the political ploys of our generation, and it can lead to arrogant judgmentalism or to self-destruction, or to both.

Scriptural truth, on the other hand, establishes that

> None is righteous, no, not one;
> no one understands, no one seeks God.
> All have turned aside, together they have gone wrong;
> no one does good, not even one (Rom. 3:10–12).[50]

All sin is the same before God. We may speak of certain people being more wicked or more unrighteous than others; but God declares that 'there is no distinction, since all have sinned and fall short of the glory of God' (Rom. 3:22–23).

God's *purer eyes* not only perceive the depths of sin in every human being in every culture (such as Judah or Babylon), but also pass judgment on all sin equally. This gradually becomes plain to Habakkuk as his dialogue with God continues, and, in particular, as he watches and waits for the core of God's revelation ('vision', 2:2) to be made known. That revelation (contained in its essence in 2:4) makes plain that in God's sight there are only two categories of people: those whom he accounts righteous, and then everyone else. There are no degrees of righteousness or unrighteousness. God does not keep league tables, with certain people high up on his lists and

---

[50] Paul is quoting Ps. 14:1–3; *cf.* Ps. 53:1–3.

others languishing in the lower divisions. There is no pass mark. There are no credits. There are no sliding or rising criteria for his decisions.

Habakkuk's problem was with the silence of God in the face of the particular wickedness of the Chaldeans (*Why . . . art* thou *silent?* 13) – not their wickedness as such, but the divine permission given to such wickedness to swallow up those *more righteous*. He can cope with wickedness 'out there', not least because it has a self-destruct device built into it – a particularly eloquent refrain in the laments and prayers of the psalmists.[51] But this Chaldean wickedness is to swallow up his own people. This is no longer out there, but in here. It is not thousands of miles away, but in our neighbourhood. And it seems to be indiscriminately destructive, without any ethical basis and without any proportion, rationale or escape.

The prophet develops this theme by means of the motif of a highly successful and prosperous fisherman (14–17). But this fisherman is a veritable fisher of individuals and nations. Again the prophet lays his charge against God: *thou makest men like the fish of the sea, like crawling things that have no ruler* (14). 'Habakkuk sees God as the ultimate source of these international atrocities.'[52] There may well also be an echo of God's creation ordinance, giving human beings 'dominion' over all other created things.[53]

Here, protests Habakkuk, is God making human beings, whom he has created in his own image and after his own likeness, like fish in the sea – fodder for a vicious, ruthless tyrant who trawls for people[54] as though they were *like crawling things that have no ruler* (14). There is a double nuance here: God is the ruler of people and of nations, especially of Judah; and human beings are intended to rule, or 'have dominion', over fish, not be treated like fish. But the Chaldean war machine inexorably and implacably moves on from country to country:

> *He brings all of them up with a hook,*
> *he drags them out with his net,*
> *he gathers them in his seine;*
> *so he rejoices and exults* (15).

'Perhaps the most repulsive element of the entire picture is the fiendish gloating of the Chaldeans. They gleefully inflict these

---

[51] *E.g.* Pss. 5:10; 7:14–16; 9:15–16; 10:2; 35:8; 37:15; 57:6; 140:1–13. *Cf.* Pr. 26:27; 28:10; Ec. 10:8.
[52] Robertson, p. 161.   [53] Gn. 1:26–28.
[54] The Assyrians, a hundred years earlier, used to drive a hook through the lower lip of their captives and string them along in single file. 'In such a diabolical manner they enforced docility' (Robertson, p. 162).

humiliating brutalities on their victims. How can this be? Is this procedure actually the right way for the Lord to deal with his own people?'[55] We have seen in our day film of similar behaviour by militia in our war zones, particularly in the ghastly killing-fields of places like Vietnam, Rwanda and Bosnia.

While God, apparently in heedless silence, looks on this merciless and endless genocide (*mercilessly slaying nations for ever*, 17), the Chaldeans start to worship their own weaponry:

> *... he sacrifices to his net*
> *and burns incense to his seine:*
> *for by them he lives in luxury,*
> *and his food is rich* (16).

Earlier, in his first reply to Habakkuk's lament, God indicated that the Chaldeans' guilt before him consisted of making their own might their god (11). This idolatry had escalated from an inner attitude of arrogant self-confidence to brazen public acts of worship: making sacrifices and burning incense are two universal and timeless practices of religious devotion. The language may be vividly metaphorical, but it depicts a rampant paganism in a highly successful and affluent nation: *for by them he lives in luxury, and his food is rich.*

To the Chaldeans, therefore, the effectiveness of their ruthless policies of subjugation and empire-building was their justification. They fought; they won. They captured prisoners and property. Through vicious appropriation of both, they boosted their own coffers and bolstered their own economy. Their lifestyle was opulent. These were boom years for the Babylonians. Like so many prosperous nations before and since, they attributed their success to their own strength and skills. They saw wealth as the legitimate reward for enterprise and effort. The more they acquired, the more they wanted. Covetousness became the driving force in their military campaigns. And 'covetousness', as we have been told, 'is idolatry'.[56]

Affluence, materialism, covetousness, idolatry – this is the essence of authentic paganism, which may or may not be accompanied by piety and religious activities. Ruthless violence can come in different guises, not just the naked imperialism of a warmongering nation like the Chaldeans. Whenever pride, greed and cruelty come together, whether in an individual or a family or an enterprise or a government, methods will be employed which are essentially no different from the violence portrayed by Habakkuk. Such violence

---

[55] Robertson, p. 163.   [56] Eph. 5:5; Col. 3:5.

towards rivals and competitors, indeed towards anyone who is perceived to be a threat or an obstacle to greater and greater success, is not infrequently veneered with religious devotion and acts of charity. But 'God is not mocked',[57] even if, like Habakkuk and many others, we long for swifter action and more visible punishment.

'The wicked consider that to be rightly done which has been attended by success. They thus dethrone God and put themselves in his place.'[58] Any version of the principle that 'the end justifies the means' veers in this direction. To the Chaldeans, the goal of prosperity and power for their own nation justified any means of achieving it: the sacking of cities, scorched-earth devastation, slaughter of women and children, desecration and despoliation of holy places, deportation of thousands into exile and slavery, and massacre of tens of thousands in battle.

As the five *Woe!* passages in chapter 2 make plain, God has a day of reckoning for such violence on the grand scale. But we, too, need to watch any unethical behaviour in our own lives, which we try to justify by the results, particularly in a culture which has increasingly replaced ethics with pragmatics, the long-term with the short-term, the highest good with the bottom line, and principle with convenience. In these and many other ways people 'dethrone God and put themselves in his place'.

Habakkuk ends his catalogue of Chaldean cruelty with another question to his God, this silent Rock, as he remonstrates:

> *Is he then to keep on emptying his net,*
> *and mercilessly slaying nations for ever?* (7)

How can God let this fisherman carry on fishing for human beings in his massive net, harvesting nations like fish, dragging them on board and chopping them up for his own pleasure and profit? 'Has not God turned loose upon a helpless mankind a voracious force that even he would be powerless to check?'[59]

Having become like wild animals themselves, the Chaldeans treat everyone else like animals. Violence begets violence. Where will it ever end? The terrorized become the next terrorists. It is true of domestic abuse as much as of tribal mayhem. If the tortured are not going to become the next torturers in an endless spiral of violence, something drastic has got to be done. And the one person who presumably can do something is asserting his own decision to make these bloodthirsty tyrants his own instruments. That is not just bizarre; it raises virtually every question ever asked about the nature and the purposes of God.

---

[57] Gal. 6:7.   [58] Calvin, 15, p. 51.   [59] Patterson (WEC), p. 159.

Habakkuk 2:1–20
2. A double vision

1. Watching and waiting (2:1)

In the film *The Remains of the Day*, based on the novel of the same name by Kazuo Ishiguro, Anthony Hopkins plays the role of an emotionally repressed butler in an English country house in the 1930s, who falls gradually in love with the housekeeper, played by Emma Thompson. The butler is incapable of expressing his feelings in any way, and the relationship remains stilted and unreal.

Often our relationship with God can remain at a similarly superficial and unreal level. We think that we dare not explode and tell God what we feel about his silences, his decisions and his ways. But God wants the kind of honesty with which Habakkuk confronted him. God wants us to trust him with our deepest fears and our wildest feelings. His approval of Job's honesty, coupled with disapproval of the pious trivia of Job' comforters, underlines this.[1] God wants us to throw everything at him, not to pretend that we do not think and feel in ways which are, for a certain kind of believer, unacceptable or shocking.

Habakkuk was free to be so blunt with God because he had plumbed the depths and found underneath the solid foundation of the everlasting 'Rock' – God's eternal changelessness (1:12). Having splurged his stupefaction and trauma before God, he takes his stand to watch and wait for God's response. There was no such statement after his first prayer of lament to God (1:2–4), but God had graciously responded to him. 'It is a wise man who takes his questions about God to God for the answers.'[2] Habakkuk expects an answer and he will watch and wait until it comes.

The role of the watchman in Israel was crucial. It was an essential ingredient of any prophet's ministry: 'The prophet is the watchman of Ephraim, the people of my God' (Ho. 9:8). God appointed his

[1] Jb. 42:8.   [2] Armerding, p. 509.

prophets and he expected them to be his people's watchmen. A watchman was like a sentinel, a sentry on duty on behalf of the people, stationed to warn them of the cost of departing from God's law and God's way.

Habakkuk's watching and waiting, however, take a different stance altogether. 'Habakkuk looks in the other direction. He wants to see how God will act in the light of the stipulation found in the covenant, to which he also is a signatory, that sin necessitates punishment.'[3] In other words, Habakkuk is watching God to see whether he will keep his side of the covenant and judge the Babylonians for their violent cruelty, particularly to his own people. He is watching and waiting for God.

Such watching and waiting constitute a fundamental ingredient of faith in God. But it is often missing among activist believers following a shredded lifestyle in a frenetic generation. We do not find it easy to watch or to wait. We are much better at talking and doing. In particular, we find it very difficult to watch and to wait for God to answer our prayers, especially the impassioned ones which are torn from broken hearts and baffled minds like Habakkuk's. So it is important to learn more about watching and waiting from the prophet.

a. Watching and waiting takes time

'Habakkuk knows that Yahweh's second respond to his complaint may not come immediately. He is prepared to wait for it … An answer will come: the prophet is sure of that …'[4] In an impatient, instant generation, where time is money, we need the reminder that it takes time to watch and wait. We may know the scripture which says that 'they who wait for the LORD shall renew their strength' (Is. 40:31),[5] but we urge God to hurry up and give us his answer quickly.

Two specific examples of men who watched and waited will illustrate the matter. Daniel set himself to watch and wait for God in intercessory prayer for his people. He had to wait three full weeks before any answer became apparent. Then, having been assured that he was a 'man greatly beloved' by God, Daniel was told: 'Fear not, Daniel, for from the first day that you set your mind to understand and humbled yourself before your God, your words have been heard, and I have come because of your words' (Dn. 10:11–12).

Jeremiah, whom the LORD instructed on several occasions not to pray for the people of Judah and Jerusalem, was approached by King Zedekiah's representatives with the request, 'Pray for us to the LORD our God.' A combination of circumstances resulted in 'many days'

[3] Baker, p. 58.   [4] Bruce, p. 857.   [5] Cf. Ps. 37:1–7.

elapsing before 'the word of the LORD came to Jeremiah' – and it was not the kind of word Zedekiah or his leaders wanted to hear. Jeremiah was prepared to take time watching and waiting until God answered his prayer.[6]

'Yahweh's response to those who enquire of him is never automatic.'[7] We have been imperceptibly conditioned by our push-button world. We can easily regard prayer as a way to get what we want, rather than the way in which our covenant relationship is expressed in watching and waiting.

b. Watching and waiting make lonely work

Habakkuk says, *I will . . . station myself on the tower* (1), pointing to the reality of solitary sentry-duty. There may have been others on other parts of the wall, doing similar work. Any two may have met from time to time, especially with the long watches of the night, unless each had his own separate watchtower. But, by its very nature, the prophet's calling to be a watchman was intensely lonely.

The record in the Old Testament of most prophetic ministry depicts individuals out on a limb for God – or, in Jeremiah's distinctly pressurized experience (as a contemporary of Habakkuk), at the bottom of a pit.[8] So consistently did such 'watchman' ministry bring isolation and ostracism at the hands of a disobedient people, especially its leadership, that to be a watchman was synonymous with announcing doom.[9]

Habakkuk's vigil, as he set himself to watch and wait for God to answer his prayer, was almost certainly solitary and unaccompanied. His dialogue with God is represented from the outset as a personal, private expression of the dark night of the soul. Even if his whole prophecy becomes part of the liturgy of the temple worship, and even if he served there as a professional prophet (as some scholars believe), his watching brief was self-imposed in the place of private prayer. Agonizing with God on behalf of an apostate church in a godless nation is, in any case, more lonely if one is within the 'establishment' and part of the institution than if one has chosen to operate as a lone ranger.

c. Watching and waiting offer an alternative option

The prophet, finding himself sinking and as it were overwhelmed in the deepest abyss, raises himself up above the judgment and reason of men, and comes nearer to God, that he may see from on

---

[6] Je. 37:1–21. [7] Bruce, p. 857. [8] Je. 38:4–13.
[9] See Mi. 7:2–4 (and exposition, above).

high the things which take place on earth and not judge according
to the understanding of his own flesh, but by the light of the Holy
Spirit.[10]

It is very easy to drive a wedge between prayer and hard thinking,
between waiting on God and wrestling with intellectual problems,
between relinquishing and refusing to give up. Imagine someone
who is very close to finding a personal faith in God. He has posed
innumerable questions of an intellectual kind, most of which have
been carefully and satisfactorily answered. But he still has one or
two which nag him and with which he nags the Christian couple
who are his friends. The questions are to do with the presence and
power of evil in a world supposed to be created and controlled by a
righteous, loving God. Eventually, the wife says: 'I'm going to
pray for you, that God right now will open your eyes to see him for
who he is and to see what he has done for you, because your intel-
lect is getting in the way of your faith.' But the husband interjects:
'There you are, ignoring the intellectual realities and escaping into
prayer!'

There is no failsafe course to steer when we find ourselves in such
a place, for ourselves or for another. But, when it comes to the ways
of God, sooner or later we all need to reach a position where we
genuinely decide to watch and wait, rather than wrestle with our
rational processes. That position, for some people, needs to be
reached later rather than sooner. But, for many others, it should be
sooner rather than later.

Job, for example, came to a place of new faith only when he
stopped arguing with his friends and with God himself, and allowed
God to take him for a walk in his garden. God did not address Job's
specific questions; but he revealed to Job more of his majesty and
creative genius than the man had beforehand ever appreciated. Job's
reaction is significant:

> I have uttered what I did not understand,
>> things too wonderful for me, which I did not know . . .
> I had heard of thee by the hearing of the ear,
>> but now my eye sees thee;
> therefore I despise myself,
>> and repent in dust and ashes (Jb. 42:3, 5).[11]

Habakkuk has said all he wants or needs to say. He has thought
through, over, under and around every side of the situation. Now
that he has emptied himself of everything, he is ready to hand it all

---

[10] Calvin, 15, p. 56.   [11] Cf. Ps. 131:1–3.

and himself over to God. That is the alternative to yet more wrestling, tussling and arguing – with God or anyone else.

d. Watching and waiting call for quietness

Sentries listen as much as they look. Especially at night, it is important to be alert to hear the slightest sound. To listen, it is necessary to have quietness, internally as much as externally. If we are preoccupied with our own problems and our minds are racing, it is very hard to hear properly. We can miss important sounds and imagine others.

Habakkuk says, *I will . . . look forth to see what he will say to me* (1). The prophet understands that he needs to look and to listen, to pay full attention to what God will say. 'Habakkuk was not looking for an audible word from heaven, but rather for that still, small voice within his heart and mind.'[12] To tune in to God in this way, we need to cultivate inner stillness. Each person will discover, probably through experimentation and within the limitations of available time and space, the situation in which quietness is best found and listening to God is most readily achieved.[13]

In Chaim Potok's novel, *The Chosen*, Danny Sanders, who lives under the terrible, disciplined silence of his father, one day says to his friend Reuven, 'You can listen to silence, Reuven. I've begun to realize that you can listen to silence and learn from it. It has a quality and a dimension all its own. It talks to me sometimes. I feel myself alive to it. It talks. And I can hear it. It has strange, beautiful texture. It doesn't always talk. Sometimes – sometimes it cries, and you can hear the pain of the world in it.'[14]

Habakkuk had been long experiencing such silence, including the silence of God. 'The silences of God – mysterious, exasperating, consoling, pregnant with meaning – require our trust at least as much as does the Word of God. God does not talk all the time and God's silence is as emphatic as his speech.'[15]

e. Watching and waiting require perseverance

Resolve and determination are essential to the watchman's work. Watching and waiting involve not only time but perseverance:

> Upon your walls, O Jerusalem,
> I have set watchmen;

[12] Goldsmith, p. 40.   [13] *Cf.* Ps. 46:10, 'Be still, and know that I am God . . .'
[14] Quoted by Cornelius Plantinga Jr, in 'Background Noise', *Christianity Today*, 17 July 1995, p. 42.
[15] Plantinga, *ibid.*

> all the day and all the night
>> they shall never be silent.
> You who put the LORD in remembrance,
>> take no rest,
> and give him no rest
>> until he establishes Jerusalem
>> and makes it a praise in the earth (Is. 62:6–7).

The thrust in the calling of these particular watchmen is rather different from Habakkuk's. As well as taking no rest themselves, they were to give the LORD no rest as they 'put him in remembrance' of his promises about the restoration and renaissance of Jerusalem after the Babylonian exile. Habakkuk is to persevere in looking and listening, rather than in pleading and interceding. But his ministry needs the same single-mindedness.

> It is not enough to open our eyes once and by one look observe what happens to us; but it is necessary to continue our attention. This constant attention is just what the prophet means by watching; for we are not so clear-sighted as immediately to comprehend what is useful to be known. Watchmen, though they hear nothing, yet do not sleep; and if they hear any noise once or twice, they do not immediately sound an alarm, but wait and attend.[16]

This quality of wholehearted, single-minded perseverance in seeking the LORD is a steady refrain in the Scriptures.[17] To be a watchman required immense self-discipline and a steely resolve not to be caught napping, not even to lose concentration. Habakkuk set himself to watch and to wait until God chose to speak to him.

f. Watching and waiting imply being open to correction

Habakkuk was not the kind of person whose insistent demands on God cease only when they get the answer they want, when God appears to have come round to their way of thinking. On the contrary, he expects God to correct and reprove him. This emerges from whatever rendering of the Hebrew text for *my complaint* (1) we adopt. It could mean either 'the argument I have offered' or 'the correction that I receive'.[18] The prophet knows that God will speak

---

[16] Calvin, 15, p. 60.

[17] *E.g.* Dt. 4:29; 1 Ch. 22:19; Ps. 145:18–19; Je. 29:11–13; Mt. 7:7–11; 21:22; 26:36–45; Eph. 6:18.

[18] So Armerding, p. 509. The verb form is used in Is. 1:18, 'let us reason together', and the context here in Habakkuk suggests a similar emphasis. Habakkuk has marshalled his 'arguments', and expects God to answer in kind.

very plainly and directly in response to his second *complaint*. His first prayer had received an extremely robust riposte, and Habakkuk had pulled no punches in his own reply. So he expected God to reprimand and correct him.

God looks not just for honesty but for humility. In the personal relationship into which he has brought those with faith in him, he intends us to be teachable as well as frank. So Habakkuk 'braces himself for the rebuke of the Lord. He had dared to question the earlier revelation of the Lord which had come in response to his complaint.'[19]

When God decides to administer reproof, rather than to meet our desires, we can easily conclude that he is not listening, because his answer is not what we want to hear. We know that if we choose to listen, our lives will have to change. Basic attitudes will have to go. Habits will have to die. We still make a virtue out of our watching and waiting, suggesting to others that God has still not spoken to us, when deep down we know that we are not ready to accept the correction God is applying to our lives.

Habakkuk's 'reaction to God's reproof would have a telling effect on his own spiritual condition and the effectiveness of his entire ministry. It was a crucial moment for God's prophet and he was to prove worthy of the test.'[20]

2. Write the vision (2:2–4)

And the LORD answered me (2). Whatever watching and waiting had entailed for him, and however long it was before God responded, the answer came to Habakkuk – in clear and unmistakable terms. Although its substance was for wider consumption and for subsequent generations, the LORD's message was personally given to him. He had besieged God with his urgent complaint, so God replied to him personally. That is the nature of God's relationship with his prophets and his people – like a father with his children.

God makes it clear to Habakkuk that what he has to tell him needs to be written down *upon tablets*, not simply to prevent its being forgotten, but to enable others to read it and then run with it. The wider and long-term significance of God's reply is highlighted by the word translated *vision*, or 'revelation' (NIV). There is an echo of the verb translated *saw* (1:1), to describe the entire 'oracle' or 'burden' of Habakkuk's prophecy. The prophet gives notice, then, that the result of his 'disciplined watchfulness'[21] is a vision or

[19] Robertson, p. 167.
[20] Patterson (WEC), p. 163; *cf.* Jb. 13:3, 12–15; 31:1–40; 38:1–2.
[21] Armerding, p. 511.

revelation from God. He had affirmed that he was going to look to see what God will say (1); as he expected, God gave him a vision in which he revealed what was in his mind.

It is impossible to be sure how much of the book should be regarded as the *vision*. The most likely interpretation depends largely on the fact that it has both a specific application to the Babylonians and an eschatological application when *the end* comes – when God's judgment on his enemies, and on the enemies of his people, is consummated.

On this analysis, the *vision* contains everything in the rest of the book that is linked with the judgment of God on human (especially Babylonian) wickedness, and with the salvation of God for all who have faith. That material might be restricted to 2:4–5. It could certainly be contained in 2:4–20. It could continue to 3:15. But 3:16–19 looks more like one prophet's response to the vision than an integral part of it. The content of 2:4, however, with its introductory summons, *Behold*, seems like the central truth on which the rest is vivid and dramatic commentary, depicting how God is going to demonstrate his irresistible adherence to the principle set out in 2:4.

Whether the vision itself was succinct or elaborate, Habakkuk was instructed to *write* it down and *make it plain upon tablets* (2). God intended the vision to be 'clearly understood, assimilated, preserved and propagated'.[22] It was the custom in Habakkuk's time and place to erect tablets, probably of wood, in public places, so that notices of general interest and importance could be fixed to them.[23] This method of publication is still common in Asia, particularly China. We are all accustomed to advertising hoardings and informal graffiti, and we can imagine, for example, a succession of large notices along the main road into Jerusalem or round the marketplace, each carrying a key phrase from the text of Habakkuk's vision in these chapters.

It was particularly important for Habakkuk to write down the vision, because by its very nature it would be some time before it came to pass. It therefore had to be preserved with accuracy. Memory does strange things with messages, especially important ones. The prophet is told to *make it plain* (2), using large letters and legible handwriting. No room must be given for confusion, error or inaccuracy.

The stated reason for this clarity is *so he may run who reads it* (2). This aphorism has been given a misleading interpretation by those who, perhaps unwittingly, turn it around to say, 'so he may read

---

[22] Patterson (WEC), p. 174.
[23] See God's instructions to Isaiah on two separate occasions: Is. 8:1–4; 30:7–8.

who runs'.[24] Its true meaning has been summarized as follows: 'Everyone who reads or hears these words is to consider himself a herald of a significant communication intended for all people everywhere.'[25] God intends this message to be passed on by every person who reads it. This is not a time-specific, place-specific or person-specific message. The message is to be passed on – whether in the casual conversations of everyday life, or under a clear mandate to announce God's word throughout the land. But whether gossiping or publicly proclaiming the message, everyone who reads it must be enabled to pass it on. An essential part of this process is making it plain.

Because the core of the message – *the righteous shall live by his faith* (4) – is the nub of the Christian gospel, the same principle of plainness and propagation applies to us today. There is a straightforward simplicity about the good news which must not be adulterated or added to. Everyone who receives the gospel is to be a herald of it. For some it is a specific calling, but for all it is a clear commission.[26]

There is another possible nuance to the word *run*. God's message was intended to galvanize those paralysed by despair at the situation in the land. There must have been many who shared the prophet's desperation at the prevalence of violence and wickedness. Others, no doubt, had cried out to God to do something about this rampant evil. They needed a word of true encouragement to continue trusting God for the future. This was that word.[27]

The instruction to Habakkuk to write the vision on tablets could be a reference to the tablets of the covenant made by God with the people through Moses at Sinai.[28] The significance of this vision is comparable to that of the Sinai covenant; in fact, the Jewish Talmud records a remark made by Rabbi Simlai: 'Moses gave Israel 613 commandments. David reduced them to eleven [see Ps. 15], Micah to three [Mi. 6:8], Isaiah to two [see Is. 56:1], but Habakkuk to one: "the righteous shall live by his faith".' 'Jewish scholars felt that these three Hebrew words fairly summarized the message of the whole Bible.'[29]

This section of Habakkuk's prophecy, therefore, looks back to the giving of the law and forward to the coming of the gospel. Indeed, Paul's treatment of the principle of faith in Romans takes the thrust

[24] So Bruce, p. 859 (also S. R. Driver).   [25] Patterson (WEC), p. 172.

[26] In Je. 23:21 the ministry of a prophet is described as running in response to God's sending his servants on his errands. When God calls, we run with the good news. *Cf.* Ps. 119:32; Is. 52:7–10.

[27] Is. 40:31. The theme of running is also taken up in the New Testament, *e.g.* 1 Cor. 9:24; Gal. 2:2; 5:7; Phil. 3:16; Heb. 12:1–2.

[28] Ex. 31:18; 32:15–16; Dt. 9:10; 27:8.   [29] Kaiser, p. 162.

of Habakkuk 2:4 right back to Abraham. When faced with an astonishing promise about the birth of a son to him and Sarah, 'Abraham believed God, and it was reckoned to him as righteousness' (Rom. 4:3, quoting Gn. 15:6).

God's assurances to Habakkuk are piled up:

> For still the vision awaits its time;
>   it hastens to the end – it will not lie.
> If it seem slow, wait for it;
>   it will surely come, it will not delay (3).

The repeated emphasis on timing brings home the gulf between our perception and God's perception of time. Habakkuk, like ourselves, wanted God to act at once. God's time is not necessarily ours. Just as, in human affairs and planning, timing is fundamental, so it is with God's purposes. 'There are times when every scrap of theology we possess suggests God ought to act',[30] but still nothing appears to happen.

This is the regular experience of every believer on the personal level. More poignantly and pressingly it is true on a much greater scale, not least in the situation with which Habakkuk was agonizing – the eradication of a nation, God's own people. Steven Spielberg's searing portrayal of Hitler's 'solution' to the Jewish 'problem' in the film *Schindler's List* is one eloquent restatement of the questions put to God by Habakkuk: How long? Why? When? The suffering of Christians under vicious regimes raises the same questions. Whenever the violent cruelty of evil people proceeds unchecked and unpunished, the same questions remain, whether the case is that of a solitary victim, or mass genocide.

The answer of God to Habakkuk, expressed in the vision, is definite and uncompromising: the vision *hastens to the end* (3). The word translated *hastens* literally refers to breathing, blowing or panting. The phrase could be rendered 'pants for the end', implying that the prophetic vision has its own inner yearning to be fulfilled. This indicates, not a self-fulfilling prophecy, but God's own passionate commitment to fulfil what he has promised. For God, it is not a matter of putting his word out in the public domain and then removing himself to get on with other matters. No, God watches over his word.[31] The Spirit of God who inspired it lives within it and will not rest until it comes to fruition. God's very reputation and honour are wrapped up in his promises. He cannot lie,[32] and therefore the vision cannot lie: *it will not lie* (3). Neither human faithlessness nor divine delays can nullify the

---

[30] Craigie, 2, p. 92.   [31] See Je. 1:11–12.   [32] See Nu. 23:19.

faithfulness of God: 'Let God be true though every man be false' (Rom. 3:4).

In the Old Testament, *the end* often refers to the termination of a period of time, such as the end of the day, or of a month or year. In context here the phrase clearly has a more pointed reference: to the fulfilment of the vision, but also to the terminus (of judgment on Babylon and salvation for God's people) which such fulfilment will demonstrate. But the end was, for prophet and people, a long time ahead. Before the end came, their troubles would increase dramatically – with invasion, devastation, deportation and slavery to the forefront. In such dramatic suffering they would need to hold on to the vision, trusting God to hasten its fulfilment.

But although 'the coming devastation of God's own people at the hands of the Chaldeans was a matter of most solemn consequence, the final resolution of the problem would come to pass only at the eschaton'.[33] There is, in other words, a double meaning to this phrase *the end* or the eschaton (the Greek word for 'what comes last' or 'the ultimate'). The end of Babylonian domination and the return of God's people from exile would be penultimate. The ultimate end is when Jesus the Messiah returns in glory and will be acknowledged by all as Lord of all. 'Then comes the end, when [Christ] delivers the kingdom to God the Father after destroying every rule and every authority and power. For he must reign until he has put all his enemies under his feet. The last enemy to be destroyed is death' (1 Cor. 15:24–26). Habakkuk's *vision*, in this eschatological sense, is still panting for fulfilment.

In such a context, it is inevitable that the working out of the vision will *seem slow* by human yardsticks. But, in God's timing, *it will surely come, it will not delay* (3). God's tardiness is largely an illusion, for two reasons. First, God does not regard or experience time as mere mortals do. He is above and outside time: 'a thousand years in thy sight are but as yesterday when it is past, or as a watch in the night' (Ps. 90:4).[34] Habakkuk may have set himself to watch and to keep on watching (1), but the prophet's long vigil is like the twinkling of an eye to God.

The second reason not to interpret delay as tardiness is a refrain in the New Testament, especially in Christ's teaching, to the effect that the fulfilment of the vision could take place at any time, and will, virtually by definition, be at a time when people least expect it. When God decides to act, he moves like lightning. To human beings

---

[33] Robertson, p. 171. For parallel language about God's sovereign control over time, and for specific references to the 'end', see Dn. 7 – 12, esp. 7:26; 8:17, 19; 10:14; 11:35; 12:4, 9.

[34] *Cf.* 2 Pet. 3:10.

his actions will seem sudden, even though they have previously concluded that he is slow, slack and late.[35]

The literal meaning of the word translated *delay* is 'be late': 'It will not miss its appointment.'[36] All kinds of events and circumstances may seem to be conspiring to wreck God's timetable, even to force him to abort his plans. But the vision will not be late, not even a moment. From our perspective, the time is running out (a revealing phrase); but God is on course and on time. Our task is to *wait for it* (3). After such a protracted time of watching and waiting, Habakkuk might well have breathed in deeply on hearing the word *wait*. But wait he must: *it will surely come* (3).

In similar situations in our personal lives, the process of waiting is as important as the moment of clarification and fulfilment. We grow in faith by learning how to wait. Because *the righteous shall live by his faith* (4), God often chooses to keep us waiting so that we learn to 'walk by faith, not by sight' (2 Cor. 5:7).

We come now specifically to the phrase which 'became the watchword of Christianity, is the key of the whole book of Habakkuk and is the central theme of all the Scriptures'.[37] There are only three words in the Hebrew text and their sequence seems significant: 'The righteous by faith shall live.' This sequence is also retained in the Septuagint, the Greek translation of the Old Testament, from which New Testament writers take this phrase in their application to Christian believers.[38] But the second part of the verse cannot be taken in isolation from the first, because together they form the core of the vision which God is bringing to Habakkuk: 'the clear distinction between two classes of men and nations',[39] as drawn by God. The crystal clarity of Habakkuk 2:4 is, therefore, a shaft of pure light in the darkness of a violent, unjust and evil world:

> *Behold, he whose soul is not upright in him shall fail,*
> *but the righteous shall live by his faith.*

In the instruction *Behold*, God is opening the prophet's eyes to foundational truth. It is not accessible to human perception or reason. Even for men and women of faith, like Habakkuk or Job, such truth can easily be obscured or forgotten in the harsh realities of living and dying. So God, in effect, repeats what Habakkuk already knows but has allowed to fade from his mind. He is given a résumé of what an individual is like without a personal relationship

---

[35] Cf. Mt. 24:36–44; 25:1–13; Mk. 13:32–37; Lk. 12:35–40; 1 Thes. 5:1–10; Rev. 3:1–3; 16:15.

[36] Bruce, p. 859–860.

[37] C. L. Feinberg, *The Minor Prophets* (Moody, 1976), p. 211.

[38] Rom. 1:17; Gal. 3:11; Heb. 10:37.   [39] Patterson (WEC), p. 178.

with God, and of what happens to someone with such a relationship.

The text of the first part is not transparent, but its essential meaning is clear. Literally rendered it reads, 'Behold, puffed up, his soul is not straight within him.' It is possible that the Chaldeans are specifically intended in this description, but it looks and feels like a general statement. Two characteristics of people without a living relationship with God are highlighted: they are 'puffed up' and 'not straight'. 'Puffed up', or 'bloated', is a more accurate rendering of the Hebrew text than the paraphrase *shall fail*. 'There are those whose heart is not right in relation to God; instead of trusting in him, they hold aloof in a spirit of self-sufficiency, trusting in themselves. Their souls are inflated; they lack either substance or stability, and a pin-prick will make them collapse.'[40]

Such conceit leads to crookedness. Instead of being straight and straightforward, self-sufficient people find that they have to pretend and put on an act. This is fundamentally because they are living a lie. They have decided to rely on themselves alone, and therefore they compel themselves, because of their pride, to give the constant impression of having got it all together and being successful. They cannot afford to fail – or, if they do, they can certainly not afford to be seen by others to have failed. They find themselves twisting and turning to avoid facing up to the truth.[41]

The other part of the verse holds out the alternative. In context, it provides Habakkuk with a clear answer to the dilemma he had expressed earlier: 'the wicked swallows up the man more righteous than he' (1:13). No, replies God, the righteous shall live by faith. They will not be swallowed up. They will not merely survive, but flourish. And the quality which produces this outcome is *faith*, or 'faithfulness' (which could refer either to God's faithfulness or a person's steady life of faith).

'The Hebrew denotes "firmness"; then, as an attribute of God, trustworthiness, unchangeable fidelity in the fulfilment of his promises; and, as an attribute of man, fidelity in word and deed; and, in his relation to God, firm attachment to God, an undisturbed confidence in the promises of grace.'[42] The word speaks of trust through thick and thin in a trustworthy God, who stands by us through thick and thin as Saviour – a veritable Rock.

This is a faith 'which strips us of all arrogance and leads us naked and needy to God'[43] – precisely the contrast between such a person (*the righteous*) and the puffed-up arrogance of those who do not admit any need of God. The righteous have manifestly not achieved

---

[40] Bruce, p. 860.

[41] See Dt. 32:5; Ps. 125:3–5; Mt. 17:17 and Phil. 2:15 for the phrase 'a crooked and perverse generation' and the implications of living in such a context.

[42] Keil, p. 73.   [43] Calvin, 15, p. 74.

their righteousness by their own decisions or actions, but have acquired it by the sovereign decision of God. In the Old Testament, righteousness always means 'right with God' (hence the variety of renderings of which it is capable, consistent with this basic truth). Instead of remaining in the arrogance of their self-sufficiency, the righteous have decided to trust in a faithful and promise-keeping God. Such people then discover what it really means to *live*.

Truly to live includes freedom from fear of God's holy judgment on all wickedness, especially conceit and crookedness. For Habakkuk, the Chaldean was the epitome of such pride and perversity, but essentially no more proud or perverse than many of his own people. So how could anyone escape God's righteous judgment and *live*? By faith, by trusting oneself to 'a faithful Creator' (1 Pet. 4:9). Faith – from Abraham[44] through the sacrificial system given through Moses[45] and on through the history of Israel – is the fundamental reality in the relationship God intended between his people and himself. God spoke his word, giving instructions and making promises. Then it was up to the people to move forward in 'the obedience of faith' (Rom. 1:5; 16:26).

This is the core of the vision, and it is this revealed truth which took hold of both Paul[46] and the writer of the letter to the Hebrews,[47] for both of whom this three-word declaration became a lodestar in understanding, explaining and applying Christian gospel truth. It is a declaration which makes sense only against the backcloth of a sinful world under judgment. If our worldview discounts or debunks the reality of God holding human beings to account for their lives, the vision can only be so many words, rather than revealed truth. Habakkuk was passionately moved both by the sinfulness of humanity and by the holiness of God. This is God's answer to his agonizing.

Judgment or salvation; pride or faith; death or life; crookedness or righteousness: these are the ingredients and the alternatives described by God in the substance of the vision he gave the prophet. Habakkuk was to *wait for it* to reach *the end*. He could appreciate a proportion of the vision's significance, that which applied to his own day. But there was more to it. That was why God told him to write down these words. Like the rest of the Old Testament Scriptures, 'they were written down for our instruction, upon whom the end of the ages has come' (1 Cor. 10:11). In Jesus Christ the end has come. The countdown has begun.

---

[44] See Gn. 15:6.   [45] See *e.g.* Ex. 29:38–46.
[46] Rom. 1:16–17; 11:1, 5, 12, 26; Gal. 3:1–14.   [47] Heb. 10:36–39

3. Words of warning (2:5)

Verse 5 of chapter 2 seems to act as a transition from the general message (4), which expresses the kernel of God's vision to Habakkuk, to the specific woes pronounced on the Chaldeans, especially their king (6–19). It is more detailed in its description of the bloated crookedness of self-sufficient people, and the details certainly describe the Chaldeans. If we accept the RSV rendering (noting that the Hebrew of the first two lines is obscure), *the arrogant man* is a personification of the Chaldean nation and of Nebuchadnezzar in particular.

The same combination of pride and greed is to the fore again. The addition of *wine*, or strong drink, seems at first sight out of place. There is, however, considerable evidence from ancient historians about addiction to strong drink among the Babylonians. Its perils are often noted in the Old Testament.[48]

The explicit link between drinking and arrogance suggests the intoxication of conquest. As the Babylonians extended their empire, so their victories went to their heads. They became intoxicated with their own success. It became like a drug: the more they got, the more they wanted. They became addicted to winning. As in any addiction, there was no such thing as enough. Addiction, also, is a power which operates in all kinds of directions; those who are addicted to, say, gambling will be prone to addiction to drugs or alcohol. This is the addictive personality. The Chaldean was that kind of person: *like death he has never enough* (5).

The classic account of Chaldean intoxication, both with success and with strong drink, comes in the dramatic story of Belshazzar's feast.[49] The account opens with drinking and ends with death – of the Chaldean king and of the Chaldean empire: 'King Belshazzar made a great feast for a thousand of his lords, and drank wine in front of the thousand.' This drinking bout led to the king calling for the holy vessels taken by Nebuchadnezzar from the temple in Jerusalem fifty years earlier, so that the drinking could continue out of these consecrated chalices. Meanwhile 'the king and his lords, his wives, and his concubines ... praised the gods of gold and silver, bronze, iron, wood, and stone'.

As this debauched idolatry continued, 'the fingers of a man's hand appeared and wrote on the plaster of the wall of the king's palace'. Terrified, Belshazzar demanded that someone tell him the meaning of the writing. Eventually it was Daniel who explained its interpretation: 'God has numbered the days of your kingdom and brought it

[48] *Cf.* 1 Sa. 30:16; 1 Ki. 20:12, 16; Pr. 23:29–35; 31:4–7; Is. 5:11–12, 22; 22:11–13; 28:1–8; 56:9–12; Ho. 7:1–7; Am. 4:1; 6:1–8.
[49] Dn. 5:1–31.

to an end ... you have been weighed in the balances and found wanting ... your kingdom is divided and given to the Medes and Persians.'

This was the end to which Habakkuk's vision was inexorably and breathlessly moving (2:3) – or, at least, the first manifestation of the end. While Daniel spoke and Belshazzar gathered his senses in his drunken stupor, the Medes were scaling the city walls and swarming through the king's palace. 'That very night Belshazzar the Chaldean king was slain. And Darius the Mede received the kingdom.'

'Strong drink does not in itself engender the pride that is so obnoxious to God. But it serves as an agent by which latent human pride comes forth in all its ugliness. Strong drink evokes expressions of bloated self-esteem inherent in the sinful mind and heart'.[50] In 'the Chaldean' this intoxication with power and possessions is highlighted by the phrases *for himself* and *as his own* (5). The word *gathers* also points back to the same word used twice earlier: 'They gather captives like sand' (1:9); 'he gathers them in his seine' (1:15). Such is *the arrogant man: His greed is as wide as Sheol*. Sheol, the underworld or Hades, 'is a place depicted repeatedly as devouring its prey'.[51]

The nations and the peoples lived in fear of the Chaldeans and of their insatiable greed and ruthless violence: *he has never enough*.[52] Like death, which 'never takes a holiday',[53] he is always looking for more. 'The Chaldeans wished to swallow up the whole world',[54] like many modern empire-builders, not least commercial entrepreneurs and multinational companies. Western nations express fears of Chinese expansionism, while western business interests hungrily establish themselves in the Chinese marketplace. Calvin recalls the insatiable appetite of Alexander the Great, 'who wept because he had not then enjoyed the empire of the whole world; and had he enjoyed it his tears would not have been dried; for he had heard that there were many worlds'.[55]

But all this greed, arrogance, violence, intoxication with conquest and addiction to hoarding, brought the Chaldean no rest and no resting-place: *the arrogant man shall not abide*. The Hebrew verb translated *abide* occurs nowhere else, but the related noun is used several times to denote pasturage or places of residence, with the basic meaning of somewhere to settle. The noun occurs, for example, in Psalm 23:2: 'he makes me lie down in green pastures'.[56] Just as the person addicted to wine cannot settle, but is edgy and restless, for ever looking for another drink, so this Chaldean addict can never

---

[50] Robertson, p. 184. [51] Armerding, p. 514. [52] *Cf.* Pr. 27:20; 30:15–16.
[53] R. L. Smith, p. 108. [54] Calvin, 15, p. 88. [55] *Ibid.*
[56] *Cf.* 2 Sa. 7:8; Is. 32:18; Je. 10:25; Am. 1:2.

settle down in one place. He is never satisfied. There can be no clearer evidence of the contrast between the restlessness of the proud and the rest of the righteous.

4. Woe upon woe (2:6–19)

The bulk of chapter 2 spells out the practical implications of the vision in historical events. In this sense it could be part of the vision itself. It certainly seems to be part of what God revealed to Habakkuk, in answer to his prayer about the way God had decided to use such a violent and ruthless nation as the Chaldeans to punish his own people. Having heard God speak plainly about the instability and the impermanence of such a conceited and crooked people, Habakkuk receives inspiration to foresee the day of reckoning for the Chaldeans and to itemize the charges which will then be brought against them.

All these (6, referring to the nations and peoples who have fallen victim to Chaldean aggression) find the tables turned. Instead of being scorned and laughed at (1:9–10), they themselves *take up their taunt against him, in scoffing derision of him* (6). Many people in many countries will take up the words in this passage, using them to bait the Babylonians and keep up their own spirits in the midst of their miseries.

A modern equivalent is the cartoon or the caricature. The theatre and the press also exercise a similar function. Most modern media provide the opportunity for the kind of commentary, political and otherwise, contained in this passage. Writers, artists, poets, dramatists, film-makers, singers and cartoonists are often the most effective protesters in a tyrannical regime: hence the determination to censor and crack down on all publications not in line with official policy in nations like South Africa under apartheid or the former Soviet Union.

This section is, therefore, subversive literature and 'prophetical in its nature and applicable to all times and all nations'.[57] All these woes are directed at those who, in one way or another, reject the principle stated in 2:4 that the righteous by faith shall live. They underline that the wicked and the arrogant have no place to settle and no place to hide. The writing is on the wall, often in caricature and needing to be interpreted, but plain and precise.

The tone of these woes can be misinterpreted.[58] It is a tone not so much of doom and denunciation as of deep sadness and lamentation. Perhaps a better English phrase is 'Alas for . . .!' The substance of the words remains devastating as a declaration of divine judgment,

---

[57] Keil, p. 77.   [58] *Cf.* Is. 5:8–23.

and the tendency to gloat is never far away. But God himself does not gloat over the destruction of the arrogant and the wicked. The evidence of both the Old and New Testaments points to his inner agony at their refusal to listen and to repent. But because persistent corruption inevitably has its human victims, God's compassion leads him to both chastisement and condemnation of its perpetrators. The heart of God is broken both by the suffering of the violated and by the sinfulness of the violator. The woes are torn from that broken heart in holy indignation.[59] It is our job, not to take the moral high ground, but to express the holy heart of God.

David Watson, leader of many missions in Britain around the 1970s, used to say that we can speak about hell and the judgment of God only with a broken heart. The American evangelist D. L. Moody once led a city mission in Chicago, which lasted ten days or so. On the first Sunday night he preached about hell and judgment and left his listeners dangling over the pit. He told them to come back on another night to hear about God's blockade on the road to hell. During the next twenty-four hours Chicago was devastated by a massive fire, in which thousands of people (including many of Moody's listeners) perished. He vowed never again to preach about hell without mentioning the cross of Christ and the broken heart of God which took him to Calvary. That is the tone and thrust of these five woes in Habakkuk.

a. The first woe (2:6–8)

Babylon was called 'the hammer of the whole earth' (Je. 50:23). *Many nations* (8) will have been hammered by the Babylonians before a halt is called. The language used in this section speaks of debts being piled up over the years, which will one day be called in. This could refer to the way the Babylonians exploited and stripped country after country of its assets. They simply took everything and everyone they wanted, without paying any regard to their value or worth. They loaded themselves with what belonged to others, heaping up what was *not* their *own* (6). They *plundered* (8) city after city, country after country.

The word translated *pledges* (6) has a double meaning: it can also mean 'a cloud of dirt', referring to the defiling nature of acquiring wealth in such a manner. The prophet pronounces a woe on people, like the Chaldeans, who operate in this unprincipled and unjust fashion; people who make capital out of the misfortunes of others and who profit from human misery.

---

[59] So Jesus; *cf.* Lk. 6:24–26; 10:13–15; 11:38–52; 17:1; 22:22. It is particularly evident in Mt. 23:13–39.

The indictment goes even wider. In a powerful phrase, repeated for emphasis (17) the prophet summarizes the Chaldeans' crimes: *the blood of men and violence to the earth, to cities and all who dwell therein* (8). The story of all empire-building is summed up in this statement, not only the sagas of territorial expansion (for example, the treatment meted out to American Indians by white settlers, or colonial exploitation of indigenous peoples in India or Africa); but also the way industrial, commercial and financial empires have been built with the blood, toil, tears and sweat of workers, and with a reckless disregard of the earth's natural resources.

Contemporary outrage about 'fat cat' packages garnered by some company directors is all part of the same debate. There are more ways to incur guilt for *the blood of men* than by committing murder. When multinationals and major banks downsize, laying off thousands in order to maximize already vast profits, while simultaneously hiking the total packages of their top people, the same principles apply.

Equally, the practices of high-street banks (and other similar financial institutions) have followed highly questionable, if not unethical, policies. Individuals and small businesses have been given incentives to take out loans far larger than was either prudent or practicable. We have been saturated with unsolicited literature, backed up by costly advertising, urging us to take out yet more loans and get ourselves further into debt. A simple trick of verbal fraud has allowed what are, in fact, debit cards to be called credit cards. Building societies have been in cahoots with banks to persuade (not merely to encourage or enable) people to take out second and third mortgages on their homes – with the result that, in many cases, these homes have represented negative equity: a phrase which is commercial gobbledegook for massive debt, sometimes with no realistic hope of repayment.

This scenario has not taken into account the murkier world of money-lending, protection money, loan sharks and money-laundering. The principles implicit in Habakkuk's words are relevant also to the matter of Third World debt and international trade. This passage refers to the *violence* done to *the earth* and to *cities*, as well as to those *who dwell therein*. Ruthless exploitation of the environment, allowed to proceed unquestioned and unchecked since the Industrial Revolution, is at last being challenged and addressed. We can appreciate Habakkuk's (and God's?) heartfelt cry: *for how long?* (6). It echoes the prophet's original cry to God about the violence in his own land among his own people.

All such exploiters and plunderers – 'the robber, the thief, the embezzler, the dishonest person, the one who appropriates for himself what belongs to another'[60] – will have their come-uppance. Those who sow the wind will reap the whirlwind,[61] because 'whatever a man sows, that he will also reap' (Gal. 6:7). By this kind of behaviour, violent people are building up a mountainous pile of debt – indebtedness to the violated and the oppressed. *Will not your debtors suddenly arise?* (7) asks the prophet with rhetorical crispness. Part of the shocking impact of this lies in its complete reversal of Chaldean thinking. They have all along regarded themselves as the ones in credit and their victims as the ones in debt. From the divine perspective, the opposite is true.

What is more, when the great reversal comes, it will come *suddenly* (7). This is the answer to the cry, *for how long?* (6), and, incidentally, to the apparent slow fulfilment of the vision (3). The exploitation and violence may continue for what seems like an interminably long time; but the reversal will happen suddenly. One is reminded of the astonishingly sudden and swift disintegration of the Soviet empire in 1989, as nation after nation called in the incalculable debts incurred by Marxist tyranny over the years. For Belshazzar and for Babylon it was the same: suddenly the armies of Darius the Mede were at the palace gates, and 'That very night Belshazzar ... was slain' (Dn. 5:30).

The reversal was equally sudden and dramatic in South Africa. Nelson Mandela remained in prison for twenty-seven years, but only four years after his release he became President. *Suddenly* everything changed, and the debts incurred by apartheid are in the process of being collected. 'God can indeed execute his judgments in a wonderful and sudden manner.'[62]

'He who sows injustice will reap calamity, and the rod of his fury will fail' (Pr. 22:8). For the Chaldeans, their hitherto demoralized and passive victims would come to life and cause them to quake in fear. 'They will shake off their apathetic lethargy and themselves shake the oppressor.'[63] They may, in sheer numbers, be but *a remnant of the peoples* plundered by the Chaldeans (8); but they will execute like for like. 'The survivors within the conquered nations indeed executed the sentence announced here';[64] the Medes and Persians were some of the peoples invaded and plundered by the Chaldeans.

This theme of reciprocal judgment, as victims turn into victors and exact retribution on a scale equivalent to their own sufferings (the so-called *lex talionis*, an eye for an eye and a tooth for a tooth),[65] runs all the way through this section. As an expression of God's

---

[60] R. L. Smith, p. 111.   [61] *Cf.* Ho. 8:7.   [62] Calvin, 15, p. 99.
[63] Baker, p. 63.   [64] Armerding, p. 517.
[65] See Ex. 21:24.

righteous judgments, particularly when these are exercised directly by his own verdict, reciprocity is an intelligible and tolerable principle. We know that 'the Judge of all the earth' (Gn. 18:25) will act justly and compassionately. We know, also, that God has entrusted all ultimate judgment to his Son, Jesus; having shared our humanity, he can be trusted to judge justly.[66]

The problem comes when victims take it upon themselves to carry out judgment on their oppressors. International courts of justice sitting in judgment on war criminals, whether German Nazis or Bosnian warlords, and basing their verdicts on the Geneva Convention – that is one thing. But vengeance on the violators by the violated, visiting equivalent violence on those now in their power – that is quite another. Such virtual vendettas achieve only a perpetuation of the violence. Yet justice must be done, and must be seen to be done. God does not turn a blind eye to any such violence; nor should we. The reality of forgiveness has to be held in tension with the law of sowing and reaping.

It is clear that anything short of God's ultimate and utterly righteous judgment, which will come only at the end and will be presided over by Jesus Christ his Son, will never solve the problems of violence, wickedness and corruption. In the meantime, however, there is an inbuilt pattern of reciprocal justice in human and international affairs. The prophecy of Habakkuk teaches us to look for it and to wait for it. In the ultimate sense, justice will come only at the full end of history; in the penultimate sense, justice is at work already. Habakkuk, in other words, is beginning to perceive a moral order in the course of human history.

b. The second woe (2:9–11)

Here Habakkuk concentrates on the almost paranoid search for privacy and security which typified the Chaldean king and his leadership. There are no watertight compartments in these first three woes: violence is the feature of all three, violence with absolutely no regard for justice and with completely ruthless execution. In the first woe the charge was that 'you have plundered many nations'; here the emphasis is similarly on *cutting off many peoples* (10).

In the first woe the prophet had indicted the Chaldean for what he had amassed for himself (6). Here he emphasizes what he was wanting *for his house* (9). This probably has a double nuance: the Chaldean king's royal palace in Babylon, but perhaps more the royal dynasty, that is, his sons and heirs. The goal of the Chaldean ruler

[66] *Cf.* Jn. 5:22, 26–27; Acts 10:42; 17:31; Rom. 2:16; 2 Cor. 5:10; 2 Tim. 4:1; 1 Pet. 4:5.

was to establish his supremacy for the next generations, indeed for ever. He wanted to make an everlasting name for himself, so that the royal house of Babylon would never be forgotten.

To achieve such a goal, he depended on two mutually exclusive achievements: *evil gain* (9) and physical security (*to be safe from the reach of harm*, 9). Gain is neutral and can be achieved fairly, as well as be shared wisely. The Chaldean's gain was *evil*, or unjust. The Hebrew phrase for getting *evil gain* is taken from the weaver's loom, literally meaning 'to cut off the threads'.[67] We use the same imagery when we speak, normally with a hint of disapproval, of people 'taking their cut' in a suspicious business deal.

'Those who get their wealth by illegal methods feel the need for security. They build their nest on some high, secluded spot guarded by every security device available.'[68] That is true today of individuals who have amassed their wealth through extortion and oppression, thereby attracting the hatred and potential vengeance of their victims. It is true also of whole groups within a society or a nation – minorities who have feathered their own nest at the expense of the rest by exploiting the system and buttressing the *status quo* – if only by doing nothing in the face of structural and institutionalized evil. This was powerfully clear, for example, in Johannesburg when I first visited the city in the early 1970s. Those who lived in the more affluent white suburbs protected themselves with an astonishing collection of security measures: gates, guards, guns, dogs, alarms, walls, fences. Unjust gain and unlimited security – measures which go together in the mind of people like the Chaldeans. But no amount of such security makes them impregnable.

The picture of an eagle's eyrie, evoked by the Chaldean's determination *to set his nest on high*, was strictly inappropriate for the royal palace of Babylon. Like Nineveh, Babylon was situated in a fertile plain at the confluence of the rivers Tigris and Euphrates. But Nebuchadnezzar, in line with proud rulers down the centuries in every culture, was an insatiable builder. He had put splendid projects in hand in other cities in his empire, but it was Babylon that he fortified and beautified with lavish buildings of all kinds.

Upon entering the city through one of its eight ornamental gates, a visitor was able to travel about the city on wide well-kept streets. Among the many impressive buildings were dozens of temples and, of course, Nebuchadnezzar's palace. The palace complex was lavishly furnished and enclosed with a wall 136 feet thick. In the outer course of the wall, Nebuchadnezzar had his name inscribed on each brick. The terraced hanging gardens are said to have been

---

[67] *Cf.* Gn. 37:26; Je. 6:13; Mi. 4:13.   [68] R. L. Smith, p. 111.

located in the north-east angle of the palace complex and were considered to be one of the seven wonders of the ancient world. It is understandable, then, that Nebuchadnezzar named his palace 'The Marvel of Mankind'.[69]

Nebuchadnezzar pursued glory for himself, his house and his empire.[70] But the greed, the pride, the injustice and the violence which characterized that pursuit spelt nothing but shame: *You have devised shame to your house* (10). The Chaldean king was utterly shameless in his policies and practices. He did not know the meaning of shame or how to feel ashamed – like so many powerful people today, who live without any boundaries and beyond any limits. Robert Maxwell was a modern empire-builder, whose career and collapse seem to epitomize this transition from shameless pride and ruthless greed to shame for his wife and family.

There is no clearer message in the Scriptures as a whole than the certain collapse of the proud. Nebuchadnezzar of Babylon experienced what is at the heart of Habakkuk's vision (4). In spite of gaining the whole world, he was told: *you have forfeited your life* (10). In direct contrast to God's revealed truth that the righteous by faith shall live, the Chaldean 'commits spiritual suicide'[71] in his headlong pursuit of power, wealth and security. 'For what does it profit a man, to gain the whole world and forfeit his life?' (Mk. 8:36). King Nebuchadnezzar was probably one of the most successful, prosperous and influential people in the history of the human race. If he, in God's perspective, forfeited his life, why do we blindly pursue similar, if comparatively paltry, goals?

The phrase translated *you have forfeited your life* could also be translated 'you have sinned against your own soul'. The stress would then fall on the deliberate perversity of the Chaldean in ignoring the inner voice of God in his soul or conscience, a voice which speaks to everyone in every generation about the dangers of pride, the call to morality, the fact of mortality and the prospect of accountability.[72] An inscription found in ancient Babylon under Nebuchadnezzar's name declared that 'one of the chief purposes for strengthening the walls of Babylon was to make an everlasting name for his reign'.[73] Nebuchadnezzar and his house ignored the dictates of conscience, thus sinning against their own souls and forfeiting their lives.[74]

Habakkuk concludes this woe with a vivid prediction: *For the stone will cry out from the wall, and the beam from the woodwork respond* (11). He is talking about the Chaldean's *nest*, his *house* which he has made as impregnable as he can, *to be safe from the*

---

[69] Patterson (WEC), p. 191.   [70] Dn. 4:29–30.   [71] Goldsmith, p. 53.
[72] *Cf.* Rom. 2:5–16.   [73] Robertson, p. 193.   [74] See Dn. 1–4.

reach of harm (9). But the *evil gain*, with which he has gathered the necessary resources to construct his citadel, has embedded itself in the walls and the beams. Those ruthlessly plundered to provide stones and wood 'live' in the very materials used to build the palace. There is something battered and bruised in its very structure. Voices of the oppressed *will cry out* from the wall in the royal bedroom, and other wounded voices will *respond* from the beams in the ceiling.[75] Images and sounds of those whom the Chaldean has tortured and ravished will haunt him at night and hound him by day. There may even be a reference to the writing on the wall at Belshazzar's feast when the end eventually arrived.

Buildings certainly can carry a spiritual presence, for good or for evil. In pastoral ministry I have, not infrequently, been called to pray in houses haunted by a violent past (through murder or suicide, perhaps). Such a history has led to various kinds of frightening activity. One such house in the centre of London was being renovated by four or five young men from Yorkshire, nearly 200 miles away, who slept in the house while the contract was being carried out in order to save costs. When poltergeist activity became so regular and intense that they could not sleep, I was asked (by the local estate agent) to 'deal with it; it's your business, not mine'. We prayed throughout the house and it was (spiritually) cleaned out, enabling the builders to complete the work.

Similarly, and on a larger scale, a castle in Austria was used in the Second World War by Himmler as his headquarters; in it he conducted numerous appalling experiments on women and young girls. Bought in the 1960s by Christians to use as a conference centre, there has been constant prayer to rid it of the spiritual 'vibes' of those evil years. As late as 1994, particularly sensitive Christian guests had been alerted in their spirits to the dark residue of spiritual forces in the castle – leading to more intensive prayer and, twelve months later, clear testimony by the same individuals to a transformation in its atmosphere.

A less haunting but equally potent interpretation of this vivid verse is provided here:

An empire founded on violence, plunder and exploitation is like a jerry-built house. It is bound to collapse because it has no inner coherence. The various parts of the structure, the walls and the beams, stand in perpetual tension with one another instead of providing mutual support. At last, the tension becomes too great and the building crashes in ruin. The creaking set up by the strains

[75] There may be a similar insight about the eloquence of inanimate creation in the assertion by Jesus, on Palm Sunday, about what would happen if his disciples stopped praising God: 'the very stones would cry out' (Lk. 19:40).

and stresses is perhaps implied by the outcry of the stones in the wall and the response of the beams in the woodwork ... The prophet's insight has been vindicated repeatedly in world history, not least in the twentieth century.[76]

c. The third woe (2:12–14)

In the first woe, the strictures were directed at an individual (6–8). In the second woe it was a 'house' (9–11). Now the target is a *city* (12). Habakkuk has already arraigned the Chaldean for his blood-guiltiness (8) and he is to repeat the charge in identical words (17). Here the word is again mentioned: *Woe to him who builds a town with blood.*

From the very beginning of the biblical record, *blood* is used in this vivid way to describe the violent death of a human being at the hands of another. After Cain had killed his brother Abel, God called him to account with these words: 'What have you done? The voice of your brother's blood is crying to me from the ground. And now you are cursed from the ground, which has opened its mouth to receive your brother's blood from your hand. When you till the ground, it shall no longer yield to you its strength' (Gn. 4:10–12).

Human blood has a voice. When it is shed, it speaks. Its voice cries out to God. God responds to human bloodshed with a curse on those he would prefer to bless. More than that, in the place where human blood is shed, the impact of that curse is expressed in barrenness and death. In Cain's case, that was the very ground which he tilled. In the Chaldean's case it was the splendid buildings (especially the royal palace) which he erected: hence the reference to the stones and wood crying out (11); hence, also, the deathly impact in places and buildings when human blood is shed today – whether the killing-fields of Vietnam, Rwanda or Bosnia, or the prisons of Auschwitz or Belsen.

There can be nothing but woe – an experience of God's curse instead of the blessing he desires to give – in any town (or enterprise or empire) built on blood. The voice of every victim cries out to God. Their agony rings through the streets and squares, through the marketplaces and corridors of power. They reach the throne-room of heaven and rend the heart of God. He, therefore, decrees that all such enterprises will be doomed to frustration and to failure:

> *Behold, is it not from the LORD of Hosts*
> *that peoples labour only for fire,*
> *and nations weary themselves for naught?* (13).

[76] Bruce, p. 867.

The Chaldean king uses the sweat and toil of slave labour from the nations he has conquered to build for himself towns and cities, but it all will go up in flames; it will all be for nothing (or 'vanity', as it says in Ecclesiastes – futility and meaninglessness).

God's curse on human violence when it becomes endemic in a nation or a society is seen, therefore, in the futility of people's daily toil. Violence had become a way of life for the Chaldeans; the phrases used (*builds . . . with blood, founds . . . on iniquity*; 12) are 'verbal adjectives, showing that the actions are not unique, but characterize those who perform them'.[77] Visitors to Babylon, and to other Chaldean towns and cities, saw unrivalled magnificence and grandeur. They were hugely impressed by what they saw, but all they could see was splendid buildings. God looked at the city and saw bloodshed. So far from being impressed, he issued a decree: all this will be consigned to fire and will prove an empty nothingness. And so it proved.

'The Lord Jehovah . . . saw only the blood of untold numbers of people who were slaughtered in ruthless warfare, in order to obtain the means which make these buildings possible. He saw only the iniquity, the perversity, the crookedness of the builders.'[78] There could be no more eloquent example of the saying: 'Unless the LORD builds the house, those who build it labour in vain' (Ps. 127:1). That last phrase, 'in vain', is the same as Habakkuk's phrase, *for naught* (14).

There is, in these words from Habakkuk, an important perspective on the widespread meaninglessness, emptiness, futility and frustration experienced today in the workplace. 'The Scriptures warn against the kind of labour that, like the Chaldeans, strives for wealth as an end in itself.'[79] Where this foolish preoccupation takes over, there can be nothing but intense human misery and anomie. 'Do not toil to acquire wealth; be wise enough to desist' (Pr. 23:4).

The drivenness and fear in today's workplace derive from an insatiable desire to get more and more – and for what purpose? Slave-drivers in Babylon or Birmingham or Bombay are essentially the same: building empires or enterprises by turning human beings into slaves by subhuman employment practices. By decreeing futility into all such activity, God speaks his word to both slave-drivers and their slaves.

Habakkuk concludes his third woe with a vision that seems to be part and parcel of the revelation which the prophet has been instructed to await with patience:

[77] Baker, p. 65.   [78] T. Laetsch, quoted by Patterson (WEC), p. 194.
[79] Patterson (WEC), p. 197.

For the earth will be filled
with the knowledge of the glory of the LORD,
as the waters cover the sea (14).

The word *Behold* (13), introducing the frustration and emptiness of peoples and nations as empires rise and fall, seems to have the same significance as before (4). As the core of Habakkuk's vision is contained in that verse, so verses 13–14 may contain another essential ingredient: the ultimate meaninglessness of all human activity in the light of what God will one day bring about: the knowledge of his glory filling the whole earth.

It is important to see God's judgment on Babylon (and on all future 'Babylons') in the context of God's glory. If the glory of God is to fill the whole earth *as the waters cover the sea*, leaving no room for anything else, then everything and everyone hostile to the glory of God must be destroyed. That essentially means the removal of all those concerned to promote their own glory. If the kingdom of God is to come in its fullness, all other kingdoms must be swallowed up.[80]

Habakkuk is given a glimpse of such a future for the whole earth. Isaiah had expressed a similar vision: 'The earth shall be full of the knowledge of the LORD, as the waters cover the sea' (Is. 11:9). In context, Isaiah's vision was given against the backcloth of Assyrian violence a hundred years earlier. It contains a vivid description of the antithesis of violence and bloodshed; a vision of pastoral peace and the end of animal violence, culminating with the promise: 'They shall not hurt or destroy in all my holy mountain.' This is a picture where human beings turn from violence. It can come only when everything and everyone created know their Creator.

Habakkuk adds the word *glory* to Isaiah's words; people will know not just the LORD, but his glory. This word 'is used of the visible presence of God, by which the pre-eminent value of his character and actions is revealed to men ... To know God in such "glory" is therefore to abandon the Babylonians' proud autonomy and to honour him as Lord, in submission and obedience, worship and praise.'[81]

The word 'know' or *knowledge* has, from the beginning (when Adam 'knew' Eve in sexual oneness and in such a way as to procreate life),[82] indicated an intimate, personal, exclusive relationship. It is not mere head knowledge, but the interaction of two people in detail and at depth. Such will be the way that God is known in all his glory, and this knowledge will fill the whole earth.[83] Instead of being polluted with blood, the earth will be permeated with glory. In the

[80] See Rev. 11:15–18.   [81] Armerding, p. 518.   [82] Gn. 4:1.
[83] God's glory is normally associated with the tabernacle and the temple; see Ex. 33:7–23; 34:29–35; Is. 6:1–6.

midst of such violence in our own day, and in the midst of the despair and the futility eating away at cities and nations, we do well to ask ourselves constantly: *is it not from the LORD of hosts . . .? For the earth will be filled with the knowledge of the glory of the LORD* (14).[84]

d. The fourth woe (2:15–17)

The theme of bloodshed and violence is carried into this section. There is also a word connection with the previous woe in the repetition of *glory* (14, 16). Here, however, the glory of the Chaldean is contrasted with the glory of the LORD. The Chaldean's glory will be replaced with *contempt* (16) and disgrace. The glory of the LORD will fill the whole earth: *shame will come upon your glory* (16).

'Babylon was seeking to glorify herself by demeaning others.'[85] Habakkuk exposes the deliberately perverse way in which she sets about humiliating others to boost her own glory. The prophet describes the situation, familiar today as in his day, where people set out to make others drunk. One of the quirks of heavy drinkers is that they like to get others to drink a lot with them – a pressure only partially minimized in recent years by strict laws and a firmer social attitude against drinking and driving.

Woe is pronounced on the Babylonians, because they make others drunk with the intention of being able to *gaze on their shame* (15). 'An alternative reading of this last word allows a possible interpretation associated with "vomit".'[86] The basic meaning of this word, *shame*, is nakedness. Vomit normally accompanies drunkenness, and is one of the most visible examples of its more anti-social and ugly aspects. Nakedness, leading to sexual immorality, is another common result of getting drunk. Inhibitions disappear and people behave in ways they would normally avoid. When they wake up after such drinking bouts, they are often astonished (and sometimes appalled) to discover what they have done and where they have been.

It was, apparently, Babylonian policy to get people drunk and to manipulate them into such compromising and degrading situations. Such cynical debauching of others, under the guise of hospitality and friendship, is common in many social situations today. It is often the intention from the outset to get drunk and to get others drunk – and then to make sure that everything is provided for sexual licentiousness. A growing curse has been the availability of drugs like crack

---

[84] These promises in Isaiah and Habakkuk were to be fulfilled in and through the coming of Jesus Christ and the spread of the gospel; see Mt. 26:28; Acts 20:28; Rom 3:24–25; 2 Cor. 4:6; Eph. 1:7; 1 Pet. 1:18–19.
[85] Baker, p. 66.   [86] *Ibid.*

and Ecstasy, which pushers thrust on people without the slightest compunction and with utter ruthlessness. The contemporary social scene, especially for young people who go clubbing, requires constant vigilance in case drinks are laced without their knowledge

Getting people drunk is likely to have been but one example of Babylonian humiliation of her defeated enemies. 'The imperial conqueror degrades and humiliates those whom he has conquered, in order to rob them of their self-respect and destroy their will to resist.'[87] Such methods, used by Nazis against Jews, are the stock-in-trade of all violent people, not least abusers of women and children.[88]

The woe declared by God through the prophet will work its way, as often in Scripture, by the tables being turned on the Babylonians – they will be forced to get drunk: *The cup in the LORD's right hand will come around to you* (16). When that happens and they are forced to drink of that potion, *You will be sated with contempt instead of glory . . . and shame will come upon your glory!* (16).

What is this cup in the LORD's right hand? It is a common theme in the Old Testament and is also found, in a dramatic context, in the New:

> . . . in the hand of the LORD there is a cup,
>   with foaming wine, well mixed;
> and he will pour a draught from it,
>   and all the wicked of the earth
>   shall drain it down to the dregs (Ps. 75:8).[89]

This cup is passed from one nation to another at the sovereign discretion of the LORD.[90]

The cup of the LORD, therefore, contains his wrath. When that cup comes round to one particular nation, there is no way to avoid drinking deep of its contents. The way that God's wrath will work itself out for Babylon is in her having to drink the wine with which she has compelled others to get drunk – a finale dramatically spelt out in apocalyptic terms in Revelation 17:4ff. So it is God himself who mixes his judgment with the Babylonian cocktail of immorality and violence, producing a powerful brew which will reduce her pride to shame and her glory to contempt: *Drink, yourself, and stagger!* (16).

The word *stagger* translates a Hebrew word which, if two letters

[87] Bruce, p. 871.
[88] Calvin (15, p. 113), followed by Craigie (p. 98), reckoned that this woe is addressed to 'the drunkenness of power'.
[89] See the whole psalm for a fuller commentary on the theme of power.
[90] See Ezk. 23:32–34; *cf.* Je. 25:12–33; La. 4:21.

were transposed, gave the word for 'be uncircumcised'. 'Of the appropriateness of "stagger" in the present context there can be no doubt, but "be uncircumcised" is also appropriate. The point seems to be that, as the oppressed has exposed the nakedness of others, so he for his part, uncircumcised as he is, will have his own nakedness exposed and be covered with shame.'[91]

Apart from the book of Revelation, there is one other reference to a cup in the New Testament (apart from 'the cup of the new covenant' in the blood of Jesus) which commands our attention: the cup presented to Jesus and which, in the garden of Gethsemane, he prayed he might not have to drink.[92] Three times he prayed to his Father: 'Remove this cup from me', the cup which contained the sins of the whole world and God's holy judgment on them. Jesus knew that the only way to bring salvation to a corrupt and violent world was for him to drain that cup to the dregs. He drank it. He drained it. His blood, shed for the world, atones for all the blood shed in the world by the world. Now he holds out the cup containing his own blood, the blood of the new covenant, 'which is poured out for many for the forgiveness of sins' (Mt. 26:28). That cup is the only alternative to the cup of God's judgment. He invites us to drink from the cup of salvation,[93] so that we do not have to drink from the other cup.[94]

There is one other dimension to this fourth woe:

The violence done to Lebanon will overwhelm you;
the destruction of the beasts will terrify you (17).

Lebanon, a distinctively luxuriant region allotted to the people of Israel by the LORD in his original mandate through Moses and Joshua,[95] was particularly renowned for its magnificent cedars. These vast forests had been systematically plundered by the Babylonians. At the same time they had slaughtered large numbers of wild animals – all in the name of conquest and empire-building, or 'progress'.

The cedars of Lebanon, evocatively called 'the trees of the LORD' by the psalmist,[96] were a constant and ready target for rulers committed to grand, if not grandiose, building projects. These splendid palaces and temples became settings for banquets of unparalleled luxury, epitomized by Belshazzar's feast on the night of Babylon's capture by the Medes. The wild animals (boar, bear, lion) became game for the hunter and food for the table.

Such *violence* directed at the created world will return to haunt its

---

[91] Bruce, p. 872.   [92] Mk. 14:32–42.   [93] See Ps. 116:12–13.
[94] See Jn. 6:53–57.   [95] Dt. 1:7; 11:24; Jos. 1:4.   [96] Ps. 104:16.

perpetrators: it will *overwhelm* (17) the Babylonians – a word which has the connotation of covering or smothering its victims. There could be a suggestion of one of those towering cedars crashing down on the heads of those who had presumed to chop them down.[97]

The verdict is clear: 'The ruthless exploitation of nature will ... incur retribution. The earth is God's creation and the cedars of Lebanon were planted by him ... But they have been plundered by the conqueror for his military equipment and for his building projects; the birds that nested in their branches have been evicted from their homes, and the animals that had their habitat there have been slaughtered wholesale.'[98] No wonder the prophet Isaiah exults at the fall of Babylon in these terms:

> The cypresses rejoice at you,
>   the cedars of Lebanon, saying,
> 'Since you were laid low,
>   no hewer comes up against us' (Is. 14:8).

e. The fifth woe (2:18–19)

In what may appear an anticlimax after Habakkuk's previous four indictments, we come to the bottom line in the prophet's declaration of God's certain judgment on Babylon:

> *Woe to him who says to a wooden thing, Awake;*
> *to a dumb stone, Arise!* (19)

The first two woes (6–11) referred to gain by violence; the second two (12–17) to rule by violence. We might have expected another pair of woes. Instead we have this climactic attack on the idolatry of the Babylonians, because (in line with the consistent perspective of the Old Testament) what we worship affects our choices and our lifestyles. The Babylonians had chosen idolatry, and their social and national life bore the inevitable trademarks of their consequent lifestyle. That is still true today. There is only one way to a truly wholesome, clean and healthy society: returning to the revealed will of God.

The idolatry of the Babylonians may have been viewed as the source of all the other atrocities previously mentioned. Because their religious orientation was wrong, their moral standards had to be perverted. As the creators of gods who could not speak, they had to make up their own standards for a way of life.[99]

---

[97] So Robertson, p. 205. [98] Bruce, p. 872. [99] Robertson, p. 207.

The prophet here testifies to the double theme about idols which is frequently mentioned in both Old and New Testaments: an idol is empty, lifeless and useless; but it wields immense power in the lives of those who worship it.[100] Habakkuk emphasizes this strange double perspective in describing something made of wood, stone or metal as *a teacher of lies* (18). It cannot speak or respond to someone speaking to it: but it is an influential teacher, imparting lies rather than truth. 'They are the tools of Satan, the father of lies, and are therefore spiritually highly charged and very dangerous.'[101] Such a perspective is frequently dismissed in a time of *laissez-faire* pluralism. Idol-worship is pagan but harmless, we feel, and it is wrong to go overboard in condemnation.

The prophet's comment corrects such a view: *the workman trusts in his own creation when he makes dumb idols!* (18). It is not mere craftsmanship or the need to make a living that moves people to spend time and skill in carving idols. Idols have a strange ability to 'usurp the place of God in men's lives, claiming a trust that belongs to him alone and giving guidance [*revelation*, 19] that can come from him alone'.[102] This constitutes the complete antithesis of Habakkuk's key truth, that the righteous by faith shall live (2:4). Instead of trusting in God the Creator, a person who turns to idols *trusts in his own creation.*

These three perspectives of Habakkuk – teaching lies, claiming trust, giving revelation – summarize the inherent power of idolatry. In each case the one true God is supplanted, a danger to which the people of Israel had been bluntly alerted in the second commandment.[103] The Babylonians looked to Bel, Marduk and the rest for wisdom, strength and direction. The Babylonian corridors of power were dominated by 'wise men', who were consulted by the king and his governors on every important matter, 'magicians . . . enchanters . . . sorcerers'.[104] When it came to the crunch, as is recorded more than once in the story of Daniel, these experts in idolatry and paganism were useless. The idols of the Babylonians amounted to 'something that not only does not perform its intended function, but in fact leads its worshippers into error by leading them away from the true and self-revealing God'.[105]

When that happens, everything becomes legitimate, particularly the appalling violence depicted in the previous four woes. 'Once violence is first considered "normal", it can soon be seen as necessary and then as legitimate.'[106] If people, especially powerful people, begin to worship something made with human hands or through

---

[100] See Is. 44:9–20; 1 Cor. 8:4–6.   [101] Goldsmith, p. 53.
[102] Armerding, p. 519.   [103] Ex. 20:4–5.   [104] See Dn. 1:20; 2:2, 27; 4:7.
[105] Baker, p. 67.   [106] Os Guinness, *The Dust of Death* (IVP, 1973), p. 159.

human ingenuity, they have launched themselves on the slippery slope of self-adulation, on which it is possible to justify anything. 'We know, from the survival of ancient inscriptions, that Babylonian emperors ascribed their successes to their gods,'[107] but these gods were idols of their own making, and it is a simple matter for sinful human beings to attribute to the gods their elementary desires and ambitions. 'Violence is inextricably rooted in the human psyche and is inevitable as an outburst of the subterranean conflict.'[108] It may be true that 'violence is an involuntary quest for identity',[109] but the Babylonians had, by their violence, let loose their true identity.

Idolatry is essentially the worship of that which we make, rather than of our Maker. And that which we make may be found in our possessions, a home, a career, an ambition, a family, or a multitude of other people or things. We 'worship' them when they become the focal point of our lives, that for which we live. And as the goal and centre of human existence, they are as foolish as any wooden idol or metal image.[110]

Salman Rushdie vividly describes Hindu idols in Bombay:

Once a year, the gods came down to Chowpatty beach to bathe in the filthy sea: fat-bellied idols by the thousand, papier-mâché effigies of the elephant-headed deity Ganesha or Ganpati Bappa, swarming towards the water astride papier-mâché rats – for Indian rats, as we know, carry gods as well as plagues. Some of these tusk 'n' tail duos were small enough to be borne on human shoulders, or cradled in human arms; others were the size of small mansions, and were pulled along on great wooden carts by hundreds of disciples.[111]

As Habakkuk says, we can dress up our idols in glittering decoration (*overlaid with gold and silver*, 19), to the point where they become *objets d'art* or tourist souvenirs. Indeed, many of the most impressive sights in countries like India or Japan are historic shrines in places of immense devotion to 'the gods'. To watch devotees offering gifts and praying to these idols is to witness the same phenomenon as confronted Habakkuk and his contemporaries in the ancient culture of Babylon. We may be nonplussed by their gullibility. We may want to echo Calvin's sentiments: 'Men are

[107] Craigie, 2, p. 99.   [108] Guinness, *op. cit.*, p. 163.
[109] Marshall McLuhan, *War and Peace in the Global Village* (Bantam Books, 1969), p. 97.
[110] Craigie, 2, p. 99.
[111] *The Moor's Last Sigh* (Vintage, 1996), p. 123.

extremely stupid, nay, they are seized with monstrous sottishness, when they ascribe a kind of deity to wood, to a stone, or to metal.'[112] But 'covetousness is idolatry' (Col. 3:5), and we are a covetous generation among whom idolatry has become endemic. With such idolatry has come violence and 'there is a beastliness in the marrow of the century'.[113] Chief Rabbi Jonathan Sacks has said, 'Idolatry always ends in the shedding of innocent blood.'[114]

5. A word to the whole world (2:20)

Verse 20's imperious summons to silence in the presence of the one true God is an apt conclusion to the questioning of the prophet, the agonizing of the people and the chattering of the pagans before their idols. It also marks the only appropriate way to respond to the LORD's pronunciation of five woes on Babylon. There is nothing more to say or to be said. In the light of God's word of judgment, it is right that 'every mouth . . . be stopped' (Rom. 3:19).

In calling for *all the earth* to be hushed in the presence of the LORD, Habakkuk was acknowledging the need for him also to stop searching and striving for an explanation of all his dilemmas. In hearing God's clear answer to his urgent prayers, he realized that there is a 'time to keep silence and a time to speak' (Ec. 3:7). He had spoken, and gone on speaking. To say any more, now that God had clearly answered him, would be to descend into paganism, to continue as if he would be heard for his 'many words' (Mt. 6:7).

Habakkuk was assured that, so far from abandoning the place of sovereign power, the LORD truly was *in his holy temple*. That word 'usually refers to Yahweh's temple in Jerusalem, but from early times the earthly sanctuary was believed to be a replica of the sanctuary in heaven'.[115] Thus the psalmist had declared:

> The LORD is in his holy temple,
>   the LORD's throne is in heaven;
>   his eyes behold, his eyelids test, the children of men
>   (Ps. 11:4).[116]

God was still on the throne and even the mighty Babylonian empire was firmly under his authority.

We live today in a spiritual climate which encourages, rightly and healthily, an honest openness (to God and to one another) about the pains and the pressures of faith, and of believing in a holy and

[112] Calvin, 15, p. 123.
[113] Norman Mailer, *Miami and the Siege of Chicago* (Signet Books, 1968), p. 194.
[114] In a public lecture in London (1996).   [115] Bruce, p. 876.
[116] *Cf.* Mi. 1:2; Zc. 2:17; Zp. 1:7.

compassionate God who remains in control of a darkening world. We therefore find Habakkuk's plain speaking and fervent praying a tonic in discouragement and a stimulant for our own walk with God. But we equally need to cultivate the room to be silent, to stop our talking and even our thinking, in order to be absolutely still and silent in the presence of the LORD.

> There is another kind of silence and that is when we willingly submit to God ... And we submit to God when we bring not our own inventions and imaginations, but suffer ourselves to be taught by his word. We also submit to him, when we murmur not against his power or his judgments, when we humble ourselves under his powerful hand and do not fiercely resist him.[117]

Habakkuk is describing, in brief, 'the total inadequacy of words when faced with the glory of God'[118] – a reality captured eloquently in one of John's apocalyptic visions: 'When the Lamb opened the seventh seal, there was silence in heaven for about half an hour' (Rev. 8:1). This was the seventh and final seal of the scroll which, in describing the sovereign authority of Jesus, underlines his control over the destinies of people and nations. Habakkuk's call for universal silence foreshadowed that ultimate thirty-minute silence. Practising the presence of God today will necessarily involve us in similar silence. To hear God speak, we must ourselves stop speaking – an extraordinarily difficult task in a noisy, hurrying, verbose and violent world.

[117] Calvin, 15, p. 132.   [118] Goldsmith, p. 54.

Habakkuk 3:1–19
3. Habakkuk's prayer

1. Habakkuk's request (3:1–2)

The introduction, content, mood and style of chapter 3 all indicate an immense sea-change in Habakkuk's approach to God and to the situation in which he finds himself. These words are expressed, not as an oracle (1:1), but as a *prayer*. The prophet has been silenced by the response of God to his agony of heart and mind. His response, having been hushed, is to turn back to God in prayer.

This response has every appearance of having later become enshrined in the liturgical worship of the people of God; notice the three occurrences of *Selah* (3, 9, 13), the ascription *according to Shigionoth* (1) and the directions *To the choirmaster* at the end (19). As such, it is possible that this chapter came to be used apart from the previous two as a suitable expression of public worship in times of national emergency or disaster. It was 'probably used on many occasions in temple worship during the autumn festival'.[1]

The prophet's prayer, strictly speaking, is confined to the striking words recorded in verse 2. But the whole chapter is a meditative comment on the prayer and gives vivid expression to Habakkuk's thoughts and feelings. During its course he moves from an awed plea for God to act now, through vivid recall of God's dramatic intervention in the past, to a strong assertion of confidence and celebration in God whatever the future holds. 'This prayer indicates that the prophet now has no further case to make. He has pleaded his cause, he has concluded his dialogue with the Almighty. Now he leads God's people to an acceptance of the just and merciful orderings which the Lord has revealed to him.'[2]

The prayer (2) is in two parts. The first two sentences express the prophet's conviction about God's work in the world. The rest of the verse is a threefold request for that work to be renewed and once

---

[1] R. L. Smith, p. 115.   [2] Robertson, pp. 214–215.

again revealed *in the midst of the years.* This striking phrase, rather dully translated 'in our day . . . in our time' in the NIV, probably has an eschatological thrust, denoting the interval between the present time and the end (2:3) appointed by God. This interval appears to Habakkuk 'as a long series of years',[3] characterized by the apparent absence of God.

We can probably identify with this notion of 'the drab flatness of time that seems never to be punctuated by the splendid acts of God . . . Faith is replaced by nostalgia, hope by despair.'[4] Habakkuk has reached a place where he knows that these 'years of barren hopelessness' can be transformed by God's fresh intervention in their affairs. Our walk with the Lord can sometimes seem to be merely a trudge through the featureless lowlands of routine and duty. There is little or no expectancy of anything new or different from the hand of God. The possibility of such an intervention is remote for us.

Habakkuk, however, is committed to this possibility because he has taken time to absorb reports of God's activity in time past. This has brought him to a new place of reverence in the presence of God: *thy work, O LORD, do I fear* (2). At the beginning of God's dialogue with Habakkuk, the prophet had been told to open his eyes to see what God was doing among the nations: 'I am doing a work in your days that you would not believe if told' (1:5). He now registers his awe at what he has seen, which he will soon indicate to be of a piece with God's activity in the world down the centuries of his dealings with the people of Israel.

If, then, God has worked in the past, not just once but on several occasions, there was good reason to trust that he would work again – a conviction expressed in similar vein by the psalmists.[5] So he prays: *'Renew* your work, LORD; do it again, make it come alive.' God may, indeed, never repeat himself, but he can be expected to do in a new way what he is in the habit of doing – bringing life. When today we read of God's work in previous days or in other places, the temptation is to want him to repeat it for us and with us, when, in fact, he is committed to doing something altogether new, something which breathes new life in the midst of our years.

If we are going to recognize and rejoice in God's work in and around us today, we, like Habakkuk, need to have our eyes opened to see him at work in new ways: *make it known.* The prayer is for divine revelation, not just for himself and for the people of God, but for everyone. Unless the LORD does open blind eyes,[6] his work remains unseen, unrecognized and unappreciated; hence the fundamental importance of Habakkuk's double plea: 'Renew your work; reveal your work.' Both are necessary.

[3] Keil, p. 95.   [4] Craigie, 2, p. 103.   [5] See Pss. 44; 89.   [6] See 2 Cor. 4:3–6.

Habakkuk's prayer is not yet finished. His final plea is based on the hard realities of what God has done in past years and what he has made plain to the prophet in recent days: *in wrath remember mercy* (2). Of one fact Habakkuk could now have no doubts: that with God there is holy, righteous anger. However long he bides his time, however quiet and distant he appears to have become, however much violence and greed he seems to bypass or overlook, there is woe and wrath for the unrighteous: 'the arrogant man shall not abide' (2:5). Habakkuk has come to see afresh that God's righteous anger is directed at all human pride, Israelite as well as Babylonian.

He knows, therefore, that in such a situation he cannot ask God to renew his work and to reveal it for all to see, unless he pleads for God to remember mercy in the midst of his wrath. The Hebrew word used for wrath here (*rōgez*) is never used elsewhere of the wrath of God. The verbal form is used in 3:16 of Habakkuk's body trembling. So we might say that the emphasis is on God feeling wrath emotionally, much as the word translated 'compassion' stresses the way God feels love emotionally.

Habakkuk knows that God is a God of wrath and of mercy. He knows that the behaviour of his contemporaries deserves God's wrath; but he has the faith to pray that mercy will permeate and temper wrath.

Habakkuk was, of course, on solid theological ground in praying like this. 'The love of God is so strong that, even when he is flagrantly ignored, deserted or rejected, he is drawn, as a husband to his wife or a mother to her child, to love in spite of the actions of the other. The wrongs are real, but so too are the compassion and the desire to forgive, if the "condition" for restoration – a renewed desire to acknowledge God – is present to allow the floods of his mercy to be unleashed.'[7] This revelation of God's eternal nature has been an article of faith from the time of Moses.[8]

The Hebrew word translated *mercy* is a form of the one used for 'womb', and 'signifies a warm love of great depth'.[9] Its counterpart in the Greek of the New Testament is also linked with the inner depths of a person's being ('bowels'), and is consistently used to describe the way in which Jesus was 'moved with compassion' in the face of all kinds of human condition – a characteristic to which the gospel writers bear witness and to which several individuals in desperate need made impassioned appeal: 'Have mercy on me . . .'[10] We, like Habakkuk, have a firm basis on which to appeal to God, in his undoubted wrath, to remember mercy.

---

[7] Baker, pp. 69–70, who cites Ho. 11:8–11.   [8] See Ex. 32:10–12.
[9] Patterson (WEC), p. 230.   [10] *E.g.* Mt. 9:27; 15:22; 17:15; 20:30–31.

2. Habakkuk's experience (3:3–15)

As Habakkuk meditates on the activity of God, his focus is inevitably fixed on the exodus, which is consistently the major theme celebrated in Israelite worship. He ponders those remarkable events on a wide canvas, from the four hundred years of slavery in Egypt, culminating in the people's deliverance from Pharaoh's control, on through the wilderness wanderings, the events around Mount Sinai, the handover from Moses to Joshua, right up to their entry into the promised land. As he reflects on these things in prayer, he encounters God at depth.

In his mind's eye Habakkuk sees the entire saga as God on the march, coming from the south in majestic grandeur. As the prophet watches this movement, he gradually changes his own attitude from that of an awed spectator to that of a personal questioner. He describes the coming of God (3–7). He questions the purpose of God's coming (9–15). What he concludes about the significance of God's coming in former times he takes as relevant for his own generation (16–19), however long it might be before things become plain.

There is, once again, an eschatological motif in the prophet's words. God has come to the aid of his people in the past; God certainly will come again to their rescue; and at the end of time God will come once and for all to vindicate those who belong to him and to exercise judgment on those opposed to him. This perspective is plain, for example, in the words, *His glory covered the heavens, and the earth was full of his praise* (3), an echo of the eschatological vision earlier: 'The earth will be filled with the knowledge of the glory of the LORD, as the waters cover the sea' (2:14).

This perspective is similar to the one described in the words of Jesus about his own second coming at the close of the age: 'all the tribes of the earth . . . will see the Son of man coming on the clouds of heaven with power and great glory' (Mt. 24:30). Then 'the vision of Habakkuk shall receive its finalized fulfilment'.[11]

Habakkuk's reinvigoration has occurred precisely because he is in communication with a God who is on the move. 'The stunning revelation about this God is that he actually "comes".'[12] The emphasis is on the coming of God himself as the source of hope for the LORD's people. We are accustomed to the twin truths of God's transcendental otherness and God's incarnational presence among and within us. But Habakkuk describes God coming to us, actually on the move on our behalf from point A to point B, *for the salvation of thy people, for the salvation of thy anointed* (13).

[11] Robertson, p. 224.　　[12] *Ibid.*, p. 222.

The prophet describes for us what he sees as God goes forth, bestrides the earth and tramples the sea (12, 13, 15). He sees God leaving his place in Sinai to come to Egypt to deliver his people from oppression.[13] Israelites normally spoke of God coming to them either from the temple, his distinctive dwelling-place on earth, or from his dwelling-place in heaven. Here he comes from *Teman* and *Mount Paran* (3), locations in Edom directly associated with the giving of the law at Mount Sinai and with the acts of God on behalf of his people in the days of Moses.[14]

However awesome such comings have consistently been, there is a divine restraint about them: *there he veiled his power* (4). The sheer incandescence of the light which shone as God presenced himself in the midst of his people had to be veiled, if it was not going to burn up everyone and everything like some former-day nuclear or chemical explosion. 'God is light' (1 Jn. 1:5) and 'dwells in unapproachable light' (1 Tim. 6:16). If, then, he decides to approach sinful human beings in salvation and blessing, he must veil the fullness of his majesty.

But even when God's power is veiled, the impact of his coming is terrifying: *Before him went pestilence, and plague followed close behind* (5). When God does come, there is necessarily a process of judgment at work. The Israelites had experienced this at first hand in the events before and after the exodus, both in the plagues which came on the Egyptians[15] and in the afflictions which hit them as a result of their own rebelliousness against God in the wilderness.[16]

As God visited the earth in succeeding generations and centuries, he consistently veiled his power (supremely in the coming of Jesus). But he gives occasional glimpses of what remains hidden, notably the reality of his purity and holiness. Enough has been made known for us to conclude, with the writer of the letter to the Hebrews, that 'It is a fearful thing to fall into the hands of the living God' (Heb. 10:31), because 'Our God is a consuming fire' (Heb. 12:29).

Habakkuk watches in his prayer of meditation, as God comes to a halt:

> *He stood and measured the earth;*
> *he looked and shook the nations* (6).

God pauses in his onward march and takes stock: 'Now the Almighty has arrived. Like a great colossus towering over the mountain peaks, the Lord God measures the earth, claiming the right of domain inherent in himself as Creator. With a glance of his

---

[13] See Ex. 3:7–8.   [14] See Dt. 32:2–4.   [15] Ex. 7:1 – 12:32.
[16] See Ex. 16:20; Nu. 11:31–34; 12:1–16; 14:36–38; 16:1–50; 25:1–18.

eye, he manifests his sovereignty in apportioning territories . . . His glance startles the nations. As a grasshopper springs suddenly with his disproportioned legs, so entire nations leap with fright when they suddenly become aware that the Lord has come.'[17]

There is a play on the word for *eternal* (6), which is used first of the mountains and hills, consistently seen as the most ancient and permanent aspects of the creation, and then of God's ways which *were of old*, or eternal – far more primeval, far more enduring than the mountains and the hills. When God arrives on the scene and makes his presence felt, not only people but mountains shake, scattered 'as though smashed by a giant sledgehammer . . . The eternal hills grovel in the dust, flattened before the Lord's majesty.'[18] Habakkuk's description is not far removed from modern accounts of earthquakes, floods, hurricanes and other so-called 'natural' disasters.

Habakkuk then sees two particular Bedouin (*tents . . . curtains*) opponents of Israel – *Cushan* and *Midian* (7) – overwhelmed with panic. Cushan was the first oppressor to contest Israel's occupation of the promised land. The Midianites were a regular thorn in her side. But Cushan had been repulsed in the time of the Judges by Othniel,[19] and Midian by Gideon.[20] As the LORD had brought deliverance in times of internal disorder and corruption in Israel through those two champions, so Habakkuk anticipates victory in his own day, as God shakes the nations.

As God stands astride everything he surveys, the prophet then begins to speak to him about his actions on behalf of his people:

> *Was thy wrath against the rivers, O LORD?*
> *Was thy anger against the rivers,*
> *or thy indignation against the sea . . .?* (8)

Almost as soon as he has posed the question, the prophet realizes that it is a rhetorical question: a purely ecological or geological explanation is plainly inadequate. To talk of God venting his anger on nature is as inappropriate as ascribing divine attributes and powers to nature, as did the people who inhabited the land of Canaan before the Israelites appeared on the scene.

'These powers are variously allotted among members of the Canaanite pantheon, but in the Hebrew scriptures they are all controlled by the one living and true God. Among the Canaanite divinities Asherah walks on the sea and Baal rides on the clouds, but the God of Israel exercises these and other prerogatives himself.'[21]

[17] Robertson, p. 227   [18] *Ibid.*   [19] Jdg. 3:7–11.   [20] Jdg. 6:1 – 8:28.
[21] Bruce, p. 882.

When we come to appreciate the gulf between Canaanite religion and Israelite worship in such matters, we can understand the unacceptability of much modern talk about 'Mother Nature' and the like.

It is noticeable that Habakkuk switches from the general word for God (Eloah, 3) to the covenant name *the* LORD (Yahweh, 8), when he begins to address this majestic figure striding through history and creation, demonstrating (in however veiled a fashion) his power over nations and nature. The prophet recognizes this holy, eternal, glorious Sovereign as the God of Abraham, Isaac and Jacob, the God of their fathers, the God of Moses and Joshua.

As Habakkuk speaks to the LORD, he returns to his original theme of wrath. The passage (8–15) is redolent of divine displeasure. Four words are used: *wrath ... anger ... indignation* (8) and *fury* (12). The imagery is of God as a warrior, riding out against his foes in order to *crush the head of the wicked* (13), because they dared to *devour the poor* (14). Clearly, this prayerful reminiscence of the way God had dramatically and decisively come to the rescue of his people in the past acts as a powerful reminder to Habakkuk in his present crisis.

Again, the imagery evokes the events around the exodus, as in the vivid description of God's *horses* and *chariot* (8) attacking the (Red) *sea* on leaving Egypt, and the *rivers* (such as the Jordan) on entering the promised land. *Thy chariot of victory* is an oblique reference to God's consuming purpose in all this activity; that is, the 'salvation' (*yēša'*) of his people. As the prophet continues to speak to the LORD, he uses terminology which recalls the work of God in creating the world from chaos. He also seems deliberately to contradict pagan versions of the origins and nature of the universe (9b–11).

Earth and sea, sun and moon all submit, stunned into silence and stillness, to the LORD's power as he uses all the weapons in his arsenal: chariot and horses, bow and arrows, spear and sword. *The deep* with its *raging waters* (10), historically and eschatologically the symbol of everything hostile to God (including Rahab,[22] the monster of chaos, and Leviathan,[23] her dragon associate), is seen holding up its hand to acknowledge defeat (*it lifted its hands on high*). There could be a specific reference, in mentioning the sun and moon standing still (11), to the events which enabled Joshua to complete his victory over the Amorites.[24]

As the prophet's meditation continues, particularly as he talks to God about his mighty acts in former times, he seems to see with increasing clarity the message of history. At the beginning of the book the prophet seemed like James Joyce's character Stephen in *Ulysses*, who declares, 'History is a nightmare from which I am

---

[22] Is. 51:9. [23] Is. 27:11. [24] Jos. 10:12–14.

trying to awake.' As this prayer unfolds, we see that 'each of the themes Habakkuk chooses ... comes from decisive chapters in the history of salvation'.[25] History has become a series of divine actions, the purpose of which cannot be doubted.

This purpose is now unequivocally stated (13–14): the *salvation* of God's people and the destruction of God's enemies. God could have stayed put, letting it all happen and doing nothing about it. That had been Habakkuk's original fear and the substance of his urgent cry to God. Now he knew better. As God had dealt with a succession of enemies, from Pharaoh onwards, so he would deal with the Babylonians under Nebuchadnezzar.

The personal reference to *me* (14) indicates that Habakkuk feels that he is the target of *the wicked* (13), *who came like a whirlwind to scatter me, rejoicing as if to devour the poor in secret* (14). 'He senses that he too must bear the brunt of the enemy's ferocity. Perhaps as the messenger of righteousness and judgment, he sees himself as the special object of their wrath, in accord with the experience of every generation of prophets. As the front man in the confrontation of truth and error, he knows that he cannot be exempt from their fury.'[26]

In describing the destruction of *the wicked*, Habakkuk not only stresses the utter finality of their demise (13), but also suggests that it is in some way self-inflicted. The Hebrew reads, 'Thou didst pierce with *his* shafts the head of his warriors' (14) – they destroy themselves with their own weapons. This had specifically happened at one point in the past, when Jehoshaphat was king in Jerusalem. The Moabites and the Ammonites, as well as the inhabitants of Mount Seir, attacked the city in overwhelming numbers. Jehoshaphat's response was to lead his people in praise and worship: 'And when they began to sing and praise, the LORD set an ambush against the men of Ammon, Moab and Mount Seir, who had come against Judah, and they were routed. For the men of Ammon and Moab rose against the inhabitants of Mount Seir, destroying them utterly, and when they had made an end of the inhabitants of Seir, they all helped to destroy one another' (2 Ch. 20:20–23).[27]

Habakkuk draws his meditation on the mighty acts of God to a close with another picturesque description of his triumphant march over the surging waters of the mighty sea (15) – a biblical refrain first sounded at the creation of the world and recurrent through the salvation history of God's people. It reaches its climax towards the end of the book of Revelation, when the seer writes of God's final triumph in the emergence of 'a new heaven and a new earth; for the

[25] Kaiser, p. 187.   [26] Robertson, p. 241.
[27] *Cf.* Jdg. 7:22; 1 Sa. 14:20; Is. 49:26.

first heaven and the first earth had passed away, and the sea was no more' (Rev. 21:1).

So the prophet's time of prayerful meditation is concluded. He has been transported in his mind and spirit to range over a variety of 'comings' by God in times past. The whole passage is 'a collage, a collecting of many images to convey an expression both of past experience and of future expectation'.[28] Habakkuk's psalm is a blend of Moses' song,[29] Deborah's song[30] and David's song.[31] The prophet has, therefore, been drawing on the resources of a rich heritage in order to reorientate himself and his people around the historic facts of God's work on their behalf down the centuries. But he does not merely recollect the past. He re-lives it and, in a deliberate act of faith, sees God doing in the prophet's own day what God alone can do.

As we watch the strengthening of Habakkuk's faith in the face of national apostasy and the imminence of Babylonian captivity, it is good to remind ourselves of the surpassing greatness of God in the context of the Nebuchadnezzars of the world. Louis XIV of France (known as Le Roi Soleil or the Sun King), who built the palace of Versailles for himself and had in his court, among others, Racine and Molière, wanted to be remembered as the greatest French king ever. So he required that, at his funeral in Notre-Dame Cathedral in Paris, all would be darkened except the one candle on his casket at the front. But when Jean-Baptiste Massillon, said to have been the only court preacher to have made Louis XIV dissatisfied with himself,[32] got up to give the funeral oration, he walked over to the casket and snuffed out the light. With that he commenced his message with the words, 'Only God is great. Only God is great.'

3. Habakkuk's transformation (3:16–19)

Habakkuk has brought his request to God in prayer. In placing it before God, he has been led into a profound experience of God's majesty, during which he has been brought face to face with God in his awesome, though necessarily hidden, power over nature and over nations. He now describes the impact of this prayer encounter with the living God. He has been profoundly challenged and, indeed, changed by this time in the place of prayer. The Habakkuk who speaks in these four verses is a very different person from the Habakkuk to whom we were introduced at the beginning of the book.

[28] Robertson, p. 219.   [29] Ex. 15:1–21.   [30] Jdg. 5:1–31.
[31] 2 Sa. 22:1–51 (Ps. 18:2–50). *Cf.* Pss. 77:11–20; 97:1–5; 114:1–8.
[32] See C. G. Thorne Jr, in *New International Dictionary of the Christian Church* (Zondervan, 1974), p. 641.

'Though Habakkuk began this encounter in dialogue and rational argument, the real turning-point in his relationship with God was the result of a vision of the living God.' There is a 'false form of piety which refuses to question God ... to exercise the mind in the attempt to solve such questions'. There is a time to stress 'the significance of the encounter with God that goes beyond the rational exercise of the mind ... Religious experience is not an alternative to rational enquiry, but it may supplement it and contribute a degree of faith in God beyond that which the mind can achieve in its own right.'[33]

Such deeper faith Habakkuk manifestly articulates in these closing verses. He begins by describing the sheer physical impact of his exposure in prayer to the majesty of God. Then he makes two firm statements of resolve: *I will quietly wait* (16) and *I will rejoice* (18). In these two statements he shows that, as a result of his profound experience of God in prayer, he has made God's word to him (2:4) his own. He now not only knows the truth about the priority of living by faith in God; he has embraced the truth in his own life, and is committed to practising it day by day, whatever may happen.

a. Habakkuk's physical turmoil (2:16a)

> *I hear, and my body trembles;*
> *my lips quiver at the sound;*
> *rottenness enters into my bones,*
> *my steps totter beneath me.*

These vivid phrases describe the impact of God's presence and power in the prophet's body in the course of, and as a result of, his time spent in prayer. Whatever the specific nature of this encounter – however much of it was subjective and the fruit of a highly imaginative response to God's word, as distinct from direct visitation by the living God revealing himself – Habakkuk was obviously left in a state of 'agitation, exhaustion and near-collapse ... The prophet's bones turn to water and he is left without strength.'[34]

The normally loquacious and articulate prophet[35] is left speechless. He trembles from head to toe – *lips, bones*, legs. The word translated *body* ('belly,' AV; 'inward parts', NASB) refers to a person's inner recesses where the deepest desires reside. Three verbs eloquently describe Habakkuk's experience: *trembles, quiver, totter.* He has lost control of his physical faculties. The reason he gives is what he has heard in this encounter with the LORD: *my lips quiver at the sound*. This indicates that, at the heart of his experience, he has

---

[33] Craigie, 2, p. 104.   [34] Bruce, p. 893.   [35] Hab. 1:2; 2:1; 3:2.

been overwhelmed with what God has had to say to him about what he calls *the day of trouble* (16).

God's word has struck deep into Habakkuk's inner being. That is why he is so shaken. 'He was not exempted from the turmoil that pervades and characterizes the chapter.'[36] God has spoken not merely into his mind, but into his 'inward parts'. He cannot stand outside this experience and rationalize its content. He cannot be purely cerebral and communicate God's word to him and to his people in a dispassionate manner. What he describes here is a vivid, personal example of what we read elsewhere in Scripture; for instance: 'the word of God is living and active, sharper than any two-edged sword, piercing to the division of soul and spirit, of joints and marrow, and discerning the thoughts and intentions of the heart' (Heb. 4:12).

Habakkuk is shaken, not least, by the sheer precision of God's word about *people who invade us* (16). He has been overwhelmed by the vicious cruelty of the Babylonians and by the horrors of invasion and imminent defeat. But now he is awestruck by the certainty of their demise. However much he has been longing for their come-uppance, he is left physically shaken by the prospect of their punishment by God. Perhaps this is partly indicated by the striking phrase *rottenness enters into my bones* (16), as though a destructive cancer takes hold of his very bones as a physical expression of God's judgment at work. 'Habakkuk's distraught body shudders to consider that he must live with the constant anticipation of God's coming judgment.'[37]

We recall at this point that all this was in response to Habakkuk's specific request to God to renew his work (3:2). Like us, the prophet did not fully appreciate what he was asking. God, who customarily answers prayer in a way far beyond our thoughts or dreams,[38] came to meet Habakkuk in the place of prayer. There he spoke with him and revealed himself to him, not simply renewing his work, but causing it to be powerfully impressed on the prophet's whole body and being. In addition, God was revealing to Habakkuk what only the prophet would know (at least at that stage) about the measure of suffering still awaiting his people at the hands of the Babylonians. 'To see such things that were veiled to his contemporaries was to experience distress.'[39]

When such factors and circumstances combine, we can expect similar physical manifestations today: deep agony of spirit for the state of God's people and of the nation, fervent intercession for the intervention of God in saving power, increasing awareness of the

---

[36] Armerding, p. 532. [37] Robertson, p. 244. [38] See Eph. 3:20.
[39] Armerding, p. 533.

inevitability of judgment and of the human suffering which accompanies it, and intense personal engagement with God's word for the present situation. All these experiences in the place of prayer can bring about an encounter with God which will shake people from head to toe, and lay them out flat on the floor, as Habakkuk suggests in saying *my steps totter beneath me*.

It happened to other individuals on similar occasions, sometimes with similar results, but sometimes with different indications. Daniel, for example, had physical reactions to powerful visions about future events in the time of Belshazzar, king of Babylon: 'As for me, Daniel, my thoughts greatly alarmed me, and my colour changed', 'And I, Daniel, was overcome and lay sick for some days; then I rose and went about the king's business: but I was appalled by the vision and did not understand it' (Dn. 7:28; 8:27).[40]

It is to be expected that an encounter between a mere mortal and the living God should make an electrifying impact on the human soul and body. Habakkuk had ventured, not only to question God insistently about his behaviour and character, but to request definite evidence of his power and authority. He asked for revival and he got it, though not in the way he had anticipated. He did not know what he was asking and he did not know what was happening to him when, in answer to his prayer, God came to him and made himself known to him.

This provides an important perspective on many of the phenomena witnessed in recent years, such as the 'Toronto blessing'. Western Christians are usually unaccustomed to physical manifestations accompanying divine activity, and consequently find them rather startling. People in other cultures witness such phenomena more regularly. For them they are 'no big deal'; spiritual discernment is normal, and sifting the true from the false is expected. Both out-and-out rejection and blanket endorsement are equally unacceptable.

b. Habakkuk's personal response (2:16b–18)

When David Hope, then Bishop of London, was asked to comment on physical manifestations taking place in times of worship in London churches, he said: 'I'm not that concerned with what happens to people when they fall down. I'm more interested in what happens to them when they stand up.'[41] That fits the story of Habakkuk. He has been shattered by his experience of the presence,

---

[40] For similarly physical reactions to the presence and message of God, see *e.g.* Ezk. 21:7 and Rev. 1:17. Robertson refers to the experience of Jesus in the garden of Gethsemane (Lk. 22:44).
[41] In an informal conversation with the author.

power and message of God. Physically he has been shaken to the core of his being. But all that impact could have been dissipated, either by reverting to his driven interrogation of the Almighty's ways and works, or by resigning himself to the inevitable misery which still lay in store for the people and forgetting the clear promises of hope and restoration.

Habakkuk responds with two firm resolutions which turn him into a living embodiment of the vision given earlier by God, 'the righteous shall live by his faith' (2:4).

His first response is: *I will quietly wait* (16). His very first words to God at the outset were: 'O LORD, how long?' (1:2). When God had spelt out the vision for the end, the prophet had been urged, 'If it seem slow, wait for it' (2:3). Now we see him, after all his agonizing and praying, transformed from an impatient prophet into a calm and expectant servant of God. God has spoken his word into his condition and circumstances. The prophet has listened, absorbed, accepted and committed himself to God's word. He is sure that it will come to pass, that it is true and trustworthy. He can base his life on it. That is what it means to allow God's word to become 'a lamp to my feet and a light to my path' (Ps. 119:105). *I will quietly wait.*

The issue for Habakkuk had been the apparently unimpeded march of violence in the land – violence perpetrated by his own people on one another, particularly by the strong and powerful on the poor and the weak; and violence at the hands of the Babylonian armies (*people who invade us*) to be launched as vehicles of God's judgment on his own people. The prophet could now see and accept the truth that such developments lay entirely within the sovereign wisdom and justice of Almighty God. *Trouble*, or 'distress', was part of the divine purpose, but had a definite terminus in *the day*.[42] For the invading Babylonians that *day of trouble* was to come at the hands of Darius, king of the Medes, in 539 BC. Habakkuk did not know the year, the day or the hour, although to the prophet Jeremiah the length of the exile in Babylon was clearly spelt out: seventy years.[43]

It requires strength to wait quietly for something for which we have God's promise but no date. This inner quietness is 'a rest of the spirit in full trust in the redeeming God'.[44] It is different from the tranquillity which, given certain outward circumstances, many people can demonstrate, but which sometimes masks an inner turmoil. This is a rest which refuses to be torn or lured away from a steady reliance on God and his word: 'In returning and rest you shall

---

[42] See comments on this theme in the book of Joel for a fuller discussion. Here the phrase is less likely to have major eschatological significance.

[43] Je. 25:11–12; 29:10.   [44] Patterson (WEC), p. 259.

be saved; in quietness and in trust shall be your strength' (Is. 30:15).[45]

Such is the first response Habakkuk makes to his experience of having been ushered into the presence of God.

Habakkuk's second response is: *I will rejoice* (17–19). Quiet patience is the proper atmosphere for true joy. Without inner tranquillity, rejoicing is manufactured, superficial and strident. It manifestly is not the joy of the LORD, which becomes our strength.[46] It is a rather noisy, even raucous, exuberance which grates and evaporates. Habakkuk's magnificent words come from an entirely different world.

Because congregational involvement was, from an early stage, a significant part of the use made of Habakkuk's words in this section, it is doubly important to appreciate the prophet's response. First of all, he faces the facts – and they are uncompromisingly unpleasant:

> *Though the fig tree do not blossom,*
> *nor fruit be on the vines,*
> *the produce of the olive fail*
> *and the fields yield no food,*
> *the flock be cut off from the fold*
> *and there be no herd in the stall . . .* (17).

One has to live in an agrarian world to begin to appreciate this appalling scenario. It describes disaster on a total scale, the impact of which is not grasped by many modern commentators. 'The failure of all these resources had serious economic and spiritual ramifications,'[47] says one. Such understatement does not do justice to the facts staring Habakkuk in the face: the ravages of war, the horrors of invasion, the devastation of nature's resources, the removal of all basic necessities.

The devastation is akin to that described by Joel[48] in the wake of invasion by a vast plague of locusts. Everything has been destroyed. There is no grain, oil or wine. There is no meat or wool. There is no food of any kind – fruit, vegetables, cereals, milk, meat. It is not simply a devastated economy. It is the end of everything that can keep body and soul together. There is nothing, absolutely nothing – and an invading army takes possession of the land, pillaging and raping with indiscriminate violence. It is Bosnia, Vietnam and Rwanda rolled into one. 'How could life be sustained at all in such conditions?'[49] Nothing to eat, nothing to drink, nothing to wear. Not just poverty, but the enemy stalking the land. Nowhere to hide.

---

[45] *Cf.* Mi. 7:7.   [46] See Ne. 8:10.   [47] Patterson (WEC), p. 260.
[48] Joel 1:6–12.   [49] Bruce, p. 893.

Those were the facts.

Having faced the facts, Habakkuk declares his decision:

> yet I will rejoice in the LORD,
> I will joy in the God of my salvation (18).

It is one thing to thank and praise God for all the good things in our lives, to rejoice in our blessings. It is quite another to rejoice in the midst of nothing, when all these blessings have been summarily and completely removed. The prophet has learned to rejoice, not in any particular quantity or quality of blessings, but in God himself. God never changes. If we learn – if we are liberated – to find our joy in the LORD, regardless of any good things we may or may not receive at his hand, then he remains a continuous source and cause of rejoicing.

This is because God is the Lord, the Creator of the universe and the covenant-keeping God, who can be known and appreciated for his unchanging characteristics of compassion and holiness. He never changes in these qualities. He remains a cause for great joy because he is who he is. Such rejoicing, of course, can never be an academic exercise. It comes as the fruit of a personal relationship in which we 'taste and see that the LORD is good' (Ps. 34:8), that true blessedness consists, not in receiving good things from his hand, but in a personal relationship of trust between an individual and his or her God: *I will joy in the God of my salvation*. He is *my* Saviour. He has saved me from the repercussions of my sin and disobedience. I belong to him and he belongs to me. We belong together. Nothing can tear us apart or keep us apart. His salvation is not simply available to all, but is precious to me. Whether, in material terms, I have much or little, everything or nothing, he is my God and I am his child. In that I will rejoice.

Habakkuk has made his decision in the light of both the facts and the promises of God. So he repeats himself for emphasis: *I will rejoice . . . I will joy*. If there is a subtle difference (which is, to say the least, doubtful), 'the former lays stress on the audible singing of God's praises, whereas the latter implies physical movement'.[50] Both ingredients are an appropriate expression of joy in the LORD, and the distinction (which seems peculiarly western) cannot be properly warranted. Habakkuk rejoices in the LORD in ways appropriate and natural for an Israelite released from bondage to fear, and from the need to understand and explain the workings of God.

Earlier in his conversation with God about his activity of old, he had affirmed God's work 'for the salvation of [his] people' (14). If

---

[50] Patterson (WEC), p. 261.

that had been a credal statement more than an act of personal commitment, he is ready now to call this God *the God of my salvation*. What was true for the people as a whole he now registered as personally true for himself in the midst of the most horrendous circumstances. It had been neither simple nor straightforward for Habakkuk to reach the point where he could make such an affirmation in his own right. But now, having faced the facts in the light of his personal experience of God in the place of prayer, he was prepared to declare his decision and to declare it twice: *I will rejoice in the LORD, I will joy in the God of my salvation.*

I recall a particularly moving experience at a clergy retreat in Cape Town in the 1970s, a silent retreat over four days, attended by about sixty people and led by the Archbishop, Bill Burnett. At the closing service of Holy Communion, he asked a retired bishop to read the appointed gospel passage for the day, which happened to be the song of old Simeon, uttered when Jesus was brought as a baby to the temple.[51] The words 'mine eyes have seen thy salvation' were read with particular emphasis – and then the bishop did a most uncharacteristic thing (for him, for all of us, and for the setting). Having finished the reading, he added, 'I would just like to say that this week, for the first time in my life, "mine eyes have seen thy salvation".' He then sat down.

The Saviour of the world wants to be recognized, known and loved as each individual's personal Saviour.

Habakkuk now proceeds naturally to the conclusion, where he shares the secret of his position: *GOD, the Lord, is my strength* (19). The prophet is ready to let anyone know the reason for his hopefulness in a bleak situation. It is not due to any innate, inherited or inwardly developed strength of his own. There is no technique to master, no guru to consult, no formula to adopt: *GOD, the Lord, is my strength*, no more, no less. He is clear that it is Yahweh, the covenant-making and covenant-keeping God of Israel, who is personally the one who provides all the strength he needs.

The prophet seems to be echoing the words of David when, according to the preface of Psalm 18, he 'addressed the words of this song to the LORD on the day when the LORD delivered him from the hand of all his enemies, and from the hand of Saul'. On that occasion David had written,

> For who is God, but the LORD?
> And who is a rock, except our God? –
> the God who girded me with strength,
> and made my way safe.

[51] Lk. 2:21–35

> He made my feet like hinds' feet,
> and set me secure on the heights (Ps. 18:31–33).

In echoing David, Habakkuk seems to be taking the shepherd king's words and giving them deeper meaning. David had composed the psalm at a time of deliverance and victory. Habakkuk uses the words to express a faith which trusts God and rejoices in him while it is still very dark. Moreover, whereas David testified to God as the One who 'girded' him with strength, like an outer layer of protection, Habakkuk declares that *GOD, the Lord, is my strength*, an inner reservoir of boundless resources.[52]

Both Habakkuk and David bear witness to the ability to move nimbly like a deer on dangerous terrain. They are given the strength, not just to stand firm and to cope in the face of immense adversity, but to rise up above it and to make swift progress – to climb, not simply to coast. Habakkuk has discovered the secret of turning the hills and mountains into opportunities to discover more of God's strength in his inner being. When he sees a climb ahead, he revels in its potential, rather than being discouraged by its problems. He is expressing the truth which Paul classically stated: 'when I am weak, then I am strong' (2 Cor. 12:10); 'I can do all things in him who strengthens me' (Phil. 4:13).

God, by his own indwelling Spirit, provides us with the strength to do what would otherwise be impossible. Many of us suffer from spiritual vertigo: faced with the prospect, let alone the presence, of high places – of scaling the spiritual heights – we grow queasy. We do all we can to avoid ending up in such threatening situations. We try to keep within what we reckon to be our areas of spiritual competence. In our own resources we have neither the head nor the feet for high places. But *he makes me tread upon my high places* – places which God has prepared for us (and us for them), places which seem dangerous and beyond our reach. Habakkuk knew that he had been taken into such a place, and that several more such high places lay ahead of him. He was prepared to be taken there and to be equipped by God to walk there.

When the Scriptures talk of *high places*, they consistently refer to places under the control of forces hostile to the LORD (over forty times in the Old Testament). High places were often places of pagan worship.[53] This worship was often assimilated into, or even taken over by, Israel's leadership.[54] King after king failed to root out these

---

[52] On other occasions and in other psalms David makes the same declaration as Habakkuk: *e.g.* Pss. 28:7; 59:9, 17. See also David's statement in Ps. 18:1.

[53] See Nu. 33:50–52.

[54] *E.g.* Jeroboam (1 Ki. 12:31–32), Rehoboam (1 Ki. 14:23), Ahaz (2 Ki. 16:4), Manasseh (2 Ki. 21:3).

places of false worship. Even kings given the accolade of doing what was right in the sight of the LORD failed to deal with these high places.[55] They are at times explicitly called the high places of Baal.[56] Jeroboam went to the depths of appointing 'priests for the high places ... from among all the people; any who would, he consecrated to be priests of the high places' (1 Ki. 13:33).

These sites were chosen for such practices because of the symbolic importance of being high above the surrounding area, and because, as such, it was believed that the people (or the deities) who controlled the high ground were effectively in charge of the neighbourhood. To walk on high places like a deer was equivalent, therefore, to taking possession of the land.[57] It involved warfare, including spiritual warfare, and it was costly and dangerous. But there was no progress to be made without walking on high places. God's strength in Habakkuk enabled him to turn the high places of others into his own – hence the phrase *my high places*. Micah had been enabled to see the LORD himself taking (re)possession of 'the high places of the earth' (Mi. 1:3), and Habakkuk knew that the LORD would enable him to share in the same victory.

Habakkuk's spiritual descendants are the church of the living God. Her Saviour and Lord has declared that 'the powers of death [or, 'the gates of Hades', mg.] shall not prevail against it' (Mt. 16:18). That is a commission to advance; to take the battle to the enemy; to see territory now in the possession (thorough, but usurped) of forces hostile to God and the church, as *high places* to be reclaimed and to be placed under the sovereign rule of God and his Christ. It means feet like hinds' feet, and it involves spiritual warfare.

The prophet's secret, therefore, is an open secret: 'the righteous shall live by his faith' (2:4). Habakkuk has been through the whole gamut of faith and doubt in the course of these three chapters. The essence of the vision given to him by God is the essence of the Christian gospel. God's word, like God himself, never changes: it endures for ever. But each person and each community has to learn in practice what it means to live by faith in the God of Abraham, Isaac, Jacob, Moses, Joshua, David, Jehoshaphat – and Habakkuk: the God and Father of our Lord Jesus Christ.

---

[55] This failure is seen as the great 'but' in the lives of Asa (1 Ki. 15:14), Jehoshaphat (1 Ki. 22:43), Jehoash (2 Ki. 12:3), Joash (2 Ki. 14:4), Azariah (2 Ki. 15:4) and Jotham (2 Ki. 15:35). Hezekiah did at last remove them (2 Ki. 18:4).

[56] *E.g.* Je. 19:5.   [57] See Dt. 33:29.